THE CONNECTICUT

D1250358

RIVERS OF AMERICA

THE
CONNECTICUT

WALTER HARD

Introduction by Erik Hesselberg
Illustrated by Douglas W. Gorsline

LYONS
PRESS

Guilford, Connecticut

An imprint of The Rowman & Littlefield Publishing Group, Inc.
4501 Forbes Blvd., Ste. 200
Lanham, MD 20706
www.rowman.com

Distributed by NATIONAL BOOK NETWORK

British Library Cataloguing in Publication Information available

Library of Congress Cataloging-in-Publication Data available

ISBN 978-1-4930-4012-4 (paperback)

♾™ The paper used in this publication meets the minimum
requirements of American National Standard for Information
Sciences—Permanence of Paper for Printed Library Materials, ANSI/
NISO Z39.48-1992.

Printed in the United States of America

Contents

Introduction

Early in Walter Hard's *The Connecticut* is the forgotten story of the Republic of Indian Stream—the short-lived nation state in northern New Hampshire formed to avoid paying taxes. While the 1783 Treaty of Paris settled hostilities between the brand-new United States and Great Britain, it was vague on the U.S.-Canada boundary line, at least as it concerned the jagged corner of New Hampshire, where the Connecticut River rises. This led to both the U.S. and Canada claiming the forested land as theirs, and as a result a double tax bill for the 300 or so citizens of the isolated northern territory. Their response was to form their own county, the Indian Stream Republic (the present Pittsburg, New Hampshire), framing a constitution and electing a president. The tiny republic was even referred to in the 1830 Census as the, "Indian Stream Territory, or so-called." But its reign was brief. In 1836, these "pugnacious opponents," as Hard calls the Streamers, were at last persuaded (with the help of the New Hampshire militia) to accept the fact "that they were United States citizens and New Hampshirites."

Hard describes the Connecticut as a "friendly stream, which invites intimacy and elicits affection," and his own affection is woven into this charming history. He tells of the attempt by the Plymouth Pilgrims to capture the lucrative Connecticut River fur trade, establishing a post at Windsor in 1633, upriver from the Dutch fort at Hartford, the "Hope of Hope." The Pilgrims were aided in their trading by the use of shell beads known as *wampumpeag* or *wampum*, whose worth among local tribes they had learned from the Dutch. However, the Plymouth group was thwarted by a fellow Englishman, William Pynchon, canny agent of the Massachusetts Bay Company, who outflanked the Pilgrims with a fur-trading post father up at *Agawam*, an Algonkian word meaning "Unloading Place."

The Dutch claim to the Connecticut was based on the 1614 voyage of Adriaen Block, the first European to explore the waterway Native Americans called *Quinatucquet* or *Quenticutt*, meaning "Long Tidal River." Block, for whom Block Island is named, had been gathering beaver skins on the Hudson River when clashes with a rival Dutch trading company culminated in the burning of his ship *Tyger*. The resolute skipper built a new ship with timbers salvaged from the *Tyger*, a 44 ½ foot sloop he christened *Onrust* or *Restless*, piloting the vessel through the whirlpool currents of Hell Gate before entering Long Island Sound. Sailing east along the coast, Block came upon the Housatonic River, which he called "River of Red Hills," from the iron-stained basalt ridge of New Haven's West Rock. The wide Connecticut River he named the *Versche*, or Freshwater River, in contrast to the brackish Hudson. Block explored the Connecticut as far up as present-day Hartford, and a little beyond. As if to confirm his successful fur trading, the town of Windsor claims Block established a fur trading post there.

There is also the sad story of Lady Fenwick, the lovely, auburn-haired Englishwoman who came to the Saybrook Colony in 1639 with her husband George Fenwick, second governor of Connecticut. Hard presents a rather homey picture of the Fenwicks setting up house in Saybrook, planting a garden with seeds brought over from England. Although Hard does not delve into this, the Saybrook venture was backed by a London joint-stock company of Puritan grandees led by Robert Rich, the second Earl of Warwick, a notorious speculator in piracy. Warwick, who had his own small navy, saw himself as continuing the freebooting legacy of Sir Water Raleigh, funding colonies with the profits from piracy and slavery. At Saybrook, the "Lords and Gentlemen," as they were known, envisioned a baronial center of landed estates for the few aristocratic sympathizers of Oliver Cromwell, who were expected to seek refuge here. But the aristocratic colonizers, which included Lord Saye and Brook, never came. Meanwhile, Lady Alice proved too delicate a flower to "stand transplanting in the bleak New England soil of Saybrook Plantation." She died in 1646 after the birth of her second daughter, buried under a brownstone monolith at the mouth of the river on Saybrook Point, called Kievet's Hook by the Dutch from the insistent cries of sandpipers on the tidal flats.

The Connecticut was first published in 1947 by Rinehart and Company as part of the landmark Rivers of America series, launched a decade earlier. Constance Lindsey Skinner, who provided the vision for the series and was its first editor, saw the American story as a "folk saga" playing out along our waterways. "The American nation came to birth upon the rivers," she wrote in an essay accompanying the first volumes. "Has the fact colored our temperament. . . . Are we in any part what we are because of rivers? Possibly only a poet would answer yes." Indeed, Skinner thought poets and novelists, not historians, were best suited to tell America's story: "If the average American is less informed about his county, cares less about its past and about its present in all sections but the one where he resides and does business, it is because the books prepares for his instruction were not written by artists." Skinner recruited top literary figures like Robert P. Tristram Coffin, Carl Carmer, Henry Seidel Canby, and Henry Beston. The Rivers series proved so popular it was extended beyond the original 24 to 64 volumes, published over thirty-seven years. *The Connecticut* was the thirty-second in the series.

The Vermonter Walter R. Hard Sr. (1882-1966) was a regionalist poet known for his images of sturdy, self-sufficient New Englanders. Born is Manchester, Vermont, Hard attended Williams College to study journalism, but was forced to leave after three years to run the family drugstore following the death of his father. He performed the job dutifully for thirty years, though he said he always found it a chore. To relieve the tedium, he began jotting down stories, bits of wisdom and observations from customers, which he worked into a column for the *Manchester Journal*, beginning in 1924. Hard would end his commentary with a few lines of unrhymed verse with no apparent scheme of meter or form, a sort of distillation of the Vermont character. His column caught on and was soon syndicated; by 1930 Hard had produced his first collection of poems, *Some Vermonters*. Carl Sandburg praised his work, writing: "The books of Walter Hard present a likeness of a land and its people that deserve a place in the gallery of the best that has been done by regionalists of the earth." Walter Hard would go on to publish nine books of poems and two prose works, including *The Connecticut*, which he dedicated to his wife Margaret, also a writer.

In her review of his 1960 book, *Vermont Neighbors*, Ella Shannon, wrote that the strength of Hard's writing "lies in his ability to bring Yankee characters to life without overdoing it . . ." Old stories, like all old stories told well, take on new importance, become dramatic and somehow near at hand. We've heard the saga of Rev. Thomas Hooker leading his Newtown flock along an old Indian trail to the banks of the Connecticut River in the summer of 1636; Hard makes us see it:

> Once at the river they turned southward and set themselves down at what is now Hartford. They drove their cattle before them. While Mrs. Hooker traveled on a litter, her husband and his lay teacher,

Samuel Stone, shared the hardships of the journey with the rest of the congregation.

Equally inspiring is the story of Rev. Eleazer Wheelock of Norwich, Connecticut. Wheelock wanted to start a school for Mohegan Indians in the years before the Revolutionary War but was unable to raise the money because of prejudice. Undeterred, the Connecticut minister travelled to England where he found a sympathetic supporter in religiously-minded Earl of Dartmouth, who not only gave fifty pounds, but persuaded his friend King George III to put up another two hundred pounds. Donations now poured in. Wheelock's Indian school on the Connecticut River in Hanover, New Hampshire proved so popular there were soon more white students than Indians, so Wheelock changed the name to Dartmouth in honor of his noble patron.

Hard is generally sympathetic to Indigenous peoples, although his depictions of Native Americans lack a certain depth. For the most part, these "first peoples" dwell at the fringes of his story, occasionally stepping forward to offer advice on planting maize or pointing to where the fish run before retreating mysteriously back into history. The contemporary reader will find jarring the use of the trope, "Red Men," as well as the phrases, "Red threat, Red menace," and even "Red lions," to describe the fierce Pequots who held sway in the river valley until they were wiped out during Pequot War of 1638. As for that that one-sided contest, when some 400 men, women and children were massacred at their Mystic fort, Hard concludes tersely: "the Pequot menace was removed from the valley forever."

By contrast, profiles of the river valley's pioneering women were ahead of their time, especially the chapter "Women and Politics," telling the story of the remarkable Smith sisters of Glastonbury, Connecticut, early crusaders for women's suffrage. Although, the largest taxpayers in town in 1873, Abby and Julia Smith had not one word to say as to how much they should be assessed or how their money was to be spent. "Quietly, and with dignity, Abby Smith told the voters what she and her sister thought about taxation without representation." There's also a fascinating portrait of the educator Mary Lyon, founder Mount Holyoke College in South Hadley, Massachusetts.

Although published after World War II, *The Connecticut*'s emotional center is the Great Depression. Indeed, the depictions of Native Americans recall a WPA mural, showing a few feathered Natives gathered up like a welcoming committee to greet the dark and somber palefaces. WPA projects for the most part, steered clear of controversy in favor of the ennobling images all could embrace. The heroic idealism of the era is especially evident in a description of a hydro-electric dam project in Pittsburg, New Hampshire, (near the Connecticut's headwaters) which reads like a brochure for the New Deal's Tennessee Valley Authority:

The exuberant and extravagant force of the newly begun Connecticut River is being controlled and conserved by what is known as the Pittsburg Project. After its wandering course through the meadows of First Lake the rivers rushes and leaps through a rocky ravine to be held and conserved in a huge dam and reservoir. The sovereign power of New Hampshire is taking a hand in the disciplining of the carefree and youthful river.

Later, in a chapter entitled, "The River's Industrial Contribution," Hard effuses over the outpourings of factories along the river:

Today, black smoke pouring from thousands of tall stacks tells the story of industrial development which has come to the valley. These tall monuments to industry, many of them in the lower reaches of the river—and scattered in small towns throughout the northern sections, have replaced the water wheels whose power came chiefly from the feeder streams which tumble into the Connecticut throughout its length.

In those years the Connecticut River was classified as, "Suitable for the transportation of sewage and industrial wastes without nuisance and for power and navigation and certain industrial uses." No one dared stick a toe in its foul-smelling waters in which raw sewage mingled with domestic chemicals and industrial outflows. The last steamboat churned away from the dock at Hartford in 1931, leaving only coal barges plying back and forth. (Commercial traffic on the river ended around the year 2000, when the last oil barges switched to more dependable tanker trucks). Even the pleasure craft that once dotted the lower river were gone. "The Connecticut River affords a horrible example of how man, left to his own devices can destroy Nature's handiwork inland, to his own ultimate injury," The *New York Times* despaired. ". . . dwellers along the banks have watched it grow filthier year by year." By 1960, the "Beautiful River," as Timothy Dwight called the Connecticut, was known as "the world's most beautifully landscaped cesspool."

Fortunately, a new generation of determined Yankees (and others) were calling attention to the river's abuse and decline. In 1952, the Connecticut River Watershed Council was formed "to promote improvement of water quality and the restoration, conservation, wise development and use of the natural resources," along the 410-mile waterway. Their efforts got a boost in 1962, when William H. Whyte, best-selling author of *The Organizational Man*, critiquing corporate culture, was asked to prepare a comprehensive plan for preserving and developing Connecticut's natural resources. Whyte described the Connecticut River as "the most underexploited resource potential in the East. . . . If pollution enforcement is really stepped up, the benefits will be incalculable." This inspired a Hartford writer and historian, Ellsworth Grant, to get out his old Cine-Kodak camera and begin making a documentary "on the river's history, beauty, and desecration."

Grant was the brother-in-law of actress Katharine Hepburn, who had a large summer house at the mouth of the Connecticut River in Old Saybrook. The Oscar-winning actress was keenly aware of the river's soiled reputation. In 1955, while filming *Summertime* in Venice with Director David Lean, a scene called for Hepburn to fall backwards into the Grand Canal. Lean called for an understudy, but Hepburn, a fine swimmer, insisted she would take the plunge herself. "David, you forget I was raised at the mouth of the Connecticut River," she quipped before tumbling into the murky green water. (Hepburn ended up doing the scene twice, resulting in a serious eye infection that plagued her for much of her life.)

For Grant's half-hour movie *The Long Tidal River*, released in 1965, Katharine Hepburn provided the memorial narration. The film enjoyed wide publicity, igniting a movement to finally clean up the river. That year, Connecticut Gov. John Dempsey formed a 100-man task force, which submitted a report with 32 recommendations for restoring the Connecticut. On May 1, 1967, the Connecticut General Assembly passed the Clean Water Act, authorizing $150 million in bonds for the construction of sewage treatment plants along the river and its tributaries. Other states followed, leading ultimately to the building of 100 secondary treatment plants along the river's length. By 1972, the Connecticut was thirty percent cleaner than it had been six years before, and by 1980 nearly eighty percent of the river was safe for swimming.

Wildlife has returned, with great blue herons and white egrets stalking the shallows with stately and deliberate moves. Ospreys nest on platforms set out for their above the reeds, while bald eagles circle overhead. The lacework of coves and marshes of the estuary region have been described by the U.S. Fish and Wildlife Service as among "the richest wetlands ecosystems" in the Northern United States. Meanwhile, the Nature Conservancy included the Connecticut River Tidelands—the last 30 miles of the waterway from Cromwell, Connecticut, down to Long Island Sound, in its list of 40 "Last Great Places" on Earth. Reverently preserving the river's rich history is the Connecticut River Foundation at Steamboat Dock, established in Essex 1974. It operates the Connecticut River Museum housed in a 19th century steamboat warehouse, where ivory from Zanzibar in an earlier time was offloaded for factories to cut into piano keys. The museum also boasts a replica of the nation's first submarine, the *American Turtle*, a hand-cranked, propeller-driven craft invented by David Bushnell of Saybrook and tested in waters off Saybrook during the American Revolution.

In the summer of 2017 some 400 years after Adriaen Block first sailed up the Connecticut River, a replica of his 44-foot sloop *Onrust*, handsomely rigged with a single mast and flying the bright colors of her homeland, made her way upriver under the steel arches of highway bridges, passing on the shore huge oil storage tanks, power plants, and docking with the modern Hartford skyline in the background. The Connecticut River is still making history.

Erik Hesselberg
Haddam, Connecticut
November 2018

THE CONNECTICUT

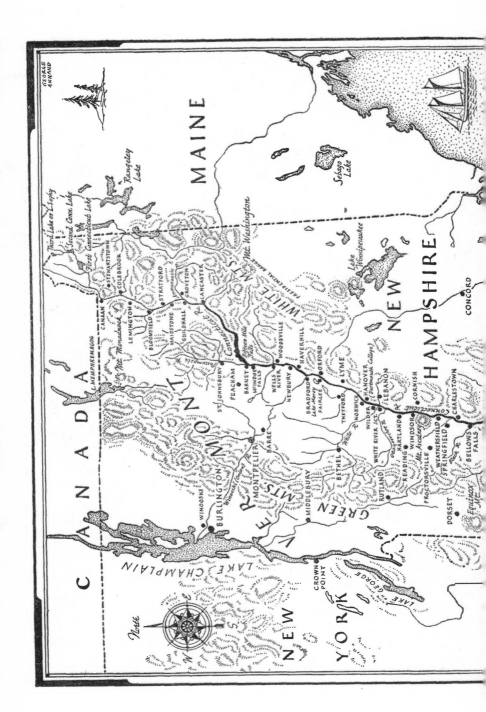

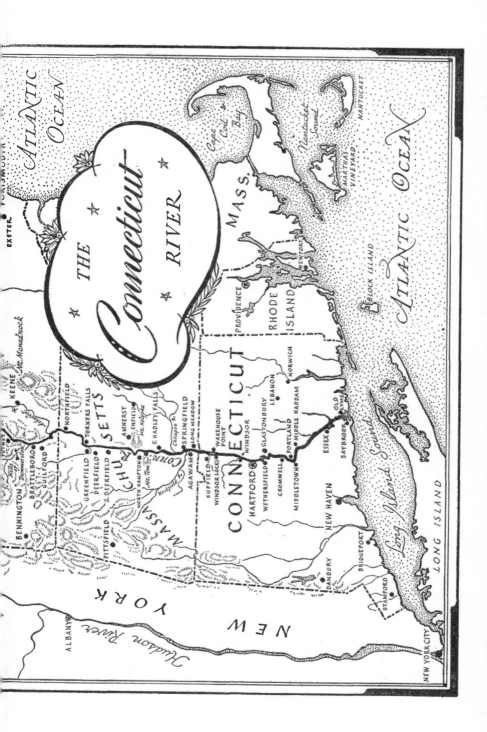

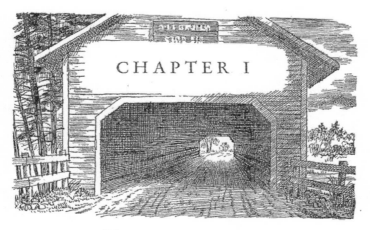

The Connecticut

THE INDIANS called the lower part of the river, where the tides rose and fell, by a name which meant "long estuary." They put an ending on the word which meant "at."

The English found it hard to get the Indian sounds into words. This accounts for the fact that there are many spellings in the old writings of the name of the river. Usually it was Quinatucquet or Quenticutt. How it came to be Connecticut nobody knows. At any rate the idea of the Indians, that it was long, is true. The Connecticut is the longest river in New England. It flows from the border of Canada, 360 miles, to Long Island Sound. Its source is 1,618 feet higher than its outlet, and it carries off the excess moisture from its drainage basin of about 11,300 square miles of Vermont and New Hampshire, Massachusetts and Connecticut.

The Connecticut is not a majestic river. It is, rather, a friendly stream, which invites intimacy and elicits affection. To be sure, it has its periods of mad haste, but somehow it gives the impression that it is merely in a hurry to get to the next area where it may wander through peaceful meadows.

Timothy Dwight, writing of his travels in 1837, was greatly moved by the beauty of the river and its valley. He wrote: "This stream may, with more propriety than any other in the world, be named THE BEAUTIFUL RIVER. From Stuart, a few miles from its source, to the Sound it uniformly maintains this character. The purity, salubrity and sweetness of its waters; the frequency and elegance of its meanders; its absolute freedom from aquatic vegetables; the uncommon and universal beauty of its banks, here a smooth and winding beach, there covered with rich verdure, now fringed with bushes, now covered with lofty trees, and now formed by the intruding hill, the rude bluff and the shaggy mountain, are objects which no traveler can thoroughly describe."

There is a marked contrast between this description of peace and beauty and the story of awesome and inexorable forces of which geologists tell us.

One of the early investigators wrote: "Of all the histories that have been written on New England, general and local, there is one that is pre-eminent. It is vast, profound, and yet simple. It is inspiring, entrancing and absorbing, for it is the history of the work of the Jehovah, written by his Amanuensis, Nature, in the rocks and strata of Connecticut Valley."

The present-day traveler, who follows a trail through the woods to the upper reaches of the Connecticut, who motors along the roads that follow its winding course to the sea, or who knows it more intimately because of exploring its length in a canoe or boat, sees chiefly its present story. He sees a river whose waters have been conserved in great dams, whose strength has been harnessed to industry. Passing along its middle miles the beauty of fertile meadow and pasture land, the peace of towns and villages, set upon wooded or open terraces, are part of that tranquil charm which characterizes this particular portion of the river and its valley.

As the river sweeps southward there are plantationlike fields where crops are raised that supply the country's markets. Suddenly there is smoke in the sky, belching from stacks of mills and factories. Here, again, the river is being held and harnessed, its waters curbed and driven by the hand of Power.

Where the river deepens at its southern tidewater there are harbors where seafaring vessels once anchored. The stream that rose above the Connecticut Lakes at the Canadian border, 360 miles away, flows past Saybrook and Old Lyme to enter Long Island Sound and the sea finally as a majestic river.

This is how the river appears to the traveler today; but perhaps the traveler is a geologist. And the geologist remembers that "a thousand years . . . are but as yesterday when it is past, and as a watch in the night." To him the river and its valley tell another tale—a tale millions of years old, which antedates all history except that which he may read in the strata of the earth that composes the river's shore line, its bed and valley, and the mountains that rise beyond it to east and west.

That story, which eternity has written in this portion of the earth's surface—which we know as the Connecticut and its valley—began aeons ago. Great chapters deal with the Ice Age, or the Pleistocene ice sheet, of a million years gone by.

Alternations of heat and cold, contraction and expansion, submergence and upheaval, befell the earth. The Ice Age removed all vegetation. Northern glaciers accumulated for a hundred thousand years or more and pushed southward. Forests fell before their onslaught. Mountain peaks were ground off and smoothed to roundness. Huge gaps and chasms were torn and gouged from their sides. The earth's surface was carved at will by the hand of the giant who held it in his grasp.

The great ice sheet crept on, burying and depressing the earth's crust under its enormous weight, sculpturing the White Mountains to glacial forms and planing off the protruding tops of the Green Mountains to less jagged summits. It deposited an untold tonnage of glacial "till" or, "drift," which it had picked up in its course, in the form of boulders, gravel, and silt.

With the coming of normal temperatures the great ice sheet "rotted" and withdrew to the north. It broke and melted into a vast sea of slowly disintegrating ice which covered what we now know as the Champlain and Connecticut valleys. After the millions of years that marked its advance and retreat (over continental North America) the mountain boundaries of the valley of the Connecticut began to thaw out and emerge.

Between these two ranges (the White and the Green) lay a "trench fault," or downdropped block of the earth's crust. It was of ancient origin and created originally by pressure upon and displacement of a portion of the earth's crust. This ancient trench became filled with sediments. These, hardening into shale and other soft rocks, were more easily eroded than the harder crystalline rocks, which formed either border of the trench; and so the river took its course in this way. This was ages before the Pleistocene, or Ice Age. When that age with its ice sheet came it also brought its own sediments, which were easily eroded.

As the ice sheet began its melting retreat it left a mass of material it had carried with it in a moraine which is now Long Island. On its back it had borne enormous quantities of debris. It left the story of its march and retirement in deep scratches upon rocks too hard to be ground and pulverized.

In the muddy strata laid down long before the Ice Age, and subsequently hardened, footprints of prehistoric reptiles have been found—footprints literally upon the sands of time.

The retirement of the ice pack was no more hurried than had been its advance. Forty-one centuries is the length of time it is estimated to have taken in its retreat from what is now Hartford, Connecticut, to St. Johnsbury, Vermont— a distance of some two hundred miles.

The enormous weight of the ice depressed the bottom of the valley between the mountain ranges. As the ice sheet "rotted," the burden lifted and the land rose once more. Naturally it rose in front of the retreating ice pack, so that for a time—a few thousand years—the valley sloped to the northward. As soon, however, as the entire valley floor was relieved it resumed its original position and southward-flowing streams again commenced their erosive action upon the accumulated silts. It was thus that some of the terraces were formed, which today are so marked a part of the valley's beauty.

As the river cut downward it "discovered" hard rock ledges across its course which it could not remove. Such falls as the Fifteen Miles Falls, above Barnet, Vermont, speak of such geologic conditions. Fifteen miles of alternating hard and soft rock strata, laid down ages ago, accounts for this scenic wonder of the river.

Today, some of the residents of the Connecticut valley have been greatly concerned lest the number of power dams built here should increase until the entire area become one enormous lake.

Our geologist traveler would tell them that there is precedent for such a state of affairs. When the giant of the Ice Age had been routed, the valley did become one long lake. Its length was 140 miles and it extended from what now is Middletown, Connecticut (where a natural dam had been formed by the accumulated debris of the retiring flow), to Lyme, New Hampshire—only a few miles from Dartmouth College, where students now study this very geologic story. In time the dam gave way and the great lake was drained. But the release of the waters of the huge lake left many smaller lakes behind banks formed by masses of debris gathered through the centuries.

Thus by catastrophic forces, and by the advance and retreat of the Pleistocene ice sheet—all of which occupied millions of years, the valley of the Connecticut River was formed. Through it flowed water, and vegetation again appeared upon the earth.

To the present-day traveler the river and its valley compose, perhaps, merely a region of entertainment and beauty—compiled of charming landscape, interesting facts, historic information, and entertaining anecdotes.

But to the geologist it means much more. He looks at the valley and the river and he sees the hand of God moving upon the face of the earth and the waters. Words come back to him . . .

"And God saw that it was good."

Today, where New Hampshire thrusts a triangle northward, shoving the Canadian line (which has been running

east and west along the tops of Vermont and New York)
into a northeasterly zigzag, there is a series of mountain
peaks. Along these the international boundary line runs, and
among them the Connecticut River is born.

So sharp is the dividing line between Canada and the
United States in this region that a shift of wind may send
the falling rain or snow north to Canada, by way of the St.
Francis River to the St. Lawrence River, or down the Connecticut River to Long Island Sound and the sea.

There, among the high peaks, in swamps and bogs,
enough water collects to make a small stream that flows into
one of a series of lakes known as the Connecticut Lakes. The
beginning river first flows into what is confusingly named
Third Lake—the lakes having been numbered from south to
north rather than from the river's source. The two lower
lakes—Second Lake and First Lake—have been enlarged by
power dams, but their wild surroundings and their great
beauty have not been spoiled.

Following the trails that surround these lakes and looking out upon their quiet waters and the untroubled wilderness expanse, it is easy to slip back in thought to the time
when this region was truly a wilderness and the red man alone
knew it. One can easily imagine the period when he first
brought adventurous French and English men from the
Province of New France to hunt with him in the deep forests,
to negotiate the mad rapids of the river, and to drift in
canoes upon the tranquil lakes. These journeys may have
eventually carried them into some of the Upper Coos country along the Connecticut, although the route commonly
used by the Indians lay farther to the west and south.

A strange story and an amazing bit of history is connected with the Indians, and their successor white men, who

occupied the great tract of wilderness land where the Connecticut rises and flows through the jagged corner of New Hampshire.

This jagged corner comprised some 160,000 acres which the red men claimed as their own. The wilderness forests, streams and lakes of the particular region had forever been their domain. Their right to it was so zealously maintained that only white men who were brought there at the invitation of Indians dared to invade the precincts. But after Major Robert Rogers and his Rangers had all but annihilated the St. Francis tribe, a few white settlers drifted in.

These settlers came at about the time that the United States government—but recently born—sent Colonel Jeremiah Eames to survey and fix the international boundary between the States and Canada. But one bitter winter in this wilderness region was sufficient to discourage their purpose of establishing a settlement, and they returned almost immediately to a more friendly situation.

However, in 1796 three intrepid adventurers from New Hampshire moved in. They bought out the last of the St. Francis sachems and set up their own particular form of government, and proceeded to ignore the rest of the world—either Canada to the north of them or the new United States to the west and south of them.

But after a quarter of a century of this sort of self-sufficient existence trouble arrived in the form of the rest of New Hampshire. That sovereign state, in looking over its affairs, was amazed to discover that it had nearly three hundred inhabitants living in the isolated region which comprised the northerly jagged corner of its territory.

When New Hampshire made it known to the small independent republic of Indian Stream that annexation of this territory was the natural right it intended to claim, there was a tremendous outcry. Some of the three hundred settlers were determined to recognize Great Britain as holding the proper claim to them as subjects. Some determined to call themselves citizens of the United States. Some refused to consider any claim. All were absolutely averse to annexation by New Hampshire.

Upon one point they all agreed. That was a desire to form an independent Indian Stream Republic. This they proceeded to do, framing a constitution and electing a president. However, as often befalls a group of so many independently minded people, there was soon more difficulty. Among the three hundred citizens of the Indian Stream Republic there was frequent and heated disagreement concerning their affairs of state. Both Canada and New Hampshire—with their eyes jealously cast in the direction of the small insurgent republic—thought this an advantageous moment to supply an entering wedge. They both sent armed militia to handle the situation. Naturally there was more trouble rather than less.

Then one faction of the Indian Streamers sent urgent appeals for help to Washington. But Washington replied succinctly: "If you are within the limits of the United States, as has always been maintained by this Government, it is because you are in the limits of New Hampshire." Thus did the federal government hit the troublesome nail squarely on the head for the benefit of one of its states.

Concord, New Hampshire, hearing of this reply, at once rushed a body of militia to the disputed territory. The president of the Indian Stream Republic fled overnight, but his constituents continued as pugnacious opponents until 1836, when they at last accepted the fact that they were United States citizens and New Hampshirites.

It is a little disappointing to know that this colorful incident, which concerned the sixty-year activities of the smallest republic in the world, had a prosaic ending. The ending was the dull naming of this picturesque township. It was named *Pittsburg*.

Yet in Pittsburg one of today's great water projects is taking place. The exuberant and extravagant force of the newly begun Connecticut River is being controlled and conserved by what is known as the Pittsburg Project. After its wandering course through the meadows below First Lake the river rushes and leaps through a rocky ravine to be held and conserved in a huge dam and reservoir. The sovereign power of the state of New Hampshire is taking a hand in the discipline of the carefree, youthful river.

Because of this project, which is a matter of both flood control and water conservation, public utilities in the Connecticut valley are able to assure mill and factory owners of necessary power—of the hydro electric power needed to operate great industries.

Running beside these dams and lakes is the new Daniel Webster Highway—U.S. 3. It makes accessible to many a region which heretofore has been chiefly known to the more venturesome traveler, camper or huntsman. Any traveler passing along the miles that flank this region of almost primitive beauty, as it carries him to or from those portions of New Hampshire forever associated with Webster, feels that it is properly named. And he must hope that the individual Connecticut Lakes will someday be given names more inspiring than numerals.

Between Canaan, Vermont, and its New Hampshire

neighbor, Stewartstown, across the river, there is a bridge. Here the Connecticut, already augmented by several feeder streams, turns southward, dividing New Hampshire and Vermont. However, it has been decreed by the courts—after long years of litigation—that all of the river belongs to New Hampshire except when it gets above normal high-water mark on the Vermont side. When the river goes on a rampage its excesses belong to Vermont.

Hills rise from a widening valley where the river slips along past Colbrook, Stratford and Groveton on the New Hampshire side, and past Lemington, Bloomfield, Maidstone and Guildhall on the Vermont side. Near Lancaster, New Hampshire, the river has its first opportunity to indulge in leisurely wanderings. Here it first shows the "elegance of its meanders." Here the drop in the river's flow is said to be only two feet in a course of ten miles.

All along this region, as well as below it, terraces rise in steps from the river's edge. Sometimes there are four or five of them, one above the other. Usually the towns that border the river stand on one of the upper terraces. The lower ones are usually rich meadow land. Looking at their verdure today, and realizing that they have always been natural meadow lands covered with lush productive growth, it is not surprising to recall how attractive they appeared to the early settlers.

Men coming up from Massachusetts and Connecticut, through this portion of the Connecticut valley, on their way to Canada or the Champlain valley were impressed. They carried the memory of these rich and abundant green meadows back with them to their homesteads in the colonies. Many of them made fresh treks and built new homesteads where life and food promised such abundance. Soldiers returning from the French and Indian Wars noted the surrounding opportunities for good crops. When they reached home they told of a green and fruitful land upon the upper river. They packed their household belongings on rafts or on ox-drawn sledges and came back to settle beside the river and its promising meadow lands.

Again turning westward the river gives to New Hampshire and takes from Vermont. It moves on into the rocky trough where it once indulged in a 15-mile orgy of foaming speed. Here are the Fifteen Miles Falls where the river drops 375 feet.

It was upon first seeing this mass of tumbling, troubled waters that DeWitt Clinton was moved to prophecy. Since he was the engineer of the Erie Canal enterprise his prophecy was highly discouraging to those canal enthusiasts who hoped that he would see a magnificent probability in their plan for a canal that should connect the Connecticut and St. Lawrence rivers. One look at the turbulent waters of Fifteen Miles Falls convinced Clinton that the proposition was utterly impractical and doomed to failure. He did, however, voice a prophecy that his hearers probably scarcely heeded at the moment. He opined that at some future day the latent power of these same falls might prove of great use to mankind. And so it has. Today the force of those waters is harnessed to produce one of the greatest power developments in the whole Connecticut valley.

Escaping from captivity the river flows more directly south. It leaves Barnet and McIndoe Falls. The peaks of the Presidential Range of the White Mountains begin to appear to the east. Mt. Washington is the highest. It lifts its head 6,000 feet into the clouds. Along the banks of the river are fields where corn grows and hillside pastures where cattle graze. This is rich dairy country. The whole landscape bespeaks an atmosphere of plenty and well-being. On the upper terraces white spires prick through the trees. Occasionally one glimpses a fine old house set among elms or maples. A high village green discloses roofs of substantial white houses built two centuries ago. Always there is the white finger of the New England meetinghouse pointing toward heaven.

The river moves on between Wells River in Vermont and Woodsville in New Hampshire. Wells River was a shipping point in the old days, when heavily laden barges used to come up the river and unload their cargoes upon its docks. The old tavern—part of which still may be seen—used to ring with the laughter of "rivermen," and in its parlor guests of a more opulent status often passed the night as they journeyed up and down the valley.

Across the river at Woodsville "freighters" (on wheels) and stages waited for those passengers who planned to make an overland journey to Maine and to have household goods accompany them.

As the river approaches Newbury, on its west bank, its course lies in the pattern of an oxbow, and the name "The Great Ox Bow" is attached to it. There on the fertile plains where the Indians used to grow their winter supply of corn the river makes an enormous loop. It covers nearly four miles and then returns to a spot less than half a mile from its original course. Below Bradford it makes another abrupt turn to the east and then flows south again.

Both Newbury, Vermont, and Haverhill, New Hampshire—diagonally across the river from each other—are steeped in tradition and history. General Washington once made his headquarters in Newbury. He must have slept through many nights in one or another of its fine old houses. The weary and harassed general, conferring with General

Jacob Bayley and General Hazen about plans of campaign, which included a possible invasion of Canada by means of the Hazen Military Road, must have welcomed the cheer and comfort these beautiful old houses extended to him.

In Haverhill there is many a romantic tale which links some one of its houses and their inhabitants to settlements on the opposite side of the river or with colonies which lay south of them in the early days of the Revolution, or prior to it. Such a story concerned the wife of Jonathan Arnold, who was the founder of St. Johnsbury, Vermont, situated on the hills about thirty miles north of Newbury.

When Jonathan Arnold took to himself a bride he stopped with her to tarry over the night with a friend in Haverhill. This break in the journey from Connecticut, where he had been married, to St. Johnsbury, where he was to settle with his new wife, proved a significant one.

As young Mrs. Arnold alighted from her horse at Samuel Ladd's house she little guessed that it was to be her future home. On the following morning when she departed on horseback with her husband, Mr. Ladd took a willow switch, which she had left by the doorway, and stuck it into the soft turf. Laughingly, it was explained to her that there was an old saying concerning a switch left by a bride at a doorway in passing. Some male inmate of the house would prove to be her second husband. In this case the saying proved true. Jonathan Arnold died after three years. Within a year his widow was being courted by Samuel Ladd of Haverhill. In time she married him and when they drove to his home he pointed to a willow bush growing beside the house—the willow switch she had left behind four years earlier, and which he had planted.

A few miles farther down the river there are more beautiful houses—old mansions in a row—so stately in architecture and setting that people journey to Orford, New Hampshire, to see them. Below Orford, on the river, history also was made. Samuel Morey—a youth intent upon invention of a steam-propelled craft—broke the Sabbath calm of the river with his steam-driven, paddle-wheel steamboat. Although Samuel Morey never received the credit that was his due, the lake near Fairlee, in Vermont, bears his name—*Lake Morey.*

The Connecticut now glides under the Ledyard Bridge, which connects Norwich, Vermont, with Hanover, New Hampshire, where Dartmouth's founder had a thought for the Indian and where Daniel Webster was once a student. Again at Wilder, in Vermont, the river's waters are impounded and put to work.

All along the upper reaches of the river feeder streams have been pouring down from the hills. These streams have the singing names which the Indians gave to them: Ammonoosuc, Passumpsic, Ompomanoosuc, and Ottauquechee.

Below the Wilder dam the river resumes its course. It passes Lebanon in New Hampshire and Vermont's Hartford. Along this section of the stream there are other towns bearing the names of older ones farther down the river: Windsor, Weathersfield, and Springfield, on the west bank, and Lyme and Charlestown on the east side, showing the home-town loyalties of the early settlers.

With all these towns historic events are connected. Not as old as the places for which they were named, they still drew history and tradition about them. Men and women who made the Connecticut valley a powerful force in the New World walked their streets. A wealth of fact and anecdote has grown up around them. Windsor—the birthplace of Vermont. Weathersfield, where Consul Jarvis "lived in almost feudal grandeur." Springfield, which has one of the greatest machine tool industries in the country—although it has no railroad depot or port. Lyme, which, like Thetford Hill across the river from it, has a beautiful common with houses, meetinghouse, and academy gathered about it. Charlestown, the famous No. 4 of early outpost settlements in the days of Indian massacres.

The river moves on through its winding valley. It slips under the long covered bridge that connects Windsor with Cornish—Cornish where St. Gaudens used to look out from his studio in New Hampshire to Mt. Ascutney beyond the river.

The river waters at Bellows Falls flow through some of the ancient canal system that was built to circumvent the madness of the falls, which were known as the Great Falls. Now, through the power generated by the subdued river—damned at the falls—electricity turns industry's wheels miles away.

Quieted, the river passes the fine old town of Walpole, on its east bank, and Westminster, on its west, where a skirmish took place almost on the eve of Bunker Hill. It passes Putney and the hills of Dummerston from which Rudyard Kipling used to look across to snow-capped Monadnock in New Hampshire.

At Brattleboro, Vermont, the West River joins the Connecticut. Here the first settlers of the state built their village around the high stockade that was to protect the valley from the aroused red man. Here printing and manufacture of the Estey organ make Brattleboro famous. Now the river is a quiet lake behind the Vernon dam below Brattleboro.

Crossing the line and starting its journey across Massachusetts, the river soon finds itself passing Northfield. This was once the most northerly settlement of the valley, and here the Indians made a last stand. On either bank are the schools which Dwight L. Moody founded.

Taking a sharp curve westward the river makes a lake which bears an Indian name—Peskeompscut. The dam at Turners Falls is its modern cause, and sluice gates have replaced ancient canal locks.

Heading south again the Connecticut flows past industrial Greenfield and the Deerfields, where history was written in blood. Now the widening valley is marked by level intervales where tobacco and potatoes, celery and onions grow in the rich soil. Women and children are working along with the menfolk in the fields, just as the families of the first settlers worked to clear the land and plant it. Many of the present workers are newcomers too. Some are from lands wrecked by war. Their sons have recently fought for this new land, on soil that was previously their home.

On through the wide valley the river flows, where Mt. Tom and Mt. Holyoke look down on what is sometimes called "The College Reach." To the east is Amherst with its two colleges—Amherst and Massachusetts State. Farther down is Northampton on the west. Here a bequest of Sophia Smith's founded Smith College in 1873. On the east, at South Hadley, stands Mt. Holyoke College, founded as Mary Lyon's Female Seminary thirty-six years earlier than Smith.

After dallying in the leisurely academic atmosphere—although there are some industries in the region—the river takes up the swifter pace of industry, stirred, perhaps, by the influx of busy waters from the Chicopee and Westfield rivers. Built at the falls of the Chicopee there is a thriving town of the same name. On the Westfield River there is also an industrial town bearing the river's title. Chicopee, Westfield: their bustle and industry are merely the forerunner of what it to be found at Springfield below South Hadley Falls.

In this region the river drops nearly sixty feet to the falls. Here the early canal (built to aid navigation of the river at this point) became the germ of the great hydraulic works that have made Holyoke famous for its paper mills, and one of the valley's centers of specialized industry.

Next, the river enters Springfield within whose borders it is the law that its waters shall not be put to work. This city of varied industries has grown up because it is at the crossway where railroads going east and west meet the valley traffic. The city which was built by the Steam Giant now protects the river whose commerce that same giant destroyed.

The river, having traversed Massachusetts, now leaves the state. It passes the border towns of Agawam and Longmeadow. From above Springfield it is deep enough to carry boats of considerable size. At Longmeadow it reaches its greatest width—2,100 feet from bank to bank. The average width through the Massachusetts reach is 1,200 feet.

Entering the state that bears its name the river is held back by another dam at Enfield Falls—the famous five miles of "white water." Escaping through the rocky bed the river passes Windsor Locks and Warehouse Point, which is on its opposite shore. It was here that the seeds for Springfield's commercial trade were planted in the early days by William Pynchon, whose keen brain and shrewd calculations laid foundations for a great city's industry when he first built his rough warehouse on the desolate point that jutted into the Connecticut below the white water.

Next the river passes historic ground in Windsor—now divided into three parts on either side of the river. As it flows along toward Hartford several streams add their waters

to it—streams with Indian names: Scuantic, Tunxis and Po-
dunk. It passes around the point where, even before the English had come to Windsor, the Dutch had built a trading
post which they called "The House of Hope," little guessing
it was to become the home of despair.

Then the river flows through Hartford, largest city of
the valley, capital of its state, and the birthplace of America's
constitutional government. Hartford is the head of the river's
navigation; here the ocean's tides are marked and from its
port craft once sailed for distant lands. Stately houses still
stand in Hartford, which contain rare and curiously beautiful relics from this long-past trade with a distant world.
Now there is little use for the river as a bearer of commerce.
The skies are marked by the smoke from many chimneys and
tall office buildings hide ancient landmarks.

The river flows on between Hartford's two parts and
takes a more irregular and changing course. The alluvial
banks give the stream a chance to vary its course by wearing
those banks away at the bends and building new shores in
other places. It has even devoured an island of considerable
length over the years.

Between Old Weathersfield and Glastonbury there is another indulgence on the part of the river in "elegant meanders." Then it again resumes its southward journey through
cultivated fields, with the primary mountains once more rising beside it. Past Cromwell and Portland it turns eastward,
perhaps where the old geologic dam broke through, and aban-
doning its ancient valley heads east for five miles. In this
bend lies Middletown, where Wesleyan University retains the
educational atmosphere of the valley amid numerous industrial enterprises. Still flowing east, the river is confined by
high ranges for about a mile so that it takes on some of its

earlier dimensions, being contracted in places to a width of 600 feet.

At Middle Haddam there is a resumption of the river's southward journey, which continues, with an easterly tendency, almost to the sea. It slips along between sloping hills to widen between Essex and Old Lyme. Along these reaches it seems to loiter, loath to leave its pleasant valley. Then at Saybrook, where once English Lords and Gentlemen planned a seat of Old World glory and where the dust of the desolate Lady Fenwick lies beneath an ancient tomb, the river widens again and sweeps majestically past these final shores to lose itself in the salty waters of Long Island Sound.

As Joel Barlow wrote of the Connecticut in 1787:

"Nor drinks the sea a lovelier wave than thine."

CHAPTER II

A White Man Comes to the River

ON A SPRING DAY in 1614 the Quinatucquet—or Connecticut—River slipped quietly along its lower reaches much as it had been doing for centuries. The untouched timber, tall and thick, stretched back as far as the eye could see, broken only by tangles of windfalls that marked the path of some heavy storm. Here and there a tree leaned out over the undermining water that rippled about its roots. There were new green leaves on the maples and beeches and on the giant oaks. They stood out against the darker green of the conifers.

It was not all dark forest. Often there were clean meadows where the river curved. These the Indians called "pocconocks," and on them they grew their crops of corn. They were the fertile fields built during geologic ages and by the floodtime changes in the river's course.

All of this scene, on this particular spring morning, was beheld for the first time by a white man. As there is silence until there is an ear to hear, so for the white race, until that day, the life of the river and its valley had gone on unknown, unseen, unheard. Then began their recorded story.

It was Adriaen Block, a determined and daring Dutchman, who first saw the river. He had been ready to set sail from the island of Manhattan to his home in Holland, carrying a rich cargo of furs, when his ship caught fire and burned. Instead of returning on a companion boat, Block, with some of his crew, elected to stay on Manhattan Island. There, during the following winter, they built a new boat which they christened the *Onrust*—the *Restless*—a most appropriate name for this small craft less than fifty feet long and carrying something like sixteen tons burden.

With this small boat, in the spring of 1614, these Dutch explorers slipped through the shallow inlet of the Connecticut River, whose mouth they had discovered. Block put it down on his chart as De Versche Riviere—the Freshwater River.

He sailed slowly up the wide, slow-moving stream, observing the forests that stretched back as far as he could see, to the low hills beyond. He doubtless saw smoke rising from Indian fires on the hills, or perhaps a canoe glided past filled with red men as silent as the surrounding forests. They may have answered the white man's salutation, but their stolid faces showed no curiosity. Considerable trading with the Indians was already going on along the coast, and the Indians on the Connecticut must undoubtedly have had some contact with European ships and have known the white man from their trade with the French in the north and the English in Massachusetts, and with the Dutch to the south of them.

But little did the Connecticut River Indians know that that particular day marked the beginning of a life-and-death struggle; that from then on the river was no longer their own.

Rounding the bend in the river at what is now Middle-town, Connecticut, the band of explorers came upon the first habitation they had seen since they had sailed from their winter quarters on Manhattan Island. On both banks of the river the Senguins—one of the larger tribes of river Indians —had placed their lodges. A few miles farther up they came on another settlement. This belonged to a different tribe, who had built, across the river from their camp, a palisade which proclaimed that all was not peaceful in that region. There were meadows by the villages. Squaws were preparing the ground for planting the maize that would help keep them through the winter.

Going ashore, Block may have learned that the fort was a protection against the attacks of the Pequots, an interloping tribe which had been conquering lands to the east. He doubtless learned too that other tribes frequently came down the river from distant places along its upper reaches. And, what was most important to the Dutch traders, he learned that these Indians came with canoes loaded with skins. Since the main business of the Dutch was to open up new trading places for the merchants of Holland, this must have been welcome information.

Re-embarking, after sharing a meal of salmon (with which the river abounded) with the friendly natives, the party continued up the river until white water ahead of them cut short their voyaging. At what later became known as Enfield Rapids, the small boat put about and slipped away. Down the river they drifted—down the winding river which, all unsuspecting, had had a most important thing happen to it upon that spring day. It had been discovered by a man who could make a record of his discovery.

Block sailed out through the river's mouth and did some more coastal surveying and mapping. Then, falling in with an old friend, who was doing some exploring in that region, he returned with him to Holland. There he laid his valuable discoveries before the authorities. His boat, the *Onrust,* he left behind him to do further duty for the Dutch in new waters.

Johannes de Laet, a Dutch writer of the time, a director of the Dutch West India Company, and a friend of the Plymouth Pilgrims, gives a summary of Adriaen Block's initial trip with the little *Onrust:*

Next on the same south coast succeeds a river named by our countrymen Fresh River, which is shallow at its mouth and lies between two courses, north by east and west by north; but according to conjecture, its general direction is from the north northwest. In some places it is very shallow, so that at about fifteen leagues up the river there is not much more than five feet of water. There are few inhabitants near the mouth of the river, but at the distance of fifteen leagues they become more numerous; their nation is called Sequins. From this place [Middletown] the river stretches ten leagues, mostly in a northerly direction, but it is very crooked; the reaches extend northeast to southwest by south, and it is impossible to sail through them all with a head wind. The depth of the water varies from eight to twelve feet, is sometimes four and five fathoms, but mostly eight and nine feet. The natives there plant maize, and in the year 1614 they had a village resembling a fort for protection against the attacks of their enemies.

They are called Nawas, and their sagamore was then named Morahieck. They term the bread made of maize, in their language, Leganick. This place is situated in latitude 41° 48′. The river is not navigable with yachts for more than two leagues farther, as it is very shallow and has a rocky bottom. Within the land dwells another nation of savages, who are called Horikans; they descend the river in canoes made of bark. This river has always a downward current so that no assistance is derived from it in going up, but a favorable wind is necessary.

On his journey home to Holland, with his friend Hendrick Christiaensen, Adriaen Block had plenty of time to look over the notes he had made on his explorations. Together they made a Figurative Map which covered their combined explorations. This map was presented as a part of Block's report to the Amsterdam Trading Company, and by that company to the States-General.

Despite the fact that Adriaen Block was a great explorer and the discoverer of a great river—the Connecticut—his only monument is the island in Long Island Sound that bears his name—Block Island. This is ironic, since it had been discovered ninety years earlier by the Italian explorer, Giovanni da Verrazano. It is the Connecticut River that should (and does) immortalize him.

For some time after the memorable day when Adriaen Block sailed up it as far as white water the river's life flowed on with no apparent change. The Indians still held possession of it, and they found the growing trade with the white man greatly to their advantage. It was in Europe, and later in Massachusetts, that the changes of importance to the river and its valley were taking place. Adriaen Block's enthusiastic report resulted in the granting of charters to trading companies by Holland. For fifteen years Dutch trade with the river's redskin tribes flourished.

It was trade that the Dutch sought, and they evidently thought there was more than enough for themselves, for they told the English at Plymouth about the river and its trading possibilities. They especially recommended the river valley as a dwelling place. They seem to have been moved to suggest this change of residence out of pity for the unhappy plight of the English colonists: "Seeing them seated in a barren quarter." That the valley along the quiet river was preferable to the stern and rockbound coast was certainly more than a promoter's dream, and the Dutch apparently thought there was room for both nations and business enough to stand division.

The English at Plymouth did not seem at all inclined to move to the new territory, but they took the occasion to warn the Dutch not to trespass on what they held was already their own property under English patent as New England.

It was an odd and trouble-brewing coincidence that at the same time that Adriaen Block, Dutchman, was sailing up the Connecticut, all unbeknownst Captain John Smith, Englishman, was coasting along the Atlantic seaboard near by. About the time that the Dutch were poring over Adriaen Block's map, Captain Smith was telling King Charles I of England about his voyage around Cape Cod. When the New Netherland authorities were marking the region, including the Connecticut, "New Netherland" on their maps, the English were putting the same area down on their charts as "New England." Since at that time there were no real settlements in the disputed region, it would seem that both nations started at scratch. However, other all-inclusive English grants no doubt figured in the matter.

There is also no doubt that the English did make the first settlements along the river's banks. But before ever the Dutch came it had been discovered by the Indians, and they had settled its banks in their own fashion before the English appeared.

Indian claims, Dutch claims, and English claims to the peaceful river were to make it the scene of struggle and bloodshed. The story of the river became the story of man's desire for her and his struggle to possess her.

But it was the thrifty Dutch who took advantage of the trading possibilities of the river for the next eighteen years. Trade grew. It is reported that they not infrequently shipped a thousand pounds' worth of furs on a single vessel.

It was several years after the Dutch had so cordially invited the Plymouth colonists to partake of the fruitfulness of the Connecticut River valley that the invitation was accepted. By then both the invitation and the cordiality had been withdrawn. Meanwhile the sachems of the Mohegan Indians, who had been ousted from their holdings along the river by the fierce Pequots, made renewed efforts to induce the white colonists at Plymouth and Boston to move to the river valley and settle.

They visited the Plymouth Pilgrims with pomp and ceremony. They brought samples of the river's products and promised food and trade. They offered to subsidize the colonists to the extent of giving them corn and eighteen beaver skins per annum. In return they asked for help in regaining their lands from the Pequots. They were pleasantly received, but they were given no assurance of aid.

Next they visited the Boston Puritans in the Bay Colony with the same proposition, but received nothing substantial in the way of assurances or promises. There was no doubt, however, that all this talk stirred up interest and curiosity on the part of both colonies. Later that very summer Edward Winslow did a little exploring along the river for the Pilgrim group of Plymouth. He was so taken with what he saw that he at once picked out a building lot.

A year and a half following this initial trip, Pilgrim ships began to frequent the river, carrying on a profitable trade with the natives. The latter continued to ask the white colonists to help them in their struggle against the encroaching Pequots and to promise all manner of inducements to gain their support.

In 1633 the Pilgrims began to go into the matter seriously. The report that the Dutch had obtained title to land from the Indians and were going to build a fort to keep the English off the river probably spurred the Pilgrims to action. They decided to try to get the co-operation of the Boston Puritans. Winslow and Bradford went to Boston forthwith and had a conference with Governor Winthrop.

The governor listened to them, but he saw lions in the path—red lions. He politely rejected their partnership. At the same time he assured them that he had no objection whatever to having them undertake the adventure alone. In his *Journal* he made mention of the menace of the Indians. He also put down, as further arguments against the scheme, the fact that the bar at the mouth of the river made navigation difficult and that the river was frozen over during seven months of the year. "So," he concludes, "we thought not fit to meddle with it."

But something changed the governor's mind. Only a few weeks after he had turned down the Pilgrims' partnership and while the Plymouth people were getting ready to send their first settlers to the river, Governor Winthrop sent his ship—the *Blessing of the Bay*—on a trading expedition. This expedition just happened to include a trip up the Connecticut River. Further evidence of a weakening in the governor's previous determination not to "meddle" is the fact that there was a simultaneous overland trip arranged by the governor

and undertaken by one John Oldham. The overland trip
carried John Oldham direct to the banks of the Connecticut.
He looked over what is the present site of Springfield, Massachusetts, and returned to Governor Winthrop with a favorable report of what he had seen.

The *Blessing of the Bay,* having investigated the river,
at once set sail for Manhattan Island (so favorable had been
the impression bestowed by its reconnoitering). It bore a
message to the Dutch director, Van Twiller, from Governor
Winthrop of the Bay Colony. In it the governor warned the
Dutch against making any settlements along the River Connecticut, since that land had already been granted by the
King of England to his subjects. In reply Van Twiller pointed
out to Governor Winthrop that the same parcel of land had
been granted some time earlier by the United Netherlands
(Holland) to their West India Company. Since there seemed
to be some dispute as to the title, the Dutch director suggested that the two interested powers get together and settle
the matter. This suggestion was delivered to Governor Winthrop upon the return of the *Blessing of the Bay* to the Bay
Colony.

But Wouter Van Twiller, without waiting for any arbi-
tration committee, went into action. Perhaps he was stirred
only by the message of Governor Winthrop. He may also
have heard another bit of news from home. A new company
of Englishmen, designated as the Lords and Gentlemen, had
been granted lands that included property at the mouth of
the Connecticut. Led by Sir Richard Saltonstall a group,
including Lord Saye and Sele, Lord Brooke, and others, had
purchased these grants from the Earl of Warwick. At any
rate Van Twiller decided the time had come to head off the
English from the valley of the Connecticut. To this end he

took possession of the mouth of the river, at what later became Saybrook Point, and nailed a sign on a tree announcing to all and sundry that the region belonged to the United Netherlands. He also went up the river, to a point near the present site of Hartford, and there built and fortified a modest trading post. He bought the land from the conquering Pequots (this being some of the same parcel of land which the ousted sachems had been urging the English to take over). Clearly, more title difficulties were in the making. With no little optimism Van Twiller named his newly fortified trading post "The House of Hope."

Meanwhile the Plymouth Colony had been astir with preparations to carry out their plans for settlement along the river. They had found the trading there good and had observed the fertility of the Indian meadows. Their experience on the rocky, storm-swept coast made the valley of the Connecticut seem doubly attractive. That they put their hearts into the venture is shown by the fact that they built a new boat for the new settlers, and put Lieutenant Holmes, one of their leading men, in charge of the expedition. They also gave him a picked crew. Not to lose any time after their arrival at their river destination, they had put on board a prefabricated house—probably the first one built in this country.

They set out accompanied by several sachems of the tribes ousted by the Pequots, from whom they had purchased the land to which they were going. They also proposed to reinstate these Indians on their lost holdings. On a brilliant autumn day (September 26, 1633) the small vessel sailed up the river with its hopeful band from the rocky shores of Plymouth. In Plymouth life had been made up of continuous suffering and struggle. The valley of the Connecticut must have looked like the Promised Land to these yearning settlers.

Suddenly they found their hopeful progress challenged. As they came around a point of land they saw the newly built House of Hope. From the shore came a challenging order to halt. Two Dutch cannon, pointed directly at them, gave emphasis to the command. But Lieutenant Holmes was not a man to be halted by any Dutchman. He kept his boat steadily upon its course. To the repeated order to halt he replied that he had business farther up the river and intended to carry out his instructions. The Dutch continued to shout their challenge, but they let the boat go without touching fuse to the cannon.

The surprised but undaunted Englishmen proceeded to the spot which later became Windsor, Connecticut. There they landed. With haste they unloaded their cargo and set up the ready-cut cabin. Aware now of the danger from the Dutch as well as of the menace of the Pequot Indians, whose enemies they were recognizing as the rightful owners of the land, they at once set to work building a protective palisade. The boat returned down the river leaving the first English settlement on the Connecticut to fend for itself.

The Dutch sent a note of protest back to Plymouth by Lieutenant Holmes. Later they made various feeble attempts to oust the English by sending men to head off trade farther up the river. This plan failed miserably. The men engaged in it were finally saved from perishing with cold and hunger by the kindness and mercy of the very settlers they had been commissioned to thwart and dislodge. Then the Dutch sent an armed force to disperse the invaders; but seeing that there would be bloodshed and perhaps remembering the saving kindness to their fellow white men during the previous winter, they withdrew without taking action. The much-molested Plymouth band of weary settlers were finally left in peace as far as their Dutch neighbors were concerned.

And in these months that they had been fending for themselves they had managed to build some sort of homes, to sustain life during the first hard winter, and to plant crops of corn as early as the spring floods and the abating cold would allow.

The partially built cabin which the Pilgrims had brought with them, ready to set up immediately upon disembarking from their boat, had behind it sound wisdom, prompted by bitter experience.

When they had originally landed on the barren and difficult shore at Plymouth, the matter of housing had presented a major problem. For weeks the women and children of the party remained on board the *Mayflower* for shelter while their men worked furiously in the forest, felling trees and making clearings for the cabins which should house them during that first terrible winter.

Alice Morse Earle gives a graphic description of the probable difficulties which confronted the first settlers on American shores, in her book *Home Life in Colonial Days:* [1]

The difficulties in finding or making shelter must have seemed ironical as well as almost unbearable. The colonists found a land magnificent with forest trees of every size and variety, but they had no sawmills, and few saws to cut boards; there was plenty of clay and ample limestone on every side, yet they could have no brick and no mortar; grand boulders of granite and rock were everywhere, yet there was not a single facility for cutting, drawing, or using stone. These homeless men, so sorely in need of immediate shelter, were baffled by pioneer conditions, and had to turn to many poor expedients, and be satisfied with rude covering.

. . . In Massachusetts, and possibly other states, some [set-

[1] By permission of The Macmillan Company.

tlers] reverted to an ancient form of shelter: they became cave-dwellers; caves were dug in the side of a hill, and lived in till the settlers could have time to chop down and cut up trees for log houses. Cornelis Van Tienhoven, Secretary of the Province of New Netherland, gives a description of these cave-dwellings, and says that "the wealthy and principal men in New England lived in this fashion for two reasons: first, not to waste time building; second not to discourage poorer laboring people." It is to be doubted whether wealthy men ever lived in them in New England, but Johnson, in his WONDER-WORKING PROVIDENCE, written in 1645, tells of the occasional use of "smoaky homes."

Though the settler had no sawmills, brick kilns, or stone-cutters, he had one noble friend—his broadax. With his broadax and his own strong and willing arms he could build a log cabin.

A favorite form of log house for a settler to build in his first "cut down" in the virgin forest was made by digging a square trench about two feet deep, of dimensions as large as he wished the ground floor of his house, then setting upright all around this trench (leaving a space for a fireplace, a window, and a door) a closely placed row of logs all the same length, usually fourteen feet long for a single story; if there was a loft, eighteen feet long. The earth was filled in solidly around these logs, and kept them firmly upright; a horizontal band of puncheons, which were split logs smoothed off on the face with the ax, was sometimes pinned around within the log walls to keep them from caving in.

Over this was placed a bark roof, made of squares of chestnut bark, or shingles of overlapping birch-bark. A bark or log shutter was hung at the window, and a bark door hung on withe hinges, or, if very luxurious, on leather straps, completed the quickly made home. This was called rolling-up a house, and the house was called a puncheon and bark house. A rough puncheon floor, hewed flat with an axe, or adze, was truly a luxury.

One settler's wife pleaded that the house might be rolled up around a splendid flat stump; thus she had a good, firm table. A small platform placed about two feet high alongside one wall, and supported at the outer edge with strong posts, formed a bedstead. Sometimes hemlock boughs were the only bed. . . . The chinks of the logs were filled with moss and mud, and in the autumn banked up outside for warmth.

The friendly Indians doubtless assisted these early settlers from Plymouth during their first months along the Connecticut. They gave them maize to be dried and eaten during bitter months of storm and cold. They probably led them to good fishing places in the river and brought game to them. But Nature, herself, was so overwhelming in her abundance in this fruitful river valley that the autumn harvest, which grew all about them, must have been eagerly gathered.

There were countless wild berries and roots to be dried and stored. When the first snow covered the land it was easy to track deer. The forests abounded in flocks of wild birds, and the river was filled with fish. In the rich, golden autumn of this riverside paradise it seemed to the settlers, freshly arrived from Plymouth, that they could never again know hunger and misery. Here, where the forests held great herds of deer; where the wild turkeys came in golden, purple and bronze flocks; where the river teemed with salmon and shad; where wild ducks gathered by hundreds; where the trees were hung with wild fruits and with nuts; and where the very grass supplied roots and herbs that were edible—how could they ever have to face hunger again?

And besides all these things there was the Indian's wonderful maize; there was wild honey stored in hollow tree trunks; and there was the marvelous sap of the "sugar tree." Yes, surely, this was a land that flowed with milk and honey!

When the next spring should come, the Indians would help them plant their crops. They would give them seed corn to plant upon the broad, fertile pocconocks. They would cultivate great plantings of it. Perhaps they would plant other seeds too. Ships coming from England in the spring would bring all manner of necessary things. Sailing sloops and canoes would bring cargoes from the big ships through the shallow inlet. They would stop by the little settlement on the beautiful river in the Valley of Plenty.

It is not surprising that these Pilgrim pioneers felt that here at last they had found something that might prove permanent in their lives. "Home," which long had been only a memory, might once again become a reality.

That their fond hopes were dashed, not by the Dutch nor by the lurking Pequot tribes—enemies of the Indians who were befriending them—but by their own countrymen was a bitter irony, which fortunately they could not foresee.

CHAPTER III

From Red to White

NOT QUITE two years after the Plymouth immigrants had settled on the lands along the Connecticut, they began to be troubled by increasing evidence of a real estate boom. It was far from being a home enterprise.

In a letter dated July, 1635, Jonathan Brewster, one of the leaders of the struggling settlement, told about his growing uneasiness over the almost daily arrival of newcomers to that particular portion of the Connecticut shore. What especially troubled him was the fact that they wanted to occupy the very same land which he and his companions had chosen.

To explain the situation fully it will be necessary to note what had been taking place in the Bay Colony among those people who, according to Governor Winthrop's earlier statement, had not thought it fit to meddle with the Connecticut River proposition.

Three towns near Boston were chiefly concerned: Dorchester, Newtown (later Cambridge), and Watertown. Each of these towns was, generally speaking, composed of a congregation which had come to the Bay Colony led by its minister. Newtown's minister did not arrive to join his people until they had been there for a year. When he did arrive difficulties started almost immediately—difficulties arising from the potent theories and convictions that filled his brain.

The Reverend Thomas Hooker had no little acquaintance with church troubles even before he had come to America. He had been educated at Emmanuel College, Cambridge, the "nursery of Puritanism." From the time of his graduation he had gathered a dissenting congregation about him. They were attracted by his learning and his brilliant preaching.

After several enforced changes in parish he had to flee to Holland. It was the congregation he had gathered together there that preceded him to Newtown in the Bay Colony. Such was his reputation among the Established Churchmen in England that when the time came for him to sail from an English port he had to resort to subterfuge to escape their detaining hands.

Now, it must be kept well in mind that all the people who came to New England came because, above all else, they wished to set up a *theocracy*. The church was their state. Of course, it was inevitable that they should still be subject to the royal government. They had to admit that their rights depended upon a charter, of some kind, from the king. It was a bitter pill, but one that must be swallowed. Some swallowed it less easily than others. And Thomas Hooker swallowed it with pain.

All settlers who came here, as groups or colonies, already had some kind of written instrument, which provided the general plans and limits under which they could make their own laws: (1) There were the patents, or charters, given to companies of adventurers. (2) There were the royal patents given to proprietors of several kinds. (3) There were the royal charters constituting a colony as a direct act of the king's prerogative.

It should, also, be remembered that all the settlers at Plymouth had to begin with, as their written instrument, were the letters patent to the Plymouth Company. The Pilgrims at Plymouth were in a peculiarly uncertain position because, by reason of landing "off-course" in New England rather than in lower Virginia as had been their intention, they found themselves without any valid instrument. New England was under the jurisdiction of the London Company. This left them with no basis of authority to settle there, which must have made them feel doubly strangers in a strange land. They immediately took the only course possible. They drew up the Mayflower Pact as an instrument to provide for their government until their settlement in New England could be confirmed by the company.

The Bay Colony came to Massachusetts with a direct charter from the crown. But they came to establish church government in which the ministers actually exercised the sovereignty, if not directly, at least by influence. The great significance of this fact was that inevitably *the type of control in a congregation eventually made the mold for the kind of government that would develop*. It also followed that the kind of control in the congregation would suit the kind of creed that particular congregation professed.

Under Calvinism there were two general types of control of congregations: (1) control by elders, as followed in the strict Presbyterian church; (2) control by the congregation at large, who elected certain church officers.

Calvinism's hatred for prelacy arose from the fact that

the whole theory of origin of authority was different in an Episcopal form of government. The bishops exercised the authority, but they were not elected by anybody in a congregation. Theoretically, their authority came to them by the laying on of hands and descended directly from Christ through St. Peter. In England this laying on of hands was controlled by the crown and Parliament, who, therefore, actually appointed those in authority in the church.

The Calvinists claimed to have gone back to a more primitive type of Christianity when the church was ruled by presbyters. The Congregationalists made another change and went a little further. They directly elected and controlled their ministers. This was what made the different New England colonies so different in their types of church government—hence, of government. But they were all varying forms of theocracies.

To Thomas Hooker, minister of Newtown, the evident connection between a crown-granted charter and the people it affected was that inevitably their rights and their church would take color from that connection. All of his past experience and all of his Puritan conviction led him to hate the situation and to become intent upon the idea of seeking a new location where he might establish the type of theocracy he believed in.

And so it happened that he had not been settled over his American flock many months when his influence began to be felt in the three townships of Newtown, Dorchester, and Watertown. Boston soon became aware of something hostile in the attitude of these three congregations. Not only did they have minor grievances, but certain fundamental differences of opinion in matters of the church, and hence of government, became more and more evident.

These opposing attitudes were made plain by statements by John Cotton, the Boston divine who had come over on the boat with Thomas Hooker, and by Governor Winthrop of Massachusetts. John Cotton came out flatly with the statement: "Democracy is no fit government for church or commonwealth." Governor Winthrop found it necessary to expostulate with Thomas Hooker about "the unwarrantableness and unsafeness of referring matters of council or judicature to the body of the people, quia the best part is always the least, and the best part, the wisest part, is always the lesser."

Replying, Hooker laid down certain fundamentals as he saw them: "I fully assent to those staple principles which you set down; to wit: that the people should choose some from amongst them—that they should refer matters of council to their councillors; matters of judicature to their judges; only the question here grows—what rule the judges must have to judge by; secondly who these councillors must be."

He then made a plea for a set of laws upon which judgment might be based: "That in the matter that is referred to the judge, the sentence should lie in his breast, or be left to his discretion according to which he should go, I am afraid it is a course wants both safety and warrant."

Citing Biblical authority for his demand for a body of law to govern courts, he continues: "Reserving smaller matters, which fall in occasionally in common course, to a lower council, in matters of great consequence, which concern the common good, a general council, chosen by all, I conceive, under favor, most suitable to rule, and most safe for the relief of the whole."

It would appear that the type of theocracy favored by

John Cotton and Governor Winthrop was of the kind in which elders or presbyters held control over the congregation; and that when it came to theorizing about government and law their ideas flowed in the same channel.

Hooker's viewpoint concerned a theocracy in which control was held by the congregation itself. Government and law, following this course, would be representative of the rights of the people as a whole.

With such opposing ideas applied to church and commonwealth, it became increasingly evident to all that living in too close proximity to one another would be difficult. In less than a year Mr. Hooker asked permission to withdraw his congregation to another location.

The reasons given for this request, as presented to the High Court, the governing body of Massachusetts, do not mention any differing opinions upon theocratic government. The people simply stated that they wanted more room for their cattle; and the High Court granted the permission to move west.

Agawam—now Springfield, Massachusetts—was investigated, but before any action was taken news came of the decimation of the Indians all along the Connecticut by the ravages of smallpox. At once another petition was put before the High Court. This time the reason for desired removal was enlarged. They not only needed more room, but the lands along the Connecticut were advantageous because of their fertility and their occupation by the people of Newtown would forestall settlement by the Dutch, and also by other Englishmen. Probably their most cogent reason was the last one they gave: "The strong bent of our spirits to remove thither."

Desirable as heading off other settlers from this fruitful valley might be, Governor Winthrop hesitated to allow the departure of so large a group, and permission for withdrawal was withheld after a day of fasting and prayer. However, the next spring Dorchester and Watertown groups were allowed to go, and by autumn, without any formal action on the part of the authorities, the people of Newtown also set out for the river valley. They had unexpectedly had the chance to sell out their local holdings to a group of newcomers to the Massachusetts settlements.

Now we may return to Jonathan Brewster and his group from Plymouth, who had been establishing their settlement along the river. It was a band of intruding settlers, under Roger Ludlow from Dorchester, who were the chief cause of trouble.

They began coming in the spring of 1633 and continued to appear in increasing numbers during the summer and fall. By then they had come into serious conflict with the people from Plymouth. These, quite naturally, looked upon the insistance of the newcomers that they had a right to settle upon land which the Plymouth group already had bought, paid for, and cleared with great effort as unfair and illegal.

Brewster argued that the Massachusetts Bay people had forfeited their chance at the land when they had refused to go into partnership with them, when first invited to do so. The flimsy excuse of the Dorchester people was that it was wicked to allow so much land to go to waste. Finally the harassed Plymouth group were forced to a very one-sided compromise by sheer weight of opposing numbers. In submitting, Brewster wrote: "The unkindness was not soon forgotten."

In October, 1635, more Dorchester people arrived and a few came from Newtown. An unusually hard winter forced many of these to abandon their partially finished cabins, and with no little suffering they returned to the shelter of their old homes in Massachusetts. Those who remained endured misery—especially the Dorchester group—living on the land they had taken from the Pilgrim settlers.

The next spring, the hardships forgotten, the real movement to the river got under way. At once the matter of titles became important. Leaving any claims of the Dutch out of consideration for the time, the land along the Connecticut had been included in the New England grant (by the king) to the Council for New England in the charter of 1620. Supposedly this southern part had been granted by the Council, two years later, to a group of Puritan Lords and Gentlemen, who were preparing a haven for themselves in case things grew too unpleasant for them in England.

While there is little evidence to show that this patent was ever really issued, there is no doubt that the grantees— Lord Saye and Sele, Lord Brooke, Lord Rich, Sir Richard Saltonstall, John Pym, and John Hampden and others, as well as many in the territory in question, believed fully in its validity.

When the settlers began to come into the valley the representative of these patentees, John Winthrop, Jr., who had been appointed as their governor, demanded that the settlers acknowledge the title he represented. They were quite willing to do this as it immediately served as a means to free them from the sovereignty of Massachusetts, and gave them title to land of their own, a fact which Thomas Hooker must have learned of with deep satisfaction.

By agreement with Massachusetts they had a right to look after their own affairs. In the matter of choosing a governor for themselves or accepting John Winthrop, Jr., they

waited for more than a year. Thus Connecticut had no governor during the first year of its existence.

Besides the settlers who had come to the Connecticut River from the Massachusetts towns of Dorchester, Watertown and Newtown, there was another group who had come from Roxbury. This party was led by William Pynchon. They settled at Agawam. For a while they carried on their affairs with their neighbors of the other towns, but two years later, when they found that their land really lay within the jurisdiction of the Massachusetts Bay Colony, they severed relations with the Connecticut group.

The great migration in the summer of 1636 was especially important. It was then that Thomas Hooker and his Newtown congregation moved across the well-worn trail to the river. Once at the river they turned southward and set themselves down at what now is Hartford. They drove their cattle before them. While Mrs. Hooker traveled on a litter, her husband and his lay teacher, Samuel Stone, shared the hardships of the journey with the rest of the congregation.

Some were used to hardships, but for the pastor and his wife and teacher, the outdoor life of the trail, the dense shade of the far-reaching forest with its unknown dangers, was something of a test. The arrival at the river and the sight of smoke rising from friendly fires must have brought joy and thankfulness to the hearts of the weary travelers.

By late autumn these three settlements along the river and the one farther up at Agawam were firmly established. We can tabulate them for convenience as follows:

Windsor—the earliest settled—made up of the group migrating from Plymouth, and later of the congregation from Dorchester.

Wethersfield—settled at about the same time as Windsor—made up of the congregation migrating from Watertown.

Springfield (Agawam)—next settled—by the group from Roxbury under the leadership of William Pynchon.

Hartford—last settled—made up of the congregation from Newtown led by Thomas Hooker.

When their year under the home-authorized commission was ended, the Connecticut towns severed their relations with their original home towns of Dorchester, Watertown, and Newtown and became Windsor, Wethersfield, and Hartford. Agawam, it was later discovered, was in a different situation owing to the land belonging within the jurisdiction of Massachusetts.

They, with Agawam, now sent three delegates each to represent them in a General Court at Hartford. Thus they began immediately to govern themselves.

At once the leaders stood out. Chief among them was Thomas Hooker, who had brought to the river something much more valuable than a desire to build a prosperous trading post, though he was not averse to that. He had in his mind the establishment of a theocracy which would be much more liberal in its affairs than that of Massachusetts. The ideas he had expressed in his debates with John Cotton and Governor Winthrop might now take form.

When the delegates met at Hartford there were nearly a thousand people settled along the river. At Hartford the settlement centered around the church. This was a temporary structure, later given to Mr. Hooker for a barn. After a time better meetinghouses took the place of the cruder ones, but from the beginning these buildings served not only for worship but also as town meeting places.

Near the meetinghouse were the market and those accessories considered necessary for the enforcement of law and order: the stocks, the pillory, the whipping post, and gaol. In civil as well as religious matters, punishment for wrongdoing was considered the greatest incentive to right living.

Punishment, not hereafter but now, was evident to any attendant at Mr. Hooker's church. The results of evil, expounded by him and Mr. Stone, could be plainly seen when the listeners departed from the service. For it was during meeting time that the culprits were given their punishment.

According to the law: "He is to be sette on, a lytle before the beginning [of church service] & to stay thereon a lytle after the end." On a Sunday churchgoers might have been edified by the sight of one Walter Gray being publicly corrected for "labouring to inuegle the affections of Mr. Hoocker's Mayde." Perhaps these public lessons in morality, fully as much as the eloquence of the preachers, may have accounted for the large attendance at public worship in those days.

While these thoughts of a more representative theocracy were occupying the mind of Thomas Hooker, the average settler in the three towns along the river was concerned with the land and its cultivation. But up at Agawam, dominated by another forceful personality, there were constantly increasing plans for trade along the river. These plans, carried forward, ultimately built the small settlement of Agawam into a center of trade and still later into the great industrial city of Springfield, Massachusetts.

The man who had this commercial vision for the little

settlement was William Pynchon. He and his son John seem to some extent to have dominated the river trade for years. William was the man who had first spied out the land around Agawam as an especially advantageous spot for settlement. It was here that he led the group of people from the Bay Colony who had Deacon Chapin (in his vast Puritan cloak) as their spiritual leader.

Two years after their coming to Agawam they received the rather disconcerting news (as has already been mentioned) that, according to correct boundary lines, they were not, after all, within the Connecticut colony. It thus became necessary for William Pynchon and his companions to set up a more or less independent government for themselves under the eye of Massachusetts. This they did despite the vigorous protests of Thomas Hooker.

Apparently it was admitted that Agawam might lie within the rather uncertain western boundary of the Massachusetts patent, but the Connecticut towns felt that the fact that Agawam had participated in the general election held in 1638 bound them to their Connecticut neighbors.

In writing to John Winthrop, Sr., governor of Massachusetts, Thomas Hooker spoke his mind about William Pynchon. Referring to the election of 1638, held at Hartford, he points out that:

The committees from the town of Agawam came in with other towns and chose their magistrates, installed them into their government, took oath of them for the execution of justice according to God, and engaged themselves to submit to this government, and the execution of justice by their means, and dispensed by the authority which they put upon them by choice . . . If Mr. Pynchon can devise ways to make his oath bind him when he will, and loose him when he list; if he can tell how, in faithfulness, to engage himself in civil covenant and combination (for that he did by his committees by his act) and yet can cast it away at his pleasure, before he give in sufficient warrent more than his own word and will, he must find a law in Agawam for it; for it is written in no law or gospel that I ever read.

Edwin Bacon calls attention to more of this letter in which the Reverend Thomas Hooker seems quite to enjoy laying out the Bay people for the way they have treated the new settlements along the river. If his sermons were as alive as this letter is, few of his flock would have been likely to fall asleep. He goes on to say:

I confess that my head grows gray and my eyes dim, yet I am sometimes in the watchtower; and if the quaere be, Watchman, what is the night, as the prophet speaks, I shall tell you what I have observed, and shall be bold to leave my complaints in your bosom, of what is beyond question. . . . What I shall write are not forged imaginations and suppositions carved out of men's conceits, but that which is reported and cried openly and carried by sea and land. Secondly, my aim is not any person, nor intendment to charge any particular with you; because it is the common trade that is driven among multitudes with you, and with which the heads and hearts of passengers come loaded hither, and that with grief and wonderment; and the conclusion that is arrived at from these reproaches and practices is this, that we are a forlorn people, not worthy to be succored with company and so neither with support.

I will particularize. If enquire be, What be the people of Connecticut? the reply is, Alas, poor rash-headed creatures, they rushed themselves into a war with the heathen, and so had we not rescued them at so many hundred charges, they had been utterly undone. In all which you know there is not a true sentence; for we did not rush into the war [war with the Pequot tribes], and the Lord himself did rescue before friends.

If, after much search made for the settling of the people and nothing suitable found to their desires but toward Connecticut; if then they will needs go from the Bay, go any whither, be any where, choose any place, any patent—Narragansett, Plymouth—only go not to Connecticut. We hear and bear.

Immediately after the winter, because there was likelihood that multitudes would come over, and lest any should desire to come hither, then there is a lamentable cry raised, that all their cows at Connecticut are dead, and that I have lost nine and only one left and that was not likely to live (when I never had but eight and they never did better than last year). We hear still and bear.

And lest haply some men should be encouraged to come because of any subsistance and continuance here, then the rumor is noised that I am weary of my station; or if I did know whither to go, or my people what way to take, we would never abide; where as such impudent forgery is scant found in hell; for I profess I know not a member of my congregation but sits down well apayd with his portion, and for myself, I have said what now I write: if I was to choose I would be where I am.

But notwithstanding all this the matter is not sure, and there is some fear that some men will come toward Connecticut when ships come over; either some have related the nature of the place or some friends invited them; and therefore care must be taken, and is by this generation, as soon as any ship arrives, that persons haste presently to board them, and when no occasion is offered or question propounded for Connecticut, then their pity to their countrymen is such that they cannot but speak the truth: Alas, do you think to go to Connecticut? Why do you long to be undone? If you do not, bless yourself from thence; their upland will bear no corn, their meadows nothing but weeds, and the people are almost all starved. Still we hear and bear.

But may be these sudden expressions will be taken as words of course, and therefore vanish away when once spoken. Let it therefore be provided that the inkeepers entertain their guests with invective against Connecticut, and those are set on with the salt, and go off with the voyder. If any hear and stay, then they are welcomed; but if these reports cannot stop a man's proceeding from making trial, they look at him as a Turk, or as a man scant worthy to live. Still we hear and bear. . . .

That's in New England: but send over a watch a little into Old England; and go we there to the Exchange, the very like trade is driven by persons which come from you, as though there was a resolved correspondence held in this particular; as the master and the merchant who came this last year to Seabrook Fort related, even to my amazement, there is tongue-battle fought upon the Exchange by all the plots that can be forged to keep passengers from coming, or to hinder any from sending a vessel to Connecticut, as proclaimed an utter impossibility.

Sir, he wants a nostril that feels not and scents not a schismatical spirit in such a framer of falsifying relations to gratify some persons, and satisfy their own ends. Do these things argue brotherly love? Do these issue from spirits that either pity the necessities of their brethern, or would that the work of God should prosper in their hands? or rather argue the contrary. If these be the ways of God, or that the blessing of God do follow them, I never preached God's ways nor knew what belonged to them. . . . Worthy Sir, these are not jealousies which we needlessly raise; they are realities which passengers daily relate, we hear and we bear; and I leave them in your bosom; only I confess I feel it my duty, and I do privately and publicly pray against such wickedness; and the Lord hath want to hear the prayers of the despised.

While this letter strays from the Agawam question and anticipates some of our story's events (as in the reference to Connecticut's war with the Pequots), it explains how Thomas Hooker could differ violently with his fellows and yet keep their affection. For this he did. His perfect frankness was disarming, and the refrain "Still we hear and bear" makes it probable that he had a faculty for presenting his case in a manner to stir the consciences of his opponents.

But no arguments moved Massachusetts' determination to keep Agawam, and William Pynchon seemed satisfied to go on in his more or less free way.

His way was to keep his eye on the river and on the

canoes that glided down it loaded with rich furs. The Indians, coming from their northern hunting grounds, either maneuvered the Swift Water below Agawam, or carried their canoes around it. Pynchon, watching them, observed that they always made their camp at a point of land just south of the Swift Water. That point, he decided, was the best place to build a warehouse and to start trade on a substantial scale.

It wasn't long before the great warehouse was built and crammed full of goods. Likewise it wasn't long before the point where it stood became known as Warehouse Point.

Somewhat south of the Agawam settlement William Pynchon also built a fort that should protect the trading post. In the little village houses began to be built. Presently it comprised forty dwellings. William Pynchon's was the only one built of brick. The rest were wooden, mostly with thatched roofs. The Pynchon house was the principal one of the three fortified houses in the town. They spread along a single thoroughfare, later the main street of the settlement.

There lived courageous, hardheaded men upon whom William Pynchon depended. At first it was the Reverend John Moxon who accompanied the group, but presently Deacon Samuel Chapin appeared also to keep an oversight of their spiritual welfare. So powerful a figure did he prove, in Agawam annals, that he has been immortalized as "The Puritan" by Saint-Gaudens's statue, which stands in Springfield today.

Things in Agawam were too absorbing for William Pynchon to feel any great concern because Thomas Hooker, down at Hartford, was indignant that he should be withdrawing from the Connecticut towns and managing things pretty much as he chose at Agawam.

While using the river mostly for his trading enterprises, Pynchon did quite a business in cattle, which were driven overland to New London, Connecticut. Owing to the small number of ships, lacking largely because of the scarcity of capital, most of the trading was confined to what could be carried on by small boats, which took goods to Boston and brought back the river settlement's needs. Exports besides the beaver skins, which were in great demand, were pipe staves and provisions. These were taken not only to England, but to the West Indies where they were exchanged for sugar and molasses. That later was made into rum for which there was a ready market, not only at home but in New Amsterdam and Boston as well.

A Hartford storekeeper's books show a variety of trade in 1647. It also is clear that his profits were not always certain. There are such items as: "In skins and debts upon a voyage to Virginia, in anno 1647, yet due 67." or: "In oyle, soape, vinegar, and other goods for Delawar, ye last year 30." Several other entries end with the words: "which are haserdous" or "very haserdous." His inventory includes a variety of things, which suggests that the wants of the early settlers were not altogether few or simple. There are: ammunition, various skins, hoes, hatchets, shoes, nails, pins, paper, shot, fishhooks, blades, looking glasses, pewter, bottles, brass ladles, bells, thimbles, boxes, knives, scissors, combs, jew's-harps and brass kettles.

Other towns on the river had storehouses but none was as active as the one on Warehouse Point. The genius of William Pynchon and his sons seems to have overcome the difficulties that kept other centers of trade from developing so rapidly. And of these difficulties, which beset both the older and the newer settlements along the river, the chief, outside of disease and the elements, was the menace of warrior Indians.

When the elected delegates met in Hartford, with the six assistants, most of whom had been members of the Massachusetts-appointed commission and were experienced in matters of colonial government as carried on by the Bay Colony, they at once tackled the Indian problems confronting them. They found themselves facing the need for united action against the Pequot Indians, who were threatening to retake the lands the new settlers had bought from the original owners, the Mohegans.

One other plantation on the river now joined the upriver forces against the Red Threat. This was Saybrook Fort, the small settlement at the mouth of the river, established under the patent granted to the Lords and Gentlemen and represented (as will be recalled) by John Winthrop, Jr. This group, planning on unpleasant eventualities in England for the Puritans, had grandiose schemes of palatial mansions to be built on the heights above the river. To head off any further encroachments by the Dutch (doubtless they had noted the Wouter Van Twiller sign nailed to a tree, as well as other Dutch activities) they had sent out an engineer to look over conditions. Under John Winthrop's supervision he built a fort at what is now Saybrook Point.

To this fort came the forces sent out under orders from the Hartford Council. They joined Gardiner, the fort's commander, in an expedition against the Pequots. This newly gathered force comprised ninety men—half the military strength of the towns—under the leadership of Captain John Mason of Windsor. Both the leader of the upriver towns and Gardiner at the fort felt that the Massachusetts Bay Colony government was really responsible for the uprising of the Pequots, but action was necessary—wherever the blame lay—if the settlements along the river were to survive.

The expedition was successful. The Pequots' village was destroyed, and with it most of its four hundred men, women, and children. A later action against the remnants of the Pequots was equally victorious. The Pequot menace was removed from the valley forever.

However, embers from these fires smoldered, to break out in menacing flames along the river fifty years later.

CHAPTER IV

Thomas Hooker Plants New Seed Along the River

THE leading spirit in the civil affairs of the three river towns of Connecticut was Thomas Hooker. With John Haynes, also of Hartford, and Roger Ludlow, of Windsor, he had been working on a plan for the frame of government they would deem best when the troubles with the Pequots had demanded their attention. That menace having been (as they supposed) completely settled, they once more turned to drafting a system of laws and government for the new colony of Connecticut. The general opinion seems to be that the moving spirit was Thomas Hooker, while the documents eventually drawn up show the legal hand of Ludlow.

The first gun in the campaign was fired by Thomas Hooker from his pulpit before the assembled General Court. In this sermon he undertook to outline in a general way his conception of the form and purposes of government.

Since some historians have considered this statement, and the final development of a form of government resulting from it, as most important in the evolution of American Democracy, we present all that is extant of this epoch-making address.

Hooker's sermon was not preserved, but Dr. Benjamin Trumbull's discovery of some notes taken by a contemporary gives us the general outline.

Doctrines:

1. That the choice of public magistrates belongs to the people by God's own allowance.

2. The privilege of election, which belongs to the people, therefore must be exercised not according to their humors but according to the blessed will and law of God.

3. They who have the power to appoint officers and magistrates have it in their power also to set the bounds and limitations of the authority and place of those whom they call.

Reasons:

1. Because the foundation of authority is laid, firstly, in the free consent of the people.

2. Because by a free choice the hearts of the people will be more inclined to the love of the persons (chosen), and more ready to yield (obedience).

In these doctrines and reasons we can clearly observe a point stressed in the preceding chapter; namely, that it was theocracy, primarily, and not democracy that the colonists of the period were bent upon establishing; and that they came to establish Church government in which the ministers actually exercised the sovereignty—if not directly, at least by in-

fluence. It is also very clear, in this particular case of Thomas
Hooker and his sermon to the General Court of Connecticut,
that the type of control he favored in his own congregation
was to be made the mold for the kind of civil government
that would be decided upon for the new settlement.

Just how much of a stir these pronouncements aroused,
it is hard to tell. The men in Hartford had been sent there by
the freemen of the several towns as their representatives. No
doubt they knew something of what was in the wind, although the average citizen was too engrossed with his struggle
to get established in the new colony to pay much attention
to such matters.

In the autumn of the same year—1638—the final draft,
embodying the principles set forth by the Reverend Thomas
Hooker seven months before, was given to the commissioners.
The following January it was adopted by them as the form
of government under which they should live.

This "first written constitution known to history that
created a government" has come down in history as "The
Fundamental Orders of Connecticut." Many students of government have put this document down as the initial step
taken in this country toward democracy and the basis of our
constitution. But, as was earlier explained, all new groups,
or colonies, had some instrument bestowed upon them by
patent or charter which indicated the means and extent by
which and to which they were to be allowed to make their
own laws. Since Connecticut was free of the authority of
the Bay Colony, bestowed by royal charter, it was incum-
bent upon it to frame its own instrument—or constitution—
and this followed along the lines of Thomas Hooker's particular conception of a more liberal theocracy; although there

is reason to believe that it was Roger Ludlow who, actually, was the author of the Orders.

Mr. George M. Dutcher, of the Committee on Historical Publications, under the Tercentenary Commission of the State of Connecticut (in 1934), has this to say:

Among the many valuable records preserved in the office of the secretary of the state at Hartford none is more precious than the volume containing the earliest minutes of the General Court of Connecticut from April 1636 to December 1649. Consequently there exists no contemporary official account, and there is no contemporary unofficial one, of the circumstances attending the adoption of the Fundamental Orders on January 14, 1639. The Orders as reproduced [here] are taken from pages 220 to 227 of this same volume of records where they were entered, at an unknown date, in the handwriting of Thomas Welles, secretary of the Colony, 1641-1648. The only early manuscript copy of the Orders to survive appears in the second volume of General Court records, but is incomplete, dates from 1650 or later, and shows some amendment of the original text. The Orders seem to have been first printed in two scarce works, the first issued at New Haven in 1804 and the other at Hartford in 1822.

In the minutes for the General Court for December 1, 1645, appears the following phrase: ". . . the generall Orders formerly made by this Court . . ." There can be little doubt that this statement means the Fundamental Orders were adopted by the General Court and not by an assembly of "all the free planters" as Reverend Benjamin Trumbull declared, on what authority cannot be surmised, in his valuable HISTORY OF CONNECTICUT written more than a century and a half after the event. As at least eight of the members of the General Court in 1645, including the secretary, Thomas Welles, were probably members in 1639, the statement would seem to afford authentic first-hand evidence.

It has been customary to ascribe the general character and content of the Orders to Reverend Thomas Hooker of Hartford, who preached before the General Court on May 31, 1638, a memorable sermon on the text, Deuteronomy 1:13 [Take you wise men, and understanding, and known among your tribes, and I will make them rulers over you] which is presumed to have presaged the Orders. The legal phrasing of the Orders on the other hand indicates the work of one trained not in divinity but in law. So far as is known the one individual at that time resident in the three Connecticut River towns who possessed such training was Roger Ludlow of Windsor, to whom it may be presumed the actual authorship of the Orders should be credited. To what extent Hooker and Ludlow may have conferred and cooperated, and what contribution, if any, was made from other sources can only be pure surmise. The earliest recorded use of the phrase "Fundamental Orders" to designate this document is found in the minutes of the General Court for November 10, 1643. The Fundamental Orders, with some amendment, served the settlers of Connecticut as their constitution until they received the charter from Charles II in 1662.

There seems to have been no question whatever about the sovereignty that was to rule in the colony of Connecticut. No mention was made of any except that which came from the people themselves. There is not a word about fealty to England, nor to Massachusetts. The three small towns on the west bank of the quiet river, little more than plantations with a total popualtion of less than a thousand souls, stepped out alone, to all intents, as an independent republic.

By their fundamental document only the governor was required to be a church member. This was a step away from the type of theocratic control exercised in Massachusetts. There only church members in good and regular standing had the franchise.

However, in spite of this progressive omission, there were other ways by which practically the same end was accomplished.

Voters were admitted by each town by the consent of the body of voters, and restrictions on those eligible for admission included what seems very like a demand for church membership. On becoming voting citizens they had to take an oath that they held orthodox, trinitarian beliefs and were neither atheists, Quakers, nor Jews. The very preamble to the constitution included recognition of churchly control. It states as the object of the instrument "to maintain and preserve the liberty and purity of the Gospel of our Lord Jesus Christ, which we now profess, as also the discipline of the churches, which according to the truth of said Gospel, is now practiced among us."

If the legal phrasing of the Orders indicates the work of one not trained in divinity but in the law—such a one as Roger Ludlow—then it would appear that the phrasing of this preamble to the Orders likewise indicates the work of one not trained in law but in divinity—such a one as the Reverend Thomas Hooker.

Furthermore, the very evident fact of the most intimate connection between religion and every act of living, as set forth in the Orders, makes it seem probable that separation of the church from government was never contemplated. It would certainly seem strange that believers in the total depravity of the individual and the salvation of the few would feel safe in giving the unregenerate any considerable power in government. The few saved ones were not going to turn things over to the sinners.

Discounting all the fervid pronouncements of some of the earlier historians in regard to the Fundamental Orders and their intentional democracy, we still have something which was a decided advance over the closely controlled government of the mother colony in Massachusetts. James Truslow Adams points this out. He says: "American thought has been moulded to a very great extent by two ideals: unre-

stricted competition in exploiting the resources of the continent, and of a democracy fostered by the semi-isolated and
self-reliant life of the frontier . . ." He continues to show that
these river settlements were the new frontier and that the
people coming to them were those who were unable to live
in the more restricted atmosphere of the older settlements.

Here, he says, "we are concerned with one of the earliest
manifestations of one of the most potent forces in American
history. The more tolerant attitudes of these groups, with a
few others of like nature, were really repudiations of the basic
ideas of the Bay Colony."

Much as we acknowledge the advance which the Connecticut colony was making in matters of theocratic government, we must not fail to realize that in questions of religious
tolerance she did not stand as first among the colonies. If we
turn to the pages of Charles and Mary Beard's *Basic History
of the United States* we find these illuminating paragraphs:

The first English colony in America to grant general religious
liberty as a matter of law and principle was an offshoot from
Massachusetts, at first called the Rhode Island and Providence
Plantations. It was not founded by settlers coming directly from
England but by inhabitants of Massachusetts who rebelled against
the teachings and practices of Puritan preachers and magistrates.
In 1636 Roger Williams, ordered to conform or get out, fled with
a few friends into the wilderness and founded the town of Providence at the head of Narragansett Bay. Two years afterward Anne
Hutchinson, also outlawed by the Puritan clergy of Boston for her
religious and general independence, took refuge with her companions for a while at Portsmouth on Rhode Island.

Both Roger Williams and Anne Hutchinson believed that the
government should not force any form of religion by law on anybody; that every person should be free to worship God according
to his conscience. This rule of broad tolerance, extended to Quakers
and Jews, was retained in the Providence and Rhode Island planta-

tions after all the townships were united in an independent colony —by charter from Charles II granted in 1663. It made Rhode Island unique among the colonies.

No such general religious liberty was permitted in the second offshoot from Massachusetts, the colony of Connecticut, founded at about the same time as Providence. The expedition of Puritans who built the towns of Hartford, Windsor, and Wethersfield in the Connecticut River Valley was led by a preacher rightly deemed broad-minded for his time, Thomas Hooker. But neither he nor his companions accepted the liberal toleration proclaimed by Roger Williams and Anne Hutchinson. Likewise strict in their views of religious discipline under government control were the Puritans who made settlements in New Haven and other places on Long Island Sound.

Before and after the two groups of towns were united in a single colony as Connecticut, under a charter granted by Charles II in 1662, the Congregational Church was the established church in each town, and it remained so established by law through the Revolution down to 1818. Catholics, Protestant dissenters of various kinds, especially Quakers, and even members of the Church of England encountered hostility in Connecticut. Immigrants, who were not Congregationalists in faith, filtered into the colony here and there, but full toleration and equality were not accorded to them as a matter of principle and law.

A wide, though not complete, religious toleration was adopted in Pennsylvania under the leadership of the Quaker proprietor, William Penn. By his faith Penn was committed to the principle that religion is a matter of the conscience of the individual and is not to be imposed on anybody by law and government officials. But from the beginning of his settlement in Philadelphia in 1682 Penn opened his colony only to immigrants who professed belief in God. As a proprietor Penn, like Lord Baltimore, was eager to have immigrants settling in his colony, buying farms carved out of the land granted to him by the King, and engaging in lucrative commerce. In his quest for settlers he made special efforts to encourage the migration of Scotch-Irish Presbyterians and German Protestants, a hardy folk with skills and crafts.[1]

[1] A BASIC HISTORY OF THE UNITED STATES, by Charles and Mary Beard, copyright 1944, reprinted by permission of Doubleday & Company, Inc.

Thomas Hooker's life was a short life in his Connecticut colony—only ten years. Yet those ten years were a goodly span as measured by the years allotted to the men or women either, who came to the frontier colonies when one considers how besieged they were by pestilence, drought, famine, fire, flood, and Indian wars.

From the days when he had been preaching to small groups of dissenters in England, Thomas Hooker had shown an ability to attract men by both his preaching and his personality. Judged by the standards of the present, his doctrine was narrow. Compared to the beliefs of the men in the Bay Colony, he was a liberal. Usually he was opposed to the ideas of John Cotton and Governor Winthrop. Yet he kept their friendship. In the important matters of dealing with the Indians he constantly advised the course that would make them friends—and this at a time when the Bay Colony leaders were taking the attitude that led inevitably to trouble.

In the trials for heresy, and the resulting punishments, Thomas Hooker was invariably inclined to the more liberal judgment. That he could be aroused to fierce anger, there is no question. But as one of his contemporaries said, "he had ordinarily as much control of his choler as a man has of a mastiff dog on a chain; he could let out his dog, and pull in his dog as he pleased."

When Thomas Hooker died in his home in Hartford in 1647, Governor Winthrop, who only a short time before had been carrying on an acrimonious debate with him over the separation of Springfield from the river group, wrote of him:

". . . who for piety, prudence, wisdom, zeal, learning and what else might make him serviceable in the place and time he lived in, might be compared with men of the greatest note."

CHAPTER V

The Lords and Gentlemen and the Dutch Leave the River

Not long after the three Connecticut towns had formed their political union under Thomas Hooker's theocratic leadership they became a part of an expansion movement which greatly enlarged the influence of the Fundamental Orders.

The settlement at the mouth of the river—Saybrook Fort—had played its part in the Pequot War and in heading off the Dutch from further settlements on the river. On the other hand, Saybrook as a settlement for a group of Lords and Gentlemen had turned out to be a complete failure; and this notwithstanding the fact that Lion Gardiner, who had built the fort under the supervision of John Winthrop, Jr., had worked feverishly to prepare the site for the expected personages of nobility and influential standing.

Lion Gardiner was an astute frontiersman and of hardy

physique, both of which attributes fitted him to deal with the problems presented by this wild holding at the mouth of the Connecticut River. His wife was a sturdy Dutchwoman whom he had married in Holland. She bore him two sons in the rude fort on Saybrook Point, and the elder was the first white child to be born in the Connecticut colony.

Gardiner was also a brave captain and he proved of invaluable assistance to Captain John Mason and his militia of ninety men who had gathered from the upper river towns to stamp out the menace of the Pequot Indians.

Of all the Lords and Gentlemen for whom Lion Gardiner had prepared, only George Fenwick had arrived in the summer of 1636. Perhaps it seemed so fair a spot to him then that his dreams of a home there, where he should eventually find peace and plenty, did not appear too sanguine. At all events he spent the months until autumn making plans for such a future. When the fall came he set sail for his estates in Northumberland. There he sold his properties and once more made arrangements to return to the river-mouth wilderness, which he called Saybrook in honor of Lords Saye and Brooke.

A number of other "figures of distinction" had made ample preparations to accompany Fenwick to the Saybrook Plantation. There was just one preparation they had failed to accomplish. That was some manner in which to avoid being detained by the powers in England, who were hot on the scent of these men suspected of treachery against the throne of Charles I.

There appears to be good reason to believe that among these men were Sir Arthur Hazelrigg, Sir Matthew Boynton, and the commoners Pym, Hampden and Cromwell. Several early writers have referred to the circumstances of their attempted journey to the Saybrook Plantation. Their authority is the reported story as given by Dr. George Bates, the personal physician of Charles I, Cromwell, and Charles II, respectively.

Fact or fiction, it is a picturesque tale and we may feel that it must have had considerable probability behind it since one of the most interesting paragraphs concerning it was written by Macaulay.

Cromwell, Hampden, and the rest had successfully embarked on one of the ships in a fleet of eight. It was the spring of 1638 and they were ready to set sail. Suddenly the vessels were ordered not to leave port. All the passengers, their belongings, and their provisions were put ashore. Macaulay's report of the event follows:

Hampden determined to leave England. Beyond the Atlantic Ocean a few of the persecuted Puritans had formed in the wilderness of the Connecticut a settlement which has since become a prosperous commonwealth . . . Lord Saye and Lord Brooke were the original projectors of this scheme of emigration. Hampden had been early consulted respecting it. He was now, it appears, desirous to withdraw himself beyond the reach of oppressors who, as he probably suspected, and as we know, were bent on punishing his manful resistance against tyranny. He was accompanied by his kinsman, Oliver Cromwell, over whom he possessed great influence, and in whom he alone had discovered under an exterior appearance of coarseness and extravagance, those great and commanding talents which were afterward the admiration and dread of Europe. The cousins took their passage on a vessel which lay in the Thames, and which was bound for North America. They were actually on board when an order of council appeared, by which the ship was prohibited from sailing. . . . Hampden and Cromwell remained; and with them remained the Evil Genius of the house of Stuart.

One historian of the Connecticut River valley remarks, "How wondrously different might history have read had

Cromwell got here, and established himself at the mouth of the River!"

At this time George Fenwick was still in England. It very probably was he who had made the arrangements for the passage of the Lords and Gentlemen as agent for the patentees. When the new Connecticut government was inaugurated he was still abroad. But sometime during the next summer he set sail for the Saybrook Plantation.

With him he brought his wife. Lady Alice was a gentlewoman, born Alice Apsley, the daughter of Sir Edward Apsley. She was widow of Sir John Boteler when she married "Master Fenwicke," who was a lawyer at Gray's Inn and a man of substance, the accounts say.

Their baby son, who also shared the voyage with them, was constantly the recipient of the combined attention of his lady mother and his two maiden aunts, who were accompanying their brother George and his wife upon this daring adventure into the colonial wilderness.

What must have been their sinking of heart when they viewed the wind-swept salty marshes of Saybrook, with the crude log fort, the seemingly endless stretches of unknown forest, and the river beyond!

But, delicately bred as they were, they were courageous. When the time came they settled themselves in what was described in 1641 as "a faire house well fortified."

Inside this fortified manor house Lady Alice and her sisters-in-law did their best to establish some of the features of their English home in a pioneer wilderness. Within the palisade they made a garden. They planted all the flowers known to the home gardens in England—those, at least, which they thought were hardy enough to survive the new climate. They had jealously guarded these packets of seeds in their journey across the ocean. They would surround the new home with constant reminders of the old one. As though any reminder was needed! And, also, in this palisaded manor house Lady Alice bore her husband two daughters. Births more difficult, we can imagine, than those of the two sons of Lion Gardiner by his robust Dutch wife.

But six years of hardships, terrors, and unassuaged loneliness finally took their toll. Shortly after the birth of her second daughter, Lady Alice died. She was too delicate a flower to stand transplanting in the bleak New England soil of Saybrook Plantation.

George Fenwick watched his wife laid in her grave inside the palisade. A great sandstone monolith was placed above the burying spot. Into the grave with her went all of George Fenwick's hopes and love for this new land. Despondent and heartsick he left his wife's grave in care of a friend, entrusted his children to his sisters, and went back to England never to return. He sold his rights to the land on Saybrook Point to the Hartford government.

Uncertain as those rights were, Hartford paid a flat sum for them and allowed George Fenwick the right to a tariff on all exports of certain commodities from the river for ten years.

As it happened, this tariff collection caused a short but wordy battle with Massachusetts when she, in retaliation, collected on goods from the river entering the bay. It was not long before a free-trade agreement was mutually accepted.

It is estimated that George Fenwick's total income from this source would not show any large amount of commerce on the river at that time.

Nearly three hundred years later it was necessary to open Lady Alice's tomb. Her bones were to be removed to the old burial ground on Saybrook Point. There, in earth which had once afforded her too stern a habitation, her dust could now mingle with that of seven generations of her descendants buried there. It seemed as though earth and time relented in their harshness. When the bones were disinterred, they were found completely enshrouded in the masses of her red-gold hair.

The amalgamation of the lower part of the Connecticut River group with the Hartford group became sure some years after Fenwick's departure. In 1661, at the time of the Restoration in England, John Winthrop, Jr., was governor of Connecticut. He was chosen as the colony's agent to present their petition to Charles II for a charter under the royal seal.

No more auspicious choice could have been made. He was Connecticut's foremost man. He had been governor of the colony in 1657. In 1658 he was deputy governor. In 1659 he was once more chosen governor, and continued in the executive office by annual election from that time until his death in 1676.

In culture he surpassed his remarkable father, we are told. He was a fellow of the Royal Society of Philosophical Transactions at its foundation in London. And this was in a day when modern science was little more than born. Dr. Benjamin Trumbull tells us that he "was amiable, large minded, and tactful in affairs"; and that he "noiselessly succeeded in all that he undertook" is vouched for by the American historian, George Bancroft.

His own father, Governor Winthrop of Massachusetts, spoke of him with pious satisfaction: "God gave him favor in the eyes of all with whom he had to do." And surely he seems to have been worthy of all these encomiums in relation to his approach to Charles II and his success in obtaining the desired royal charter for his colony of Connecticut.

In London he enlisted the powerful influence of Lord Saye and Sele (now the sole survivor of the noblemen who had held the Lords and Gentlemen's patent), and the Earl of Manchester, who was now chamberlain of the king's household.

The king, it is recorded, received him and the plea for a royal charter "with uncommon grace and favor." There is an engaging piece of legend in this connection which claims that John Winthrop, Jr., secured the genial and kindly attention of the king through an adroit and charming gesture of courtesy.

It appears that among his other possessions young Governor Winthrop owned a beautiful and remarkable ring. It had been given to his grandfather by King Charles I. John Winthrop, Jr., now slipped this ring from his hand and insisted upon presenting it, with its story, to Charles II. Whether or not this act was accountable for the king's finally deciding to give him the royal charter he desired for his colony, no one can say. It is, at any rate, a nice bit of legend.

He did secure the royal charter without any doubt. It passed the seals April 20, 1662, and confirmed to the Connecticut Colony the territory covered by the Lords and Gentlemen's patent and the right to govern themselves—precisely as they had been doing.

There seems to have been but one fly in the ointment of satisfaction accorded by the colony to this piece of news. And that fly buzzed around furiously from the summarily annexed colony at New Haven. The thriving group around New Haven was a tight little theocracy. Its protests now were loud. It termed itself "disfranchised," but it was of no avail. There was nothing to do but to come in under the new charter.

The charter seemed predestined to be a source of discord even after those days when it first aroused such a disturbance in New Haven. For it was the same charter that a quarter of a century later was hidden from Governor Andros of New York in the Charter Oak, and the historical duplicate of which is framed in wood from the historic tree and now is displayed at the Hartford State House.

Covering almost the exact period as that from the first ventures of the Lords and Gentlemen at Saybrook Plantation in 1633 until the granting of the royal charter to the colony of Connecticut in 1662 was the continually troubled life of the Dutch at the post of the House of Hope. There, on a point of land that was so soon to be encroached upon by Hartford, they maintained their fort amid the distresses they constantly received at the hands of the English.

It will be recalled that Wouter Van Twiller had anticipated trouble in 1633, although all his country's original approaches toward the English had been friendly. Had the Dutch not invited the English to the river? In sympathy they had extended the hand of compassionate friendship to the Pilgrims of Plymouth. "Seeing them seated in a barren quarter," they had urged them to come to the river they had discovered. There was space and plenty for all, they felt.

But the English had rebuffed the Dutch in regard to this invitation. When they did decide to accept, it was the result of secretly made decisions rather than of frank and open consultations with the Dutch. In fact it seems as though the original invitation was belatedly accepted in a shabby and uncordial fashion.

Wouter Van Twiller, having heard rumors of possible

settlement by the English at the mouth of the Connecticut and having been the recipient of a brusque letter from the governor of the Bay Colony as regarded encroaching on *English* holdings, sat down to take thought.

He must have found those thoughts decidedly troublesome and disillusioning. He represented a people who were by nature slow to anger, the entire intent of whom had been nonaggressive and friendly. It looked to him now as though the English did not wish to be friendly. By their rude neglect of his messages and by reason of their curt statements, it seemed as though they would not be averse to unpleasant eventualities.

Wouter Van Twiller arrived at the conclusion that he should be prepared for such eventualities. It will be recalled that hurrying to Saybrook Point he nailed a sign to a tree. It was a "Keep Off the Grass" sign although that was not exactly what it said. It said that these lands were the property of the United Netherlands.

He then made a trip up the river to what is now known as Dutch Point in the area of Hartford and conferred with the conquering Pequot Indians. From them he bought a parcel of land that commanded a fine and extended view of the river. Upon it he built a trading post. A little later he decided to fortify it and to maintain a garrison there. He called this fortified post, ironically enough, the House of Hope.

As the years went on and more and more English settlers came to the river, the hope that existed on Dutch Point was dashed and turned to bitterness. During all the fifteen years that the commanding officer and his garrison struggled against English encroachments, the Dutch never authorized any armed intervention that could have altered matters.

Either the United Netherlands believed that they were too hopelessly outnumbered by the English or they were too greatly absorbed in their other holdings in the New World to send any adequate help to the officers and garrison at the House of Hope. To threaten and protest was all they did.

The English settlers, like unruly and disobedient children who have learned that they may disregard the threats and admonitions of an easygoing, ineffectual parent, kept on in their own way.

That way was a hard and humiliating way for the inmates of the House of Hope. Immediately upon the setting up of the new colony of Connecticut in 1639 the English became even more obnoxious in their treatment of the Dutch. There were almost constant embroilments. Finally after the first inauguration in the colony had taken place a Dutch representative of importance visited the garrison at the House of Hope for the purpose of deriving some true impression of what the existing difficulties were and in the hope of arriving at some better understanding with the English neighbors on the river.

The man who came upon this mission was David Pietersen De Vries, who was a seasoned soldier and also a believer in colonial enterprises. He came up in his yacht from New Amsterdam, on a pleasant summer cruise, and conferred with the small garrison at the House of Hope and with their commissary Gysbert Op Dyke.

By this time the town of Hartford had taken a firm foothold in the Dutch domain. De Vries could see a fine church and over a hundred houses. Some of the English had plowed up the land about the fort for their own planting. Protests on the part of the soldiers had resulted in their being "cudgelled" by the determined farmers of Hartford.

De Vries could plainly see that this was a situation that called either for military strength or diplomacy. He chose the latter. He sought out Governor Haynes and called upon him. He was pleasantly received and invited to stay to dinner. In his journal he makes mention of what transpired:

"I told him that it was wrong to take by force the company's land which it had bought and paid for. He answered that the lands were lying idle; that though we had been there many years we had done scarcely anything; that it was a sin to let such rich land which produced such fine corn lie uncultivated; and that they had already built three towns upon the river in a fine country."

Whether De Vries really accepted these arguments as satisfactory does not appear. At all events things went on in the same frustrating fashion for the commissary. And the Hartford settlers continued in their attitude that possession was nine points of the law and that to have was to hold.

There is one entry in De Vries's journal which casts an interesting light on a previous description of the Reverend Thomas Hooker's church and the punishment of offending members of society—we doubt that they were members of the church—outside its doors.

Among the incidents which happened while I was here was that of an English ketch arriving here from the north with thirty pipes of Canary wine. There was a merchant with it, who was from the same city in England, as the servant of the minister of this town and was well acquainted with him. Now this merchant invited the minister's servant on board the vessel to drink with him; and it seems that the man became fuddled with wine, or drank pretty freely, which was observed by the minister. So they brought the servant to the church, where the post stood, in order to whip him. The merchant then came to me and requested me to speak to the

minister, as it was my fault that he had given wine to his countryman.

I accordingly went to the commander of our little fort, or
redoubt, and invited the minister and the governor, and other leading men with their wives, who were very fond of eating cherries;
as there were from forty to fifty cherry trees standing about the
redoubt, full of cherries, we feasted the minister and the governor, and their wives also came to us; and as we were seated at
the meal in the redoubt, I together with the merchant, requested
the minister to pardon his servant, saying that he probably had not
partaken of any wine for a year, and that such sweet Canary wine
would intoxicate any man. We were a long time before we could
persuade him; but their wives spoke favorably, whereby the servant
got free.

Meanwhile quarrels between the English and Dutch
farmers continued and ill will on both sides grew, well seasoned by self-will on the part of the English and the necessity to accept the situation willy-nilly on the part of the
Dutch; for still the party at the House of Hope received no
real support from their superiors in New Amsterdam and
Holland. Ground which the Dutch prepared for planting was
seized during the night and sown with corn by the English
and thereafter held by them. Standing peas were cut down
and the earth planted with corn instead. The ropes of a plow
were cut in pieces and the plow was pitched into the river.
On the side of the House of Hope which faced the land they
built a high palisade so that entrance to it was blocked except from the water edge. The director of New Netherland
made a sharp protest, but only by word of mouth.

Trouble continued, and finally in 1642 David Provoost
was sent to take command of the fort at Dutch Point. Five
stormy years ensued and relations between the English of
Hartford and the Dutch at the fort became more and more

hostile. Now the New Netherland's director sent an order to the fort which prohibited all trade and commercial intercourse on the part of the Dutch with the people of Hartford. This, of course, was a purely retaliatory measure. As in any situation, when a basis of pure retaliation has been reached any constructive solution of the problem is practically impossible.

Later someone of a more reasoning turn of mind must have tried to take a hand in straightening out the snarl. Connecticut sent delegates, empowered by the General Court, to New Netherland to try to buy out the Dutch company's interest in the land around the fort. But by this time the Dutch had become bitterly stubborn. They clung to their rights and grievances as a dog to a bone. Nothing would persuade them to sell.

This attitude finally led Provoost to commit a rash act, compounded of defiance and compassion, in the face of the Hartford authority and law. He gave refuge to a captive Indian woman who had escaped from her owner. Refusing to agree to the demand of magistrates that he hand her over to the law he rushed into an armed brawl with the Hartford "watch" sent to enforce it.

Eventually the Dutch limits on the river were defined by a provisional treaty—the Hartford Treaty of 1650. This resulted from a friendly meeting, at last accomplished between Peter Stuyvesant and the council of the United Colonies at Hartford. Stuyvesant arrived from New Amsterdam with an impressive group of burghers to support him. The Dutch, nevertheless, got the little end of the bargain and their "happy peace" did not last long.

In 1653 England and Holland were at war in the Old World. In the New, New Netherland and the Connecticut

Colony longed to be at each other's throats. There were all manner of unfounded rumors: the Dutch were plotting with the Indian tribes to destroy all the English settlements along the river; Stuyvesant was accused of complicity in the plot. After a fierce battle of charges and denials the little House of Hope was quietly abandoned.

In July there was news of peace between England and Holland. The treaty stipulated that each side should continue to hold what it had taken. Along the Connecticut River the English colonists had long since taken the area occupied by the Dutch. Their last foothold on the Beautiful River, discovered by their countryman Adriaen Block, was finally broken. Even the river assisted in closing the chapter. Long years of its flowing have worn away the site upon which the House of Hope once stood.

At the mouth of the Connecticut let us remember George Fenwick with his gentle dream of a transplanted feudal England; at Agawam, farthest north of those earliest settlements on the river, William Pynchon with his fond scheme of trade and enterprise; and at Hartford, about half way between Saybrook Point and Agawam, Thomas Hooker with his firm hope of a new form of government. Of them all Thomas Hooker proved the most profound.

CHAPTER VI

Settlements Spread Along the River

ALREADY the townspeople in Hartford, Windsor, Wethersfield, and Agawam thought of themselves as well established. They were no longer frontier settlers and pioneers in their own eyes. There were clapboarded and brick houses in their villages. White meetinghouses dominated the little communities, and a few comfortable household articles began to be procurable at stores and warehouses.

Everywhere they were clearing land and raising crops. Industry and hopefulness filled the air. The dread of Indian difficulties was pushed into the background. Had not Captain Mason, Lion Gardiner of Saybrook Fort, and their own brave men stamped out danger from the Pequots? That had been such an overwhelming victory that all fear of future danger could be discounted, they thought.

Their sons and daughters, with the hunger for land born in them, were most often the ones who moved to new frontiers to establish new homes. So the movement spread up the river from Agawam, and down the river from the three Connecticut towns. From these substantial little towns, where some white houses that were almost mansions had been built, went adventurous young people to live lives of danger and hardship in a wilderness not many miles away.

Much of the land above Agawam was controlled by a group of land speculators, including William Pynchon who was sure to have his hand in any promising project. He may have invested the profits accruing from the Warehouse Point enterprise in opening new areas such as Northampton and, later, Hadley. The sites of these two places had been bought from the Indians by Pynchon and his company of speculators. The Indians who had sold the land were apparently friendly and, although they had made a land transaction with the river whites, continued to live in the areas they had sold.

To Hadley goes the distinction of having entertained (for probably fifteen years) two men whose presence elsewhere was greatly desired by certain people in America and England. To how many people they were known in the small settlement of Hadley there is no way of telling.

Certain it is that Parson Russell knew from the start that he was entertaining the much-sought regicides, Generals Edward Whalley and William Goffe. They had fled to his remote village in the night while hunters of all who had signed the death warrant of Charles I were scouring Connecticut. Newcomers were not unusual in the settlements and no doubt the guests at the parsonage, while they must have been different in many ways from the usual pioneer, were accepted by the populace without too many questions being asked. Besides, who would suspect the parson of any wrong-doing?

Yet in these two strangers, who sat daily at Parson Russell's table, Hadley had two of the most notorious supporters of Oliver Cromwell and antagonists of Charles I and the monarchy.

During the first Civil War, when Charles I had been seized by the army, he had been entrusted to Whalley and his regiment at Hampton Court. Whalley refused to dismiss the king's chaplains at the bidding of the parliamentary commissioners and treated his captive with due courtesy. Probably Charles recalled this with especial gratitude, for after his flight he sent a friendly letter of thanks to his previous captor.

In the second Civil War Whalley again distinguished himself as a soldier, and when the king was brought to trial he was chosen to be one of the tribunal and signed his death warrant.

Besides being a supporter of Cromwell, Whalley was his kinsman. His mother was an aunt of Cromwell's and thus they were first cousins. He accompanied Cromwell in the Scottish campaign and was wounded at Dunbar, and next took part in the pursuit of Charles II and the battle at Worcester. He followed and supported his great kinsman in his political career, and in 1652 it was he who presented the army's petition to Parliament and gave his full approval to the Protectorate, when Cromwell became Lord Protector of England. He supported the "Petition of Advice" (except as regarded the assumption of the royal title by Cromwell) and in December, 1657, became a member of the newly constituted House of Lords.

We know that as Cromwell lay upon his deathbed Whalley was one of those who watched beside him. He tried to give support to Cromwell's son Richard, but to no avail.

Presently his own regiment refused his orders, the Long Parliament dismissed him from his command as a representative of the army, and suddenly disaster drew close to him.

It was then, at the time of the restoration of the monarchy, that he managed to escape with his son-in-law, General William Goffe. They fled to America and landed in Boston in the summer of 1660. The government in England did everything possible to find them and secure their arrest. Doubtless the colony of Connecticut seemed a safer refuge than Boston in the Bay Colony.

While Governor John Winthrop, Jr., was seeking the favor of Charles II in England, and petitioning him for a royal charter for the Connecticut Colony, while he was (according to tradition) presenting him with a ring and a gracious speech, two mysterious strangers sat at Parson Russell's table. They must have had long thoughts.

For at least ten years they survived in Hadley. Whalley was buried, it is said, under a stone wall between the properties of two of Parson Russell's deacons. Afterward Goffe is supposed to have gone to Hartford.

Deerfield came into being when twenty-five miles of river front above Northampton was put up as "equivalent" land to recompense Dedham for land taken from it. This was sold in the open market and one of the early landowners was Timothy Dwight—whose name was to become famous all up and down the river.

In 1673 the Pynchon interests started the frontier settlement of Northfield, and men from the neighboring towns built a palisade about it. Danger from Indians grew as the frontier stretched away from the other settlements. The palisaded blockhouse at Northfield showed that the new settlers were aware of it. At the same time these very practical pioneers seem to have been impressed by the natural beauties of the Northfield site, for they are said to have reported: "Providence led us to this place. It is indeed far from our plantations. The Canaanites and Amalekites dwell in the valley, and if they have any attachment to any spot on earth it must delight them to live here."

There seems in these words to be a slight hint of sympathy for the Indians who were in process of being despoiled of so much of their holdings through transactions they could hardly have comprehended, and through massacre and warfare. But coupled with this bit of sympathy is the usual conjecture that the Indians, being a migratory people, probably had no permanent attachments to the land.

It may not have been the scenery that interested the Indians, but they were soon to show that they did have sufficient attachment to that region to resist its seizure. And that particular spot was the place where they proceeded to say "No farther!" to the advancing tide of civilization. As a real estate venture these farthest north settlements did not thrive for some years to come.

While they were struggling to get a foothold on a new frontier, the younger generation in the lower river towns were also establishing new settlements. Land was bought from the Indians farther to the south. By 1650 Middletown was occupying the elbow where the river turns due east for a few miles before resuming its southward journey. This sudden change in direction, with the river's consequent widening, stimulated Middletown's early-developed enterprise in shipbuilding—an enterprise which continued for many years.

Lyme, across the river from Saybrook, and the Haddams on either side of the river and a little to the north, soon had groups of newcomers clearing the land and building cabins.

Today the idea of these youthful ventures at the Haddams and Lyme make us smile. Old Lyme at the river's mouth and the Haddams above it are so steeped in historic tradition and three-century associations, connected with the Beautiful River and its valley, that the portrayal of them as *young* ventures in courage and hardihood is difficult to accept.

Usually it was land hunger that led people to abandon the plantations where some degree of comfort and security had been established. To start a fresh struggle with the uncleared wilderness was a serious matter. In some instances church quarrels were at the bottom of such changes of habitation. Above Springfield (as Agawam was now named) new settlements were encouraged and fostered by the desire of the commercially minded to increase business.

Some idea of the way in which people lived in these new settlements may be gathered from an inventory listed with the will of one Thomas Nowell, who died in Windsor in 1648. Taking into consideration the fact that this was only a dozen years after the first settlers had come to Windsor, the tabulation of possessions shows, even then, that things accumulated in a household. This is the inventory as given:

An Inventory of the Estate of Thomas Nowell, late of Wyndsor, deceased, prized by us whose names are here underwritten, Febr. 22th, 1648.

	£.	s.	d.
Item: The dwelling house, barne, outhouses, with the homelott orchyard, with an addition of meadow adjoining	75.	00.	00
Item: 13 akers of meadow	45.	10.	00
Item: 66 akers upland with some additions	03.	00.	00
Item: IN THE PARLOUR—one standing bed with its furniture	17.	00.	00

	£.	s.	d.
Item: one trundle bed with its furniture	10.	00.	00
Item: one coverlitt, 4 pr sheets, 3 pr pillow beers,	06.	12.	00
Item: 3 table cloaths, 15 table napkins,	02.	18.	00
Item: 14 yds ½ new linnen, with some cotton cloath	02.	03.	00
Item: more new cloath, 5 yds ½	00.	13.	09
Item: a cubbered, a table, a chaire, a small box, 3 stoole	02.	10.	00
Item: two truncks, one chest, 15 cushions	03.	12.	00
Item: 2 Bibles, and some other books	00.	14.	00
Item: a pair of gold waights,	00.	03.	00
Item: his wearing apparrell, 11 L., Item 2 carpets,	13.	11.	00
Item: in money and plate,	34.	00.	00
Item: a pewter flagon, 2 platters, 3 saltes, 2 pintes,	01.	00.	00
Item: a pair of andirons, tongs and other things	00.	13.	00
Item: 33 yds of kersy 11 L, 5 yds ½ of searge 1 L. 15s	12.	15.	00

IN THE KITCHEN

	£.	s.	d.
Item: in Pewter	04.	00.	00
Item: in Brass	04.	03.	04
Item: 1 iron pott, one fryinge pann	00.	12.	00
Item: 2 peeces, a pr bandleers	01.	06.	00
Item: one broiling iron, one cleaver, one spittle iron, 2 spitts, one smothing iron, one gridiron—	00.	18.	06
Item: 2 pr andirons, fire shovel and tongs	00.	18.	00
Item: 2 chaffing dishes, potthookes and hanging,	00.	05.	00
Item: 1 chaire, one pr bellows, 2 linnen wheels	00.	13.	00
Item: IN THE SELLER, 2 beare barrills, 1 butter churn, 2 Runletts	00.	13.	00
Item: 1 case of bottles, 1 salting trough	00.	08.	00
Item: in porke, 2 L. 10s, Item: in tubbs and other lumber, 1 L.,	03.	10.	00
Item: 7 bush; rye, 3 bush, maulte, 2 bush; pease,	04.	13.	00
Item: 22 bush; wheat,	04.	08.	00
Item: 2 sacks, 2 bagges, 1 hogshd., some old tooles —	00.	18.	06
Item: yearne, linnen and cotton	01.	14.	00

	£.	s.	d.
Item: 14 yards okam cloath	—	00.	18.	00

IN THE KITCHEN LOFTS AND GARRITTS

	£.	s.	d.
Item: 10 bush; Ind. Corn,	—	01. 05. 00
Item: in bacon	—	01. 00. 00
Item: 1 saddle, 1 cloakbag, 1 pillion, 1 sidesaddle and pillion cloath,	—	02. 06. 00
Item: 2 horse collars and other geares,	—	00. 12. 00
Item: 3 pillowes, one blankitt,	—	01. 00. 00
Item: 3 hogshds., 2 sythes, flax and other lumber,	—	02. 00. 00

IN THE YARDES AND OUTHOUSES

	£.	s.	d.
Item: 2 horses, one colte	—	27. 00. 00
Item: 2 oxen, 2 steares	—	23. 00. 00
Item: 3 cowes, 1 heifer, 1 bull	—	18. 05. 00
Item: 3 swyne	—	02. 00. 00
Item: waine, wheels, expinns, cops and pin,	—	01. 10. 00
Item: 2 yoakes with theire irons, 2 chaines, 2 pr yoake crookes	—	01. 00. 00
Item: one plow, one harrow, one grynding stone	—	01. 05. 00
Item: 4 stocks of Bees	—	03. 00. 00
Item: more abroad 2 cowes, one steare,	—	15. 00. 00
Item: one iron crow, a saw, beetle and wedges, with some other things	—	01. 10. 00

Total sum   368. 11. 00

In spite of the difficulties of travel this would seem to prove that there must have been quite a little commerce carried on along the river by 1648 and that a fairly high standard of living had been arrived at in a short time. However, luxuries do not seem to have existed at all unless beds and "their furniture" might be so considered.

Perhaps just as important as knowing how the new settlements came into being is some information about the kind of laws they were living under. This is especially true since much unfavorable criticism has fallen on the Connecticut

Blue Laws. Some of the criticism is entirely just, but much of it is based upon failure to recognize the fact that errors are always made in the beginning of any experiment—especially in any experiment dealing with human relations.

The Reverend Samuel A. Peters published a code of Connecticut law in his history of the state in 1781, which has been widely quoted. Especially such provisions as: "No woman shall kiss her child on the Sabbath or fasting-day." Such quotations from the laws, as given by Mr. Peters, have since been proved to be pure fabrications. The laws were blue enough without being dyed to any deeper hue by this parson.

The records of the General Court printed in 1673 have an interesting preamble: "For as much as the free Fruition of such Liberties, as Humanity, Civility and Christianity call for, as due to every man, in his place and proportion, without Impeachment and Infringement hath ever been, and ever will be the Tranquility and Stability of Churches and Commonwealths; and the denyal or deprival thereof, the disturbance, if not the ruine of both . . ." showing quite conclusively that the seemingly liberal statements of The Fundamental Orders had not gone far in making any apparent separation in the affairs of church and state. Although Thomas Hooker had been dead for twenty years when these records were printed, his idea of theocracy still held in the Colony of Connecticut—the church was still the state.

Under the heading "Capital Laws" there are listed fifteen offenses for which the punishment is death. Each penalty listed refers to its Scriptural authority—chapter and verse. Blasphemy, idolatry, and the practice of witchcraft, as well as willful murder by violence or "guile," either by "Poysoning, or other such Develish practises" demanded the death penalty. Stealing or selling another man or bearing false witness for the purpose of taking life merited the same punishment.

Children over sixteen "of sufficient understanding" who "curse or smite their natural Father or Mother" could escape the death penalty if it could be proved that the parents had neglected their training or had been cruel or extreme enough in their correction to force the children to defend themselves. A disobedient son, who could not be managed by his parents, could be brought by them to the court, and upon their testimony that the child "is Stubborn and Rebellious, and will not obey their voice and chastisment, but lives in sundry notorious Crimes; such a son shall be put to death. Deut. 21, 20-21.'"

Under the heading "Children" instructions were given for their teaching in "the English Tongue," with a penalty of a fine of twenty shillings for neglect in the matter. Parents were also required to instruct their children in the "Grounds and Principles of Religion" including the catechism "so that they may answer questions without the book."

The court was also given discretion in meting out punishment to such as "exercise any cruelty towards any Bruit Creature, which are usually kept for the use of man." (This surprising anticipation of the laws enacted years later under the A.S.P.C.A.'s pressure make an amazing combination with the one relative to the death penalty for a stubborn or rebellious son.)

Under the section "Ecclesiastical" the laws applied to "and Christians so called," which might have offered some way of escape were it not that it is very evident that every inhabitant, except those later dominated as "Hereticks," seems to have been included in the "Christians so called."

For sins ecclesiastical there were fines with alternate sentences of "standing two hours openly upon a block or stool four feet high upon a public meeting day, with a paper fixed on his Breast written with Capital Letters: AN OPEN AND OBSTINATE CONTEMNER OF GOD'S HOLY ORDINANCES . . ." Such were the punishments for behaving contemptuously toward the preacher or his sermon, or for charging him falsely of error. Absences from services cost the offender five shillings after a hearing before the magistrate.

A "Quaker, Ranter, Adamite or other notorious Heretick" was listed as an expensive guest. Anyone who entertained such was fined five pounds per person and any town which allowed such hospitality to continue was subject to an assessment of five pounds a week. Further to discourage heretical friendships, anyone who talked unnecessarily with any such persons could be fined twenty shillings. Also, all "Hereticks" could be committed to jail or banished from the colony. To have any Quaker literature in one's possession made him subject to a fine of ten shillings each time he was caught with the aforesaid.

Under the heading "Lying" a distinction was made between ordinary "Lyes" and those which were "pernicious to the Publick Weal, or tending to the damage or injury of any particular person to deceive and abuse the people with false News or reports." Conviction on this count called for a fine of ten shillings or sitting in the stocks for not more than three hours.

Under "Oppression" was set forth a doctrine which has a modern sound. "Whereas Oppression is a mischievous Evil the Nature of man is prone unto, and that men may not Oppress and Wrong their Neighbors by taking excessive

Wages for Work, or unreasonable Prizes for such necessary Merchandise or Commodities as shall pass from man to man," the court was given the right to punish such offenses by fine or imprisonment at its discretion. No mention of a minimum-wage law appears, however.

The liberality of the Fundamental Orders fades again when we read the Connecticut blue laws for keeping the Sabbath. A five-shilling fine was to be assessed for profaning the day by "unnecessary Travail, or Playing thereon in the time of Publick Worship, or before or after." To absent oneself, "there being convenient room in the House," cost the offender five shillings also. Since this law was repeated twice in the records, it would appear that it was held to be especially important by the authorities.

Education was dealt with from an ecclesiastical point of view, as is evidenced by the reasons that were given for the establishment of schools. "It being the chief Project of Satan to keep men from the knowledge of the Scriptures, as in former times keeping them in an unknown Tongue, so in these latter times, by persuading them from the use of Tongues, so that at least the true sense and meaning of the Original might be clouded with false Glosses of Saint-seeming deceivers; and that Learning might not be buried in the Graves of our fore-fathers in Church and Colony, the Lord assisting our endeavors: It is therefore ordered . . ."

This section of the records went on to provide that any settlement of fifty householders should have a schoolmaster to whom all children should be sent. Each parent or "master" of the said children might pay the schoolmaster's wages, or all of the inhabitants might share the responsibility together: "Provided that those who send their Children, be not oppressed by paying much more than they can have them taught for in other Townes."

Each county town was to have a grammar school presided over by a master capable of instructing youth "so far as they must be fitted for the Colleges." There were few enough colleges to choose from and even fewer students who were able to attend. To be exact, there was only one college—Harvard in 1673.

Recalling that not more than twenty-five years before the promulgation of this one there was considerable discussion as to the need for any code of law among the Massachusetts worthies on the ground that the judges were able and competent to decide each case, since they were chosen of the Lord, a marked advance is evidenced by the adoption of these provisions by the General Court of Connecticut.

Furthermore, there is a marked improvement over the legal rules prevalent in England at the time—especially in the reduction of the number of capital offenses. It is further noteworthy that, while many of the English death penalty crimes were crimes against property, in the Connecticut code all such were eliminated. With the Fundamental Orders as a basis and a code of law such as this, a start had been made toward a government for and by the people despite the very evident theocratic control.

CHAPTER VII

Middletown, Connecticut

A<small>T THE GREAT BEND</small> in the river midway between Hartford and the small colony at Saybrook, the wide slow-moving stream turns away from what was doubtless once its southward course to the sea and flows due east.

Adriaen Block, on that morning when he made his voyage of discovery upriver from the Sound, found there a village of Sequins, of the Algonquin tribe. Sowheag, their chieftain, sold the land, which in 1651 became a new township. It was first known as Matabasett, but three years later it was renamed Middletown, probably because it was midway between Hartford and Saybrook. The new settlers, a small group from Hartford and Wethersfield, realized that their town would depend in part on its connections with the towns along the river above and the seacoast to the southward. Many years later strangers must have been amazed to see a substantial building bearing a sign CUSTOM HOUSE so far inland, but it was there proclaiming the importance of Middletown as a commercial center.

Settlements grew up on either side of one of the many streams flowing down from the hills, Little River. These came to be known as the Upper Houses and the Lower Houses. In due time the Upper Houses took on separate identities, leaving the Lower Houses as Middletown. There around the 20-foot square meetinghouse, stretching along the banks of the river, the village came into being. For the first fifty years growth was slow and life precarious mostly because of Indian troubles. Then the frontage along the river became more and more active and many boats dotted the stream. Shipbuilding and all the other businesses that go with water traffic grew apace until, by 1776, there were over five thousand souls living at the great bend in the river, and Middletown had become the largest and the richest town in all of Connecticut. Its fleets sailed to and from the West Indies and its clippers were among the fleetest in the China trade. "Here," wrote Dr. Peters, inventor of the fabled New Haven Blue Laws, "is an elegant church with steeple, bell, clock and organ; and a large meetinghouse without a steeple. The people are polite and not much troubled with that fanatic zeal which pervades the rest of the colony." And the historian John Fiske, himself a native of Middletown, wrote that Dr. Peters's remark was "testimony to an urbanity of manner which goes well with some knowledge of the world."

Numerous streams running down from the hills surrounding Middletown furnished water power for small manufacturing plants. Some authorities say that as early as the days of the Revolution Simeon North was making pistols in a factory which was making interchangeable parts and using the methods of the assembly line. There were lead mines in the hills above the river. Some of the early business establishments have continued even to this day and the variety of the products produced in both the old and the newer plants has protected the town from the sharp declines which communities suffer where industries are more specialized.

Perhaps because of the broader outlook induced by trade with the outside world, the proximity of Yale College, and the town's prosperity, cultural interests were not wholly neglected in Middletown. Richard Alsop, whose grandfather had been a merchant and shipowner, was a son of the town, one of the group later known as the Hartford Wits. He was a wit, pamphleteer, linguist and poet, a man of importance in the development of American literature. There were others, lawyers and statesmen, and, as another famous son remarked: "In the society graced by the presence of such men there was also material comfort and elegance."

When Washington College, later Trinity, was seeking a home there were people in Middletown ready to make generous offers to add the presence of an institution of higher learning to their cultural life. Hartford proved a successful competitor, however, and Middletown had to await its college. Not long after that another chance came. Captain Alden Partridge, one-time head of the Military Academy at West Point, was not pleased with the state of Vermont where, at Norwich, he had established his "American Literary, Scientific, and Military Academy." The legislative body of that state had refused to allow Captain Partridge to give degrees and he sought a more liberal atmosphere.

In 1825 the captain moved his school into buildings on High Street provided by the hopeful citizens of Middletown. There for four years he carried on. Again the captain's desire to grant degrees was thwarted, this time by the Connecticut legislature and again—the Vermont legislature having at last given the coveted privilege—he moved his students. The year 1829 found his American Literary, Scientific and Military Academy again holding sessions in Norwich, and the three-and-a-half story building with an octagonal belfry, on Middletown's High Street, now administration offices of Wesleyan University, and the lesser buildings were left tenantless.

In that same year the Methodists were seeking a site for Wesleyan University, and again the citizens of Middletown, who held the 13-acre campus and buildings in trusteeship, entered into competition. This time they were successful against competing Bridgeport, Connecticut, and Troy, New York.

The legislature granted the charter to the new university in May, 1831. It was announced by the local press that board could be had at from $1.34 to $1.50 per week. Young men in the Preparatory School, however, were boarding themselves for as little as 50 cents a week, on a light and largely vegetable diet which, it was stated, contributed greatly to their health. The trustees were offering four-year tuition, room rent and board (not including washings, fuel and lights) for $400 payable in advance.

One newspaper of that day thus described the charms of Middletown: "The site itself is beautiful. In a word it is a rural city reclining in quietude on the slope of a verdant valley washed by a stream that heads in another empire and by which it stands connected with the great and busy world around, without partaking much of the bustle of its business or the contageon of its moral corruptions. The air is salubrious and the water fine—and perhaps no place in the Union surpasses it for health."

So in 1831 began Wesleyan University, chartered and

continued as a nonsectarian institution. It has grown steadily through the years in physical endowment and in intellectual leadership so that today it stands with the best of the many educational institutions that are the pride of the Connecticut River.

Two composers of note were born in Middletown. The town's citizens have named a park in memory of one of them, Henry Clay Work. A bust has been set up within its confines to honor the author of the famous Civil War song "Marching through Georgia." Henry Clay Work wrote many other songs, among them "Father, Dear Father, Come Home with Me Now" and that old favorite of barbershop quartets, "Grandfather's Clock."

Reginald De Koven also was a native son, remembered best by his opera *Robin Hood* and the favorite for weddings, "O Promise Me." The De Koven House was given to the city some years ago and serves as a center for local welfare and civic groups.

Scattered about town are several of the old houses connected with well-known families. Some of them have been acquired by the university. Perhaps the most interesting is Russell House on High Street. With the house goes the story of the Russells, one of the earliest families and one which still continues in the life of Middletown. The Russell Company, makers of fine textiles, is the present-day representative of the old China Trading Company. Samuel Russell, founder of the Russell fortunes, was the great-great-grandson of Middletown's first minister. His father and grandfather had made their livings as shipowners and captains and one of them had had charge of the lead mine that furnished bullets during the Revolutionary War.

At the age of twenty-one Samuel, who had been left an

orphan when he was twelve and had been trained as a merchant, went to New York and was soon in the employ of a firm trading with China and India with headquarters in Spain. In 1813, when he was twenty-four, Samuel started his own exporting firm, and five years later the partnership was formed which, in time, became Russell and Company, probably the most famous and successful concern engaged in the China trade.

For nearly a hundred years this company imported tea, silks, sandalwood, firecrackers, porcelain, and carved ivory. They had clipper ships which could match those of the English for speed and could outsail the pirates who infested the China Sea. The Russell Company flag, blue and white, flew from the mast of the ship that held the record of ninety days from China to America and in 1847 one of the Russell ships broke the record from China to England. It was reported that the profit on the cargo of tea on that one trip was 60 per cent of the entire cost of the boat.

For nearly twenty years Samuel lived in Canton, China. After his return to Connecticut he founded the Russell Manufacturing Company and was also president of the Middlesex Bank, which he saved from failure with his own funds in the panic of 1857.

In 1815 Samuel Russell had married a descendant of the famous Mather family of colonial Massachusetts. She died while her husband was in China and when he returned to America, in 1823, he married her sister. Samuel returned to China and from there sent the plans and a wooden model for the Russell House. It was built in 1827-1829 and Samuel first set eyes on it when he sailed up the river in the summer of 1830, home this time to stay.

Samuel Hubbard, a friend of Russell's, later postmaster

general of the United States, was entrusted with the building of the house according to the plans sent from China. It was to be forty-four feet square and two stories high, with a basement floor below the street level. All partitions were to be of brick and wood was to be used as sparingly as possible. He figured that the cost should not exceed $5,000 but naturally it involved a much greater expenditure, for Mrs. Russell had ideas of her own which her husband eventually gave in to. The fireplace mantels of black marble cost $60 each, the window glass came from Hamburg, and the hardware was of the best. The brass lock on the front door measures nine by twelve inches and the key is six inches long.

Mr. Hubbard had an eye out for his friend's good, for he found the Corinthian columns in New Haven where they had been made for a bank which had failed and he had them brought to Middletown by ox cart.

There were twenty-two rooms in the original house. Later, about 1860, a wing was added to serve as a home for Samuel Wadsworth Russell, the younger son of the second Samuel. Other changes were made which brought the total number of rooms to forty-two.

While the Russell family lived in the house it contained much teakwood and lacquered furniture, and priceless Chinese vases, many of them gifts from Samuel Russell's firm friend, the Chinese merchant prince Houqua. There were also mementoes of Commodore Macdonough, of the battle of Plattsburg fame, who belonged to the Russell clan and lived in Middletown.

There are five acres of grounds and the boxwood hedges were brought over from England more than a century ago. If you look from the back of the house today, across the lawns toward the stables whose roofs are just visible, time easily slips back to the days of splendor when the river bore ships which sailed through far waters, bearing rich cargoes.

In these later days ships have brought richer cargoes— new peoples from across the seas seeking a new and better way of life. Middletown has proved itself a hospitable haven for them, for they have kept the wheels of her industries turning. Their sons and daughters have enjoyed the privileges of better schooling and not a few of them have become leaders in the civic and political life of the town and state.

There are three Roman Catholic churches in Middletown, one with an Irish membership, one with Polish members, and the third made up of those of Italian descent. There is also a Hebrew synagogue, as well as the churches of the Protestant denominations some of which were established as soon as the town began to be a town. That all of the new have joined with the old to carry on the life of the city is typical of many places along the river.

So here at the great bend in the river one may see the march of American civilization since the day when Adriaen Block first discovered the village of Sequins, the smoke from whose signal hill had been spreading tidings for red generations. And across the river to this day the tracks of the dinosaur are visible in the sandstone quarries, carrying the story back to the days before man came to the valley.

CHAPTER VIII

A Red Cloud Gathers

URING the winter of 1675-76 smoke from many campfires was rising in the cold blue sky along the upper Massachusetts reaches of the Connecticut. The river was a winding, smooth, white track. Only a few weeks before it had run red. The inevitable conflict between the Indians, the first inhabitants of the land, and the newcomers, who had totally different ideas of landownership and settlement, had come.

This was not a struggle against one tribe, such as the Pequot War had been. On the Connecticut there were several tribes bound together in the common purpose of retrieving their hunting grounds and of saving themselves from destruction.

They finally assembled at Northfield, of which only a short time before a white settler, spying out new land, had said: "The Canaanites and the Amalekites dwell in the valley, and if they have any attachment to any spot on earth it must delight them to live here." What had been the frontier settlement of the valley pioneers, Northfield, now became the camping ground of the rallying tribes. Camping there were the Nonatucks and Pocumtucks and the squaw sachems.

King Philip was there too. Philip, the son of Massasoit, ally of the first colonists, who had at length been driven from his father's friends by their heartless treatment. Most powerful of all was the latest comer, Canonchet, of the Narragansetts, whose friendship with Roger Williams had held him to the white men until they had tried him to the breaking point.

Gathered at Northfield about the fires of such notable chiefs where their warriors, squaws, children; and, here and there, a captive white, who remembered the shuddering days of his horror in flight from burning towns where home had been. Women were there too, whose husbands had been slain in battle or murdered as they harvested their hard-won crops. That autumn had been a time of terror in the valley, and the gathering of Indian forces portended worse things to come.

Apparently unforeseen and unconsidered by the English, this red cloud had long been gathering. The smoldering embers of the burned Pequot villages had actually never been quenched. Fresh flames from Narragansett villages now reflected a sinister, bloody glow on the Connecticut.

Following the death of King Philip in 1678, a report on the causes underlying the Indian uprising was made by a special investigator sent over by the king from England. While this report shows prejudice against New England, its author did have firsthand information.

This special investigator was Edward Randolph. He lists the reasons given to him for the bitter feeling on the part of the Indians toward their neighbors. He suggests that some think that it was due to the premature attempts to Christianize the red man and the endeavor to make him obey laws of white civilization. He found that, while the magistrates tried to force the obedience of the Indians to these unwelcome laws, the people incited them to disobedience by furnishing them liquor to which, he testifies, they are very susceptible. Having made them drunk, the white man later profited, since, unable to pay his fine, the Indian had to give ten days of labor.

Some, the report states, laid the trouble to the visits of "vagrant and jesuitical priests" who went around stirring up the sachems against the English. Still others imputed the whole trouble to the treatment of the Sachem Philip. He had repeatedly been brought up before the magistrates on various charges and each time he had lost some of the fertile soil of his Mount Hope property.

Then the report gives the government's ideas of the causes of the Indian uprisings. The official Massachusetts testimony was that they were being visited by these great evils because God had commissioned the heathen to rise against them. They were punished thus by Heaven since they were guilty of "The woful breach of the fifth commandment, in contempt of their authority, which is a sin highly provoking to the Lord; For men wearing long hayre and periwigs made of women's hayre; For women wearing borders of hayre, and for cutting, curling and laying out hayre, and disguising themselves by following strange fashions of apparell; For profaneness in the people not frequenting their Meetings, and others going away before the blessing be pronounced; For suffering the Quakers to live among them and to set up their thresholds by God's thresholds, contrary to their old laws and resolutions." Laying the cause of trouble upon Eve had Scriptural backing, and these Adams used it properly.

The complaint about coifs and fashions also has a familiar sound, though probably it has never since had such authoritative backing.

Edward Randolph concludes with a strong indictment of the English for thoroughly preparing the enemy with the means for carrying on their warfare. He says that it was they who first taught the Indians how to use muskets, and that in the case of the praying Indians at Natick (John Eliot's missionary enterprise) the church was organized into a trained band under their own officers. These men, he says, have proved the most cruel of all.

Then he makes a scathing attack upon the repeal of the 1633 law which prohibited the sale of any arms or ammunition to an Indian, with a stiff fine for breaking it. This, he says, was repealed to benefit the few who were licensed to trade with the Indians, in an effort to give Massachusetts a monopoly on the fur business. These appointed state agents were allowed to sell guns and ammunition to any Indian, for which privilege they paid a tax to the state.

The failure of the attempt of the river Indians alone to oust the Whites from the fertile valley was inevitable. However, to attain the defeat of their native foe and to scatter the once-proud tenants of the soil was costly to the intruders. "Bloody Brook" got its name from the many Deerfield men who fell there in 1675. Militia from Springfield, Watertown, and Hartford had gathered at a call for help sent out by Major John Pynchon when it became known that the Nonatucks had left their village and were once more on the warpath.

That warpath led to Deerfield and Northfield. On the first day of September the little village of Deerfield, where women and children outnumbered men three to one, was at-

tacked in the daytime by a band of sixty Indians. These were
driven off, but next day men working in the fields of the
Northfield settlement were suddenly set upon by Nipmucks,
who killed eight of them. The rest of the people in the near-by
cabins fled to their blockhouse for safety. To this the Indians
laid siege for over a week before help from the militia, gathered from the towns farther down the river, arrived to drive
off the enemy.

But even that help had suffered frightful losses on the
way to relieve the little group at Northfield's palisaded house.
Ambushed by the Indians as they were dashing northward,
all but thirteen of the Hartford militia were killed. The inability of these English soldiers at first to master the Indian
tactics of ambush attack was one of the chief reasons for their
horrible and bloody losses in their initial engagements on the
river.

When night fell, those Northfield pioneers who were left
fled back to Hadley, leaving their homes, their crops, and their
cattle to the mercy of the Indians. Thus for the time being
Deerfield became the northern outpost on the river. All of
the river militia had gathered in Hadley. Needless to say, the
small settlement could not supply sufficient food for the added
numbers. Because of necessity, as well as for purposes of security, it was ordered that Deerfield crops—some still standing
in the fields—be brought to Hadley.

Captain Lothrop, from Potapaug—the northern portion
of Saybrook lands, since called Essex—was commissioned to
take his fine group of ninety picked men on this mission. On
the trip northward they did not encounter a single Indian.
Once in Deerfield, feverish activity commenced. Corn was
gathered, threshed, and bundled as rapidly as possible into
sacks. The people and militia working far into the night did

not know that already hundreds of Nipmucks had crossed the river in the darkness and joined the Pocumtuck forces in the Sunsick Hills. They did not guess that even while they worked Indian scouts, high on their hidden posts in the hills, were observing all that was going forward.

When every cart that could be found had been loaded with the harvest, the cavalcade set forth upon its journey toward Hadley. The militia surrounded it in close formation, but the idea of having any reconnaissance troops moving ahead to spy out the land and to warn of danger was unthought of by them.

Below Deerfield the trail narrowed in swampy land through which a stream made its way. This proved so difficult a place for the heavy carts to negotiate that the militia threw their muskets upon the loaded wagons and indulged in the wild grapes that grew at the stream's edge while they waited for the carts to be pulled through the marshy land by their drivers.

Suddenly, from the surrounding woods burst the Indian forces with wild war cries and lifted tomahawks. They fell on the unarmed and unsuspecting militia, murdering sixty-four of the ninety men. The stream was soon filled with decapitated and mangled bodies. The terrible screams of the dying and the noise of the terrified cattle finally reached the ears of Captain Moseley's soldiers who were tracking the Indians in the region. They came as quickly as possible but the Lothrop party was all but annihilated. It was only after a bitter fight, which lasted many hours, that the Indians finally withdrew as night closed down on the terrible scene of Bloody Brook.

Next day while Moseley's men were attempting to bury the bodies of the Bloody Brook victims, the Indians returned and swept down on the town of Deerfield. They were soon driven off, but by this time the remaining inhabitants were so shattered and terrified by their recent horrible experiences that they were glad to leave everything behind them and go down the river to safer towns, under the protection of Captain Moseley and his men. Deerfield soon dropped back into a wilderness tract in the Pocumtuck Valley.

Now winter with its cold and hunger swept down upon both Indian and settler along the river. Only a month after the Deerfield tragedy at Bloody Brook, the town of Springfield was burned by the Indians. Major Pynchon had gone north with a picked group of militia, but those left, along with the other inhabitants of Springfield, barricaded themselves in the warehouse built by William Pynchon. Under its steep-pitched roof they huddled together. From its small-paned windows shots were fired, and the men and women watched their beloved village being burned to the ground. When Major Pynchon finally came rushing back to defend his town he found only the brick trading house and a few houses near it left standing.

In October there was an attempt on the part of the Indians to take the winter stores of food at Hadley; but by now all the river forces were so gathered and reinforced that the Indians were circumvented. The deep winter settled down, and with it the beset settlements gathered to make military plans that should assure what now seemed their questionable survival.

This plan eventuated in what was to become known as the Great Swamp Fight—which was one of the most savage and decisive battles ever fought between Indians and whites in this country.

The Narragansett tribes had their stronghold in an enormous blockhouse situated in the midst of thick swamps that lay in lower Rhode Island. To this fort a large force of colonial militia marched in December of 1675. They surprised the Indians and terrible slaughter ensued. The losses to the Puritan militia were heavy but the Indians finally fled leaving over a thousand dead as well as their entire winter store of corn—of infinite value to the conquering colonists.

While this terrible engagement was the blow that finally broke the supreme power of the red man in the river valley, there were continual terrors from small and isolated parties of Indians who returned over the well-worn trails from their northern villages in Canada and along the Missisquoi to harry different small settlements. This continued, off and on, for the next fifty years.

During this period the Indians became tools of a new potential enemy of the valley settlers. France was quarreling with England. While actual declared war did not break out until seventy-five years later (1756-1763) the Indians were clever enough to realize that any white captive they could carry north to Quebec might be sold or ransomed to advantage. As a result there were constant night attacks upon little villages along the river and in its valley. Morning saw the terrible march of captives begun.

But the Indian had really lost forever the land he had always believed belonged only to the Great Spirit, to be used only by his people. For the next seventy-five years the quarrels of Europe reflected in the New World brought such death and destruction to the Connecticut valley as it had little dreamed possible after the Great Swamp Fight and the flight of the Indians northward.

There was a special reason for this. The Connecticut was the highway to Canada, and down it again came the red man

—the St. Francis tribe from Canada along with some of the scattered Connecticut tribes which had taken refuge there. It was this alliance of Indians and Frenchmen that now menaced the river. And the hot flame of the hatred of the Indians was further intensified by the promises of scalp-rewards from their French allies. The Indian had already become a destructive weapon in the hand of the Frenchman. The French had somehow learned how to master this Indian and make him a friend, while the English had antagonized him and made only a fearful enemy of him.

In this period between 1675 and the commencement of the declared French and Indian Wars in 1756 there was a continual advance and retreat in settlements along the river. Clouds of smoke often rose from burning English villages and their surrounding fields ripe for the harvest. The trail north was worn hard by the feet of bands of captives being marched off toward Canada. In winter the ice-covered river was a snowy track marked with the checkered web of many snowshoes. All along the way tragedy had dogged the steps of these processions made up mostly of women and children.

Deerfield had again been built into a small settlement, during the quarter of a century that had elapsed from its destruction in 1675. But now its snowdrifted stockade offered easy access to the lurking foe. In 1704 it was a little village of substantial houses. On a calm, and supposedly peaceful night, the hidden Indian forces from Canada suddenly fell upon it. The massacre that followed marked one of the darkest hours of suffering and death in the river valley. One hundred sixteen captives started the march north through the snowy woods. More than half of them were under eighteen and fully forty were less than twelve. Women, with newborn infants, who failed to keep up in the march were killed or left to die while their babies were thrown to freeze or to be devoured by wild animals in the forest.

Sometimes to facilitate more rapid progress children were placed upon sleds pulled by dogs when the juncture of the Wantastiquet and Connecticut rivers was reached. Thence to the St. Francis fort was a long and terrible journey of cold and hunger. It was only the hardiest in body and soul who ever managed to reach it in company with their Indian captors.

The few left alive in Deerfield after this second sack of the little settlement might well have given it over once more to the wilderness, as had been done some twenty years before, but this would have left the lower valley of the river even more open than before to Indian attack. A new garrison was sent to restore the fort and stockade, and the few heartbroken inhabitants stayed on.

There were intervals of peace between these Indians attacks on the river valley settlements. When land-hungry men would return to their blackened cabins and scenes of previous terrors, they still had the courage in many instances to build on the ruins of a past habitation. Then when fresh quarrels arose between England and France they sometimes found themselves once more the victims of the marauding Indians and French.

Yet in spite of the ever-threatening foe there was a steady advance up the valley, and townships were laid out on both sides of the river. There was a fort built near what is now Brattleboro, Vermont—Fort Dummer. It was supposed to guard the northern settlements along the river and also protect the lower valley towns. But steadily an increasing number of daring souls moved farther north along the shores.

With 1725 came a sudden relaxation from constant foreboding of Indian attacks along the river. In December the English and the Indians signed a treaty of peace in Boston. For the next twenty years the valley settlements were able to draw a long breath of security.

But by 1745 another war had broken out between the English and the Indians, egged on by French support. Once more marauding Indians appeared at frontier settlements and carried off captives to Canada after murdering many members of families before the long heartbreaking march was begun.

Hurriedly No. 4, the settlement farthest north on the New Hampshire side of the river, was fortified. A garrison under Captain Phineas Stevens occupied the fort. All summer the little stockade endured spasmodic attacks from the Indians. One or two men were killed, captives were carried away, and the sawmill was burned. When winter came the few surviving people deserted No. 4 for safer villages.

In two years the settlers thought it safe to return to No. 4. It was April. Down the valley there suddenly poured an army of invading Indians under the leadership of the French commander, Debeline. Families rushed to the fort for safety, but it was instantly surrounded by wildly yelling Indians. For five days they continued their terrifying destruction. Cabins were burned and the palisade about the fort seemed ready to go after repeated attempts to fire it. However, want of food and ammunition eventually caused the attacking forces to withdraw.

Finally in 1749 the English and French signed a peace treaty in the Old World. As a result the French stopped fighting with the colonists in the New World.

But the peace was short-lived. By 1753 there was another colonial involvement in Old England's quarrels. Once again

No. 4 bore the brunt of it. In 1756 the French and Indian wars with the colonists were resumed in terrible earnest.

Other parts of New England suffered too, but the river was the chief highway of danger and horror. No. 4 (now Charlestown) was its outpost. It became headquarters for the colonial militia of the river valley, and for Major Rogers and his famous Rangers.

It was also the point from which the military road to Crown Point, New York, started. The road was laid out beyond the Black River trail, over the Green Mountains to the Champlain valley. This particular section of the road between No. 4 and the Green Mountains was not completed until 1760. By that time Major Rogers and his Rangers had made the valley safe forever from attacks of the St. Francis Indians. At last Charlestown was a secure place of habitation.

Next came the taking of Quebec by the English, and the acquisition of Canada in 1763. The Peace of Paris was signed. Along the Connecticut, and in the New World, French power was ended. Ended, too, was the history of the Indians in the Connecticut River valley.

Mrs. Johnson Remembers

T HERE are several firsthand accounts of life in the frontier settlements along the river during those troublous times. Most of them deal particularly with the long march up the river to Canada following an Indian raid. All these narratives are filled with tragedy. Details of terror and sudden death, of stark and hideous suffering, are so appalling as to make it remarkable that anyone survived to rehearse such experiences.

The story of Mrs. Johnson, wife of Captain James Johnson and daughter of Lieutenant Moses Willard—who had been one of the first settlers of the frontier on the river—is fairly typical. In it we find the story of life in the struggling settlement at Charlestown, New Hampshire, at about 1745.

Mrs. Johnson tells of a trip to No. 4 when she was about fourteen years old (she was then Suzanna Willard). Starting from Leominster in Massachusetts, she tells of the journey "thro' the gloomy forest" guided by marked trees. Her frequent references to the gloom of the forest are not to be wondered at when it is remembered that it was virgin forest, whose primeval growth made a thick and continuous roof above travelers, a roof so heavy and dense that even the cheering rays of the sun were darkened. It was a "boundless contiguity of shade." And shade that held constant terror of a possible attack from the Indians with its horrible outcome of death, torture, and captivity. Mrs. Johnson recalls: "Our passage was opposed now by 'the Hill of Difficulty' and now by 'the Slough of Despond.' A few solitary inhabitants, who appeared the representatives of wretchedness, were scattered on the way." The impressionable and terrified girl of fourteen easily drew a parallel between this journey through the wilderness and that of Bunyan's famous Pilgrim.

Arriving near her journey's end her first impressions of No. 4 are not bettered by finding a party of Indians indulging in a war dance, stimulated by rum "which the inhabitants had suffered them to partake of." She says that she went "tremblingly by" and entered the settlement which then consisted of nine or ten huts housing as many families. She found that the Indians were associating—at the moment —with the settlers upon friendly terms. She was, however, overwhelmingly impressed by the loneliness and terror of the surrounding wilderness and by the primitive mode of life as compared with that in the more settled region from which she had come.

One event she recalls with evident pleasure. That was the celebration held upon the building of a sawmill for the little community. To mark this event there was a dance. The participants stepped their best on the first boards turned out by the new mill.

But having had enough pleasure in this momentary recollection, she at once reverts to the great uncertainties and dangers of the situation at No. 4. She mentions the probability of another Indian war, for it was generally believed that the Indians would join the French in their warfare on English colonists. All these uncertainties and terrors prevented the tilling of any amount of land, Mrs. Johnson explains, "and retarded the progress of refinement and cultivation."

She tells of the erection of a fort at No. 4, and of the recurring, and sudden, attacks of Indians which resulted in the death of several of the defenders of the little settlement. Some of the inhabitants were taken captive and started upon the long and bloody trail up the river. She notes the arrival, from time to time, of small companies of armed men from the older settlements, and she refers to the courage and ability of Captain Stevens, who defended the No. 4 settlement. Finally, worn and exhausted, the settlers left No. 4 to the mercy of the foe and the elements.

Later Suzanna Willard married Captain James Johnson and they both decided to return to look after his property in the northernmost part of No. 4. This was in 1749. In the Old World peace had just been declared between the English and French. "Mr. Johnson's enterprising spirit was zealous to remove to Charlestown," says his wife. So they undertook the "hazardous and fatiguing journey" in June. At the fort they found only five families and again Mrs. Johnson became lonely and fearful. "The gloomy forest and the warlike appearance of the place made me homesick." And well she might be amid the intolerable gloom of the ancient and somber forest.

Soon after the arrival of the Johnsons at old No. 4 the warlike appearance of the little community was somewhat lessened. The Massachusetts authorities sent orders for their troops, which had been stationed at the outpost, to withdraw. It was thought a wise move in an attempt to avoid any slightest appearance of hostility on the part of the colonists. But the wisdom proved doubtful.

Rejoicing in the return of peace, the day after the withdrawal of the soldiers Ensign Sartwell went out to cultivate some corn, taking the young son of Phineas Stevens to ride the plow horse. They had no sooner started work than the Indians suddenly burst from the forest. They killed Sartwell and took the Stevens boy captive.

Mrs. Johnson tells of her agony of mind following this renewal of danger. Her husband was away on trading business and her father and brother were working in a meadow when the attacking Indians appeared. Confined within the fort with six other women and four men she suffered a night of agonized suspense.

The next day her husband returned in safety, but her anxiety for her father and brother was not relieved for twelve days. Then they finally returned along with troops sent for their protection from Fort Dummer farther down the river on its west bank.

Followed a period of comparative peace in which Mrs. Johnson has an opportunity to write down a few "Cursory Notices." Since Charlestown was then the frontier settlement on the river, she must have portrayed life along its upper reaches, in 1750-1754, fairly accurately. "A detail of the miseries of a 'frontier man' must excite the pity of every child of humanity. The gloominess of the rude forest, the distance from friends and competent defense, and the daily inroads and nocturnal yells of hostile Indians, awaken those keen apprehensions and anxieties which conception only can picture. If the peaceful employment of husbandry is persued, the loaded musket must stand by his side; if he visits a neighbor, or resorts of Sundays to the sacred house of prayer, the weapons of war must bear him company; at home the distress of his wife, and the fears of lisping children often unman the soul that real danger assailed in vain."

Mrs. Johnson criticizes the rulers, at the same time excusing some of their mistakes by "the infancy of our country." Governor Shirley of Massachusetts was asking England for a fleet and an army, while "Benning Wentworth, the supine Governor of New Hampshire, obeys implicity the advice of his friend Shirley, and remains inactively secure at his seat in Portsmouth." She describes the draining of the "thinly inhabited state of New Hampshire of most of its effective men" to undertake the attack on Louisburg [Maine] and other visionary and less successful schemes of Governor Shirley, which "keep the best soldiers embodied in some remote place, such as the attack on Crown Point [New York] and the conquest of Canada." Thus, she goes on to say, the frontiers are left open to shift for themselves and to suffer from the attacks of savages until places like Charlestown are well-nigh deserted. "Only the zeal of Captain Stevens kept the fort and offered shelter for the few intrepid settlers." It is to be noted that Mrs. Johnson's interests were not exclusively domestic, although her household duties must have been extremely strenuous.

Finally the peace inaugurated in 1749 took on some appearance of being real and "the Indians expressed a wish to traffic, the inhabitants laid by their fears, and thought no more of tomahawks nor scalping knives." Only then did Mrs. Johnson and her husband feel it safe to move from the fort to their farm on the outskirts of the settlement. Mr. Johnson engaged in trade with the Indians, who brought in furs to exchange for blankets and other things they needed. He often extended them credit and "in most cases they were punctual in payment."

So the Johnson family settled down to live a fairly normal life for the first time and "the new country began to assume the appearance of cultivation." In the spring of 1754 Mr. Johnson, evidently an irrepressible trader, set out on a business trip to Connecticut. There had been a rumor of more trouble between England and France over the Canadian line, and Mrs. Johnson's life was made miserable during her husband's absence by stories of the approaching enemy. She began to be "trembling alive" with fear, and to "see a savage in every dark and shadowy place."

Her anxieties were relieved by the return of Mr. Johnson in August. He admitted that there was war in the air, but no immediate danger. He had made arrangements, however, to move down the river to Northfield "as soon as our stock of hay was consumed, and our dozen of swine had demolished our ample stores of grain," which would help to secure his family from the miseries of war, as far as meat was concerned at any rate. He had also made plans to place their eldest child, a son then six years old, in school in Springfield.

Mrs. Johnson was delighted with the large quantities of goods her husband brought back with him for it enabled her to have some company. "The neighbors made frequent parties at our house to express their joy at his return, and time passed merrily off by reason of spirit and a ripe yard of melons." Unfortunately Mrs. Johnson could not enter fully into the merriment: "as I was in the last days of pregnancy I could not join so heartily in their good cheer as I otherwise might." Still, she was not really downhearted. "The return of my husband, the relief from danger, and the crowds of happy friends, combined to render my situation peculiarly agreeable." Thinking perhaps of past days in older settlements, she adds: "Yet in a new country pleasure is often derived from sources unknown to those less accustomed to the woods." For a moment the sun broke through the gloomy forest.

The last of the pleasant parties had been especially gay. It was the 29th of August and that evening watermelons and flip had made the hours pass quickly. By midnight all the guests had gone leaving only "a spruce young spark, who tarried to keep company with my sister."

The small house was well filled. Besides Mr. and Mrs. Johnson and their sister, Miriam Willard, who was sitting in the firelit room with the "spruce young spark," there were three children, six, four and two years old, and two hired men.

At what no doubt seemed an unearthly hour, a neighbor, Peter Larabee by name, disturbed the slumbers of the household by knocking loudly on the door. He had engaged to do some work for Mr. Johnson and he believed in getting an early start.

Unknown to him a band of Indian warriors were in ambush nearby. Mr. Johnson, hearing the loud rapping, slipped into his clothes and went to the door, ready to greet his early-rising neighbor. He slid the bolt and opened the door. At once the room was filled with madly yelling savages. They bound Peter Larabee and Mr. Johnson and one of the hired men and rushed through the house. They dragged Mrs. Johnson, Miriam, and the children naked and terrified from their beds.

When night fell the family, which only a few hours before had been in the midst of a gay party, were ten miles up the river, on the opposite side from their home, and

surrounded by savages whose intent they could not know.
"Captives [Mrs. Johnson wrote years later] in the power
of unmerciful savages, without provisions, almost without
clothes, in the wilderness where we must sojourn as long as
the Children of Israel did, as far as we knew . . ."

The family, with Mr. Larabee and another neighbor,
were parceled out among their eleven captors. After crossing
the river they halted and food was prepared by the Indians,
who shared it with their captives. Some compassion was shown
when Mr. Johnson was allowed to capture a neighbor's horse,
which was wandering in a field, and place his wife upon
its back. The beast, a neighborhood pet, was known as Old
Scroggins. Following the brief meal the march was resumed.

Mrs. Johnson recalls her emotions: "To leave my aged
parents, brothers, sisters, and friends, and travel with savages
through a dismal forest to unknown regions, in the alarming
situation I then was in, with three small children . . ."

Her fourteen-year-old sister, who had been entertaining
the young man, also was in the company of unhappy people.
Mrs. Johnson was distressed, too, over neighbor Larabee, who
had been very kind and whose agony of mind must be great
since he had left behind him his wife and four small children.

That night they camped "with the sky for a covering
and the ground for a pillow." The men in the party were
bound with splints so that they should not escape. Miriam
Willard lay roped to the ground between two Indian guards.
Mrs. Johnson and the children were allowed blankets and
were left unbound. There was little possibility that they
would make any attempt to get away.

After going a few miles the next day, Mrs. Johnson was
overtaken by the pangs of childbirth. In a booth of boughs
and vines prepared by her captors, attended by her husband

and her young sister, she gave birth to a daughter. The child was later named Captive Johnson. Two tablets beside the road, between Weathersfield and Reading, Vermont, recall the birth of this baby although the spot where the booth stood is some distance away in the town of Cavendish.

The mother was allowed to rest for the remainder of the day. On the next day she was placed on a litter which the Indians had contrived. Finally the litter-bearers gave out by reason of weakness because of their scant amount of food. Rather than be left alone to die in the wilderness, Mrs. Johnson begged to be lifted, once more, to the back of Old Scroggins, that previously had borne Miriam and the six-year-old boy while the captor Indians had carried the two little girls on their backs.

Mr. Johnson led the horse, and by resting every hour for a few moments, Mrs. Johnson managed to keep on with the terrible journey. Peter Larabee carried the newborn infant in his arms, giving it occasional sips of "water gruel."

After days and nights of indescribable hunger, fatigue, cold and fear, the party eventually arrived at the shores of Lake Champlain. At one time Mrs. Johnson had fallen from exhaustion in a state of swoon. When she opened her eyes a savage was standing above her with a raised tomahawk. She was saved by the Indian who was her special captor. He wished to carry her to Canada where he might sell her as a servant in some French household or ultimately receive a good ransom for her in money. When the party was near to dying from hunger Old Scroggins was killed for food. After that Mr. Johnson carried his wife in a sort of pack slung across his back.

Half starved and nearly dead from exposure and exhaustion, the party was met by the French at Crown Point.

Though captives of war, they were treated politely by the French, who gave them "brandy in profusion, a good dinner, and a change of linen." After further days of hardship they finally arrived at their destination—the Indian village of St. Francis. Here they were separated.

Mrs. Johnson was exchanged for her son, the six-year-old Sylvanus, by her captor, who would rather have the boy to serve him in the hunting grounds. She and her infant daughter Captive were taken into the family of the son-in-law of the grand sachem and the others were sold as servants in Montreal. Luckily they all had considerate masters. Mr. Johnson was under a prominent French citizen, while Suzanna, the elder of the two little girls, was taken by three French spinsters, who lived in affluence and became devoted to her. The other little girl, Polly, was bought by the mayor of Montreal for his wife's pleasure, and Miriam Willard, lovely and spirited, was taken into the influential Du Quesne family. In spite of the pangs of separation, after the terrors and hardships of the journey which had brought them to Canada, the lot of the Johnson family was not altogether an unhappy one.

In time Mrs. Johnson and the woods-born Captive joined the others in Montreal. After four years of varying fortunes Mrs. Johnson, Polly and Captive came back to the Connecticut River valley by way of Quebec and England. Mr. Johnson was redeemed the next year. Mrs. Johnson tells of his arrival in Boston while she was traveling to the home of a friend in Springfield, Massachusetts. But, still dogged by trouble, Mr. Johnson was thrown into prison upon false charges. Later, when the charges were proved to be unfounded, the General Court sought to make amends by giving him one hundred dollars.

Mrs. Johnson relates: "After his dismission from the guards in Boston, he proceeded directly toward Charlestown. When within fifteen miles of Springfield he was met by a gentleman, who had just seen me, who gave him the best news he could hear. Although it was then late at night he lost not a moment. At two o'clock in the morning of the first of January, 1758, I again embraced my dearest friend —a happy new year; with pleasure would I describe my emotions of joy could language paint them sufficiently forcible; but the feeble pen shrinks from the task."

Finding that their dream of return to Charlestown could not be safely brought to pass, owing to the continued depredations of the Indians, they went instead to Lancaster, Massachusetts. After a few days together, Mr. Johnson set out for New York to settle some of his Canadian accounts. On the way he met Governor Pownall who persuaded him to accept a captaincy in the forces bound for Ticonderoga. Mrs. Johnson's record says: "He was killed on the 8th of July following, in the battle that proved fatal to Lord Howe, while fighting for his country. Humanity will weep with me. The cup of sorrow was now replete with bitter drops." It was indeed.

Her sorrow was somewhat relieved by the appearance that same summer of her son Sylvanus, who had come back to the Connecticut valley with the Caleb Howe family, including Jemima Howe, "The Fair Captive." At first mother and son were not quite comfortable in each other's company. Life with the Indians had changed Sylvanus. He knew no English and only a little French. He spoke volubly in the Indian tongue. He spent his later life as a fisherman in Walpole, New Hampshire. He was never able to give up the free habits of his Indian days.

Suzanna was the next to rejoin her mother. She came back with members of the Willard family, who had taken the long northward trail just before the fall of Montreal. At first things were a bit awkward for her too. She did not know her mother and could speak only French.

Charlestown was still home to Mrs. Johnson. At last, in the autumn of 1759, when the trees cast bright reflections in the river, she went back to it. "The sight of my former residence afforded me a strange mixture of joy and grief, while the desolation of war, and the loss of a number of dear and valuable friends, combined to give the place an air of melancholy."

She tells of how the settlement struggled back to life. There is included in her record a simple and dramatic reference to the arrival of Major Robert Rogers, who with his Rangers had removed forever the menace of the St. Francis Indians from the Connecticut River valley.

Major Rogers's dramatic march from Lake Champlain to the village of the St. Francis tribe on the St. Lawrence had ended in his total destruction of the town and most of the tribe. The Rangers, with Rogers leading them, had fled, pursued by the French and what Indian allies they could muster.

A small party of the Rangers with Rogers became separated from the rest. After untold suffering they arrived half dead at a junction of the Connecticut River. Here a commissary detachment, under orders from General Amherst, was supposed to meet them with provisions sent on from No. 4.

Through mistaken conclusions that the Rangers had either been destroyed or were making a different trek, the commissary finally gave up waiting for them and went back down the river to Charlestown. Almost at the exact time the starved and exhausted men reached the place only to find the smoking embers of a fire left by the supposedly relieving party, but no food.

While the rest were ready to give up to starvation and to lie down to die, the indomitable Rogers managed to fashion a raft, and with one of his Rangers and Captain Ogden he set off down the Connecticut for sorely needed food for his men.

Overcoming one mishap after another, he arrived at Charlestown. Hardly waiting to nourish his own famished body, he arranged for food to be instantly dispatched to the starving men he had left behind at the mouth of the Ammonoosuc where it made its juncture with the Connecticut. After a couple of days of rest he set out with additional supplies for the companions of his ordeal. A brief extract from his own account of his perilous journey down the river in the final desperate attempt to save his starving men gives something of a realization of the desperation and agony of that expedition.

The current carried us down the stream in the middle of the river where we kept our miserable vessel with such paddles as could be split and hewn with small hatchets. The second day we reached the White River falls, and very narrowly escaped running over them. The raft went over them and was lost; but our remaining strength enabled us to land and march by the falls. At the foot of them Captain Ogden and the Ranger killed some red squirrel and a partridge, while I constructed another raft. Not being able to cut the trees I burnt them down, and burnt them at proper lengths. This was our third day's work after leaving our companions. The next day we floated down to Watoquichie [Water-Queeche] falls . . . Here we landed and Captain Ogden held the raft by a withe of hazel bushes while I went below the falls to swim in, board and paddle it ashore; this being our only hope of life, as we had not strength to make a new raft. I succeeded in securing it; and the next morning we floated down within a short distance of No. 4. Here we found several men, cutting timber, who relieved and assisted us to the fort.

Rogers and his two companions looked like skeletons to the people of Charlestown. Provisions were instantly assembled and for two nights, we are told, Major Rogers slept in a feather bed. Then, as strength returned to his famished body, he set out to follow the party who two days before had been dispatched with food to the mouth of the Ammonoosuc.

Everyone at the No. 4 fort must have waited with deep concern and excitement for the survivors of that terrible experience. Two weeks elapsed before the little garrison at the fort saw canoes coming down the river. It is easy to imagine with what grateful rejoicing the surviving Rangers were received in the little settlement and nursed back to health by the women of the community.

Mrs. Johnson says: "Soon after my arrived Major Rogers returned from an expedition against the village St. Francis, where he destroyed and killed most of the inhabitants."

She was shortly delighted to discover that one of the Indians who came down the river with the surviving Rangers on their momentous trip was her "Indian brother," who had brought in the cows for her when she had been a captive in the town now desolated by Rogers and his men.

Several years later Mrs. Johnson married an old friend, John Hastings, and began a second family. By her two marriages she gave birth to fourteen children. In closing her story this brave pioneer woman says that her children and grandchildren like to gather about her to hear her tell of the days of her suffering and "to wonder at their magnitude."

Captive grew up to marry Colonel George Kimball of Charlestown and to become the mother of four children.

"And now, reader," Mrs. Johnson's account of her life concludes, "after sincerely wishing that your days may be as happy as mine have been unfortunate, I bid you adieu. Charlestown, June 20, 1798."

Her life's eventful journey ended at the age of eighty.

CHAPTER X

Eleazer Wheelock Meets the Allens Along the River

IN THE LATE 1760's the Reverend Eleazer Wheelock moved his Occum Indian School up the Connecticut River, from Lebanon, Connecticut, to Hanover, New Hampshire.

The school had begun with one student in 1735. That student was a young Mohegan Indian named Samson Occum. He had gone to the house of Parson Wheelock and asked to be given an education. During the four years that he lived in the Puritan clergyman's household he accepted Christianity. Later he became a minister.

These events so impressed the Reverend Eleazer Wheelock that in 1759 he decided to open an Indian school and name it in honor of his original pupil. By 1763 he had twenty Indian students.

It now became a problem as to how the school, fast becoming an institution, should be supported. The General

Assembly tried to assist by levying a tax upon every Connecticut parish. But prejudice was quick to raise its head in the colony of Connecticut. Pay out good money to help Indians? Indians who had been the cause of years of terror and death! The fact that the Mohegan-Nehantics had consistently fought on the side of the colonists during the French and Indian Wars was overlooked in the general hatred of Indians.

Finally the minister at Norwich, Connecticut, had a bright idea. He took Samson Occum, who was by then a minister, to England. There the handsome and eloquent Indian minister at once procured a hearing. The cause he represented immediately received attention. An institution to educate Indians? Of course! It not only was wise to promote such a cause, it was Christian as well!

One of the people most moved by this belief was the religiously minded Earl of Dartmouth. He contributed fifty pounds and persuaded the king to give four times as much. Money began to pour in for the enterprise. Presently ten thousand pounds had been received. More than enough to start a college.

With such a sum Eleazer Wheelock could afford to ignore the indifference and disapproval of Connecticut. He took his Indian school up the river to Hanover, New Hampshire. There, before long, he had more white students than Indian ones. And there he made a gesture of gratitude to his patron by renaming his school Dartmouth.

Besides his school, Mr. Wheelock brought with him some firmly fixed ideas about government. He found neighbors on both sides of the river who were ready to fall in with his ideas. Many of these people had also come up the river valley from Connecticut. They had even brought the names of the older towns to repeat them on their new signposts. On the east

bank of the river there were Lebanon and Lyme. On the west
bank there were Hartland, Windsor, and Norwich.

By 1775 Eleazer Wheelock's school was firmly established as Dartmouth College. In 1771 it had had its first
commencement exercises. Governor John Wentworth had
attended them. But in 1775 feeling toward the crown ran
high in the colonies. John Wentworth had to flee back to
England, and New Hampshire had thereby its last royal governor.

By this time Eleazer Wheelock had become the center of
a group of people who were ready to tell the legislature of
New Hampshire that they were not satisfied with its government. They wanted more representation for the river valley.
They felt that the government was continuing to be run very
much as it had been when New Hampshire was a royal province. The upshot of it all was that they began to plan for
a new state. They were getting no satisfaction from the officials in Exeter, assembled for the New Hampshire Provincial
Congress.

There was much to consider. The old Mason Line,
twenty miles east of the Connecticut, which marked the old
boundary between New Hampshire and "the Grants," suddenly became important. By clever argument they insisted
that the Green Mountains, which formed a bulwark on the
west of the river, should be the boundary of their new state.
It was entirely logical, they declared. The Mason Line to the
east and the Green Mountains to the west.

But before the Dartmouth group had done more than
talk and plan they suddenly got wind of something stirring
to the west of the very mountains they were contemplating
as the western boundary of their new state. They heard the
names of Thomas Chittenden and the Allen brothers, Ethan

and Ira, most frequently mentioned. Soon they discovered that calls were being made by these men upon the people who lived in the villages on the west bank of the Connecticut. Invitations were being given to these towns to send delegates to a convention to be held in Dorset, west of the Green Mountains.

There too people were revolting against the authorities. They didn't like the undemocratic atmosphere of New York, where there were manorial estates with tenant farmers. But more than all else, they refused to recognize any right on the part of New York to rule over them. These men, of what was commonly spoken of as "the Grants," were as determined in their intentions regarding independence and representation as were Eleazer Wheelock and his group.

The trouble about the Grants arose in this wise: When Benning Wentworth was governor of New Hampshire, a crown province, he had assumed that his domain extended westward from the Atlantic coast to Lake Champlain, and to a line twenty miles east of the Hudson. By saving out a choice acreage in each township he granted, he had managed to collect no little territory for himself, and he continued thus to grant townships west of the Green Mountains, and later along the Connecticut well up toward its source.

Belatedly New York woke up to what was going on. She insisted that her east line boundary was the Connecticut River. Therefore the townships granted beyond the Connecticut by Governor Wentworth of New Hampshire were illegal and invalid. Those lands, said she, were not his to grant. They were New York's.

There were appeals to England, delays, court actions, and finally a decision by the crown that New York was right. Nevertheless, there was war, without bloodshed, between the

west-side settlers on the New Hampshire Grants and those
from New York, who claimed the territory was under New
York rule. Most of the owners of land under New Hampshire
titles, signed by the wily Benning Wentworth, refused to pay
for new titles under New York. They didn't like the type of
rule provided by New York officials and they didn't intend to
be pushed around by them. So on both sides of the Connecticut there was dissatisfaction with older authority. Eleazer
Wheelock and his group wished to be rid of New Hampshire,
while the Allens and their Green Mountain Boys wanted to
shake themselves free from New York.

The settlers west of the Green Mountains, however, were
not like those of the Connecticut valley region. The latter
were from stable communities lower down the river. They
brought with them new ideas of government, but conservative ideas of religion and modes of living. On the west side
of the mountains many of the settlers had brought only a
desire to be free. In matters of religion Deists and Separates
abounded. For the most part living was less marked by the
amenities. They were a people who were adventurous, willing
to take a chance, and to try anything.

Under the impetuous Ethan Allen and his statesmanlike
brother Ira, they were ready to take things into their own
hands. These, then, were the men who were the leaders of the
movement for an independent state west of the Green Mountains. Only a few months after they held their first meeting
they decided to journey over the mountains to Westminster
and then up the Connecticut to Windsor to get the support
of those river towns for their plan for a new state.

It was true that there had been some revolt against New
York authority in the river valley but sentiment was divided. Also, the Dartmouth men were now making their own

plans for an independent state. And the leaders of the Dartmouth people looked askance at the wild and irreligious settlers west of the Green Mountains. To the south, on the river, the towns of Brattleboro and Guilford, notably, adhered to New York rule. By and large, most of the settlers in the river valley, east of the mountains, had made their titles sure by securing regrants from New York. They were primarily interested in holding the land they had settled, and they meant to make sure of it.

However, there was a revolt against New York justice in Westminster. In that uprising a man had been killed only a few weeks before Lexington and Concord. It was in that particular town that the delegates from the Grants chose to meet when they came over into the river valley with their west-of-the-mountains scheme for a new state.

Moving on up the river to Windsor they again gathered for a meeting. "We must have a constitution," a delegate, who had been to Philadelphia to sound out Congress, had said. Thomas Young had suggested that they look over the constitution of Pennsylvania. So they did. They added clauses forbidding slavery and allowing manhood suffrage without property qualifications. Then they met in convention and adopted their new constitution. Even then Burgoyne was moving up Lake Champlain from the north with flashing banners, menacing the very homes of some of the west-side delegates.

On March 3, 1778, Thomas Chittenden was elected governor of the new state, which was first called New Connecticut and then Vermont. Following the March 3 election another meeting was called for March 12, upon which occasion the machinery of government was set in motion.

Previous to this, in August of 1777, John Stark of New

Hampshire had marched with his men to the Battle of Bennington and helped Seth Warner and his Green Mountain Boys defeat Baum. Baum had been sent out by Burgoyne, who was on his way to Saratoga, to make a little detour. He was to gather the honey of arms and munitions stored at Bennington. But when Baum tried to stick his hand into the hive he was badly stung. These men of the Grants who were struggling to build up a state—and they had immediately petitioned Congress to be admitted as such—were not failing to help that new Union of States against their common foe, even while their petition was being weighed in the balance and remained ungranted.

The Dartmouth group, seeing their valley neighbors getting interested in this west-of-the-mountain movement for statehood, decided at last that they had better get on the band wagon somehow. So, meeting at Cornish, they sent delegates to Windsor. The legislature was having its first meeting there, under the new name of Vermont. The Dartmouth delegates asked to be taken in.

At first glance it would seem "the more the merrier." But the statesmen—and they were just that—who were guiding the new state's launching saw rocks ahead. Next to being an independent unit, they wanted to become one of the United States. New York, naturally powerful in the new Continental Congress, was fighting with might and main to retain or to have restored land which she continued to say was rightfully her own. It was hardly likely that she would second the petition of Vermont to be admitted as the new fourteenth state in the Union! In fact it was perfectly clear that she would do everything possible to prevent it.

All this was perfectly well known to the Allens. It was also perfectly evident to them that should the Dartmouth faction try to take the towns on the east side of the Connecticut away from New Hampshire, to join Vermont, then the fat would really be in the fire.

New Hampshire, which now looked mildly upon the attempts of Vermont to become a state and free of the domination of New York, would feel quite differently when the shoe of independent determination was fitted upon her own foot, and she found towns in what she considered to be her own territory, east of the river, trying to join Vermont. Instead of having one powerful antagonist to deal with in the Continental Congress, Vermont would find she had two—two authoritative states voting and working to persuade others to vote against her admission to the Union.

There was a referendum which made a delay, but it didn't succeed in preventing the action feared by the Vermont leaders. Sixteen New Hampshire towns under the Dartmouth group came in. So Vermont, now declaring herself free from all domination at home, or in Europe, had her boundaries beginning twenty miles east of the Connecticut and extending westward within twenty miles of the Hudson.

The expected repercussions occurred. There were hurried visits to Congress, where the Vermont emissaries found New Hampshire members frothing at the mouth. It was none other than the redoubtable Ethan Allen who was sent off to sound them out. He had been enjoying enforced exile in Great Britain for three years following an ill-advised attempt on Montreal. His reputation as the hero of Ticonderoga's earlier capture had, perhaps, established too much self-confidence. He had had time only to be delivered, a free man, in New York, dash off to see General Washington, and then back to Vermont, when this new mission sent him tearing off again to Philadelphia.

His report to the new Vermont legislature resulted in
the dissolution of the recently formed union with New
Hampshire towns east of the Connecticut. They, in turn,
forthwith took some of the west-of-the-river towns with
them—about half the members of the Vermont legislature,
to be exact! The ten east-of-the-river towns and their neighbors across the river at once decided to apply for statehood,
and failing that to become part of New Hampshire.

This move left the struggling infant, Vermont, in the
position of sadly needing a friend. Instead, she had a hostile
Continental Congress refusing to open the door and take her
it. And Congress was now playing with the idea of cutting
Vermont in half along the ridge of the Green Mountains, thus
giving one half to New Hampshire and the other to New
York. This, of course, would mean sheer annihilation. Meanwhile, to the west lay her mortal enemy, New York, waiting!
"We've struggled with the English for four years now, and
why should we be handing over such hard-won liberty to
New York or any other state?" So said one of the Vermont
letters to the Continental Congress.

In this period it was the eastern of Vermont's two counties—Cumberland—that made the trouble. The upper towns
of Cumberland County were of the Dartmouth persuasion,
but the towns near the Massachusetts line were still loyal to
New York. They now sent up a cry for help that was heard
in Albany.

New York, however, did little to help them. But they
did, achieve something for which they had not asked. They
succeeded in attracting the attention of the returned Ethan
Allen and arousing his ire. He was doubtless delighted to get
into uniform and to rush over the mountains to enjoin these
towns to a stronger loyalty to the new Vermont. Nor in the

course of these activities did he hesitate to inform the Vermont Superior Court, sitting at Westminster, of his doubts concerning the ability of its young state's attorney, Noah Smith.

Smith was conducting a prosecution against a group of recalcitrant Yorkers. Ethan, seated in the rear of the courtroom, soon became convinced that Noah Smith was by far too lenient and vacillating. He strongly disagreed with his manner of conducting the case. As Mr. Attorney Smith paused to look up some point in his Blackstone, Ethan, deeply irritated, strode to the front of the room. He then addressed the court, and turning to the amazed state's attorney thundered, "I would have the young gentleman know that, with *my* logic and reasoning from the eternal fitness of things, I can upset his Blackstones, his whitestones, his gravestones, and his brimstones." And he proceeded to do so.

Later, in the same county, he berated the inhabitants of Guilford. They were refusing to embark upon the Vermont ship of state. He cried: "I, Ethan Allen, do declare that I will give no quarter to man, woman or child, who shall oppose me, and unless the inhabitants of Guilford peacefully submit to the authority of Vermont, I swear that I will lay it as desolate as Sodom and Gomorrah, by God!"

While Ethan was thus breathing out threats and brimstone and doing some little persuading, events were moving forward. Two members of a Congressional committee visited Vermont following a complaint from New York anent Ethan's visit to Cumberland County. Governor Chittenden of Vermont dropped a note to Congress in regard to New York.

"The free born citizens of this state can never so far degrade the dignity of human nature, or relinquish any part of the glorious spirit of patriotism, which has hitherto distinguished them in every conflict with the unrelenting and long-continued tyranny of designing man, as tamely to submit to his mandates, or even to be intimated by a challenge by him."

Modern propaganda methods were resorted to when Ira Allen, armed with a broadside of arguments for the Vermont side, visited various state legislatures—especially those of smaller states. Some began to think that more small states might offset too much influence by large ones in the Continental Congress. And the very dogged determination of the small, struggling, independent mountain republic also moved members of Congress toward a more lenient attitude. Even New York members were ready to come to terms, but Governor Clinton blocked the way. Massachusetts, which earlier had urged similar claims, agreed to put them aside if Congress would take Vermont in, and even New Hampshire urged her delegates in Congress to press for some early solution.

But nothing happened. So, up started the New York crowd in Cumberland County once again! They joined with the valley people on both sides of the river, northward, in the renewal of the idea of forming a new state with the ridge of the Green Mountains as its western boundary line.

January 16, 1781, saw Charlestown, New Hampshire— old No. 4—filling up with delegates to consider this new plan. When the votes were counted it was found that a large majority had voted to annex the entire territory of New Hampshire. That left Vermont as only a small sliver of land, too small and too poor for a state, west of the Green Mountains, with close-pressing, powerful New York ready to swallow her up.

Ira Allen was the only west-of-the-mountain delegate at the convention in Charlestown. But he proved to be enough. Reassembling the next day, the convention (its members persuaded by Ira Allen overnight) reversed its decision. Turning its back on the established government of New Hampshire, it voted to annex the Dartmouth group of towns, on the east side of the river, to Vermont. This time, Ira assured them, Vermont *would* take them in. Not only did this new area, including sixteen New Hampshire towns, become a part of the state now fighting for its life, but fourteen towns east of the Hudson, whose inhabitants didn't like New York ways, asked to be received also, and their request was granted.

Vermont, with a growing population, extending from a line twenty miles east of the Connecticut River and westward to Lake Champlain and the Hudson, suddenly played a trump card. Only a few leaders were in on the game, and the delicate maneuvers were chiefly carried out by Ethan and Ira Allen with Thomas Chittenden as a wise adviser. The famous Haldimand negotiations with the British in Canada, in regard to possible annexation of Vermont, were adroitly begun. All at once Congress saw a buffer state playing out of her hands.

England had offered individual colonies peace terms. Vermont was in a most favorable geographic position to become part of Canada. She was being rebuffed by Congress. New York and New Hampshire were her enemies. Perhaps, after all, under British rule she might approximate that freedom she so greatly desired.

How far the Allens really intended to go with this scheme can never be known, but it is very doubtful that they ever meant actually to sell out to the British. They were profoundly weary of dickering with Congress. Perhaps here was an opportunity to win statehood by means of a rare ruse. Or, the Allens may well have simply been keeping open a door of escape if and when all else should fail. Conclusions about their absolute intent will have to remain a matter of conjecture.

England had an army of ten thousand waiting to strike from the north. Vermont had no protection as far as military force went. She did, however, have some wily statesmen. For months they kept the British army from descending on the new and harassed nation. Ethan was determined that this fact should be recognized in Philadelphia. He wrote a letter to Congress in which he enclosed the first offer sent from Canada suggesting negotiations. He stated that he felt Vermont had a perfect right to carry forward such discussions and negotiations with England, since Congress persisted in refusing to recognize her. But he added: "I am as resolutely determined to defend the independence of Vermont as Congress is that of the United States, and rather than fail will retire with hardy Green Mountain Boys into the desolate Caverns and Mountains, and wage war with human nature at large."

The Allens were busy men. Presently General Haldimand of Canada began to get suspicious. Ira had to journey to Canada for a couple of weeks, giving as his ostensible purpose the necessity to arrange for the exchange of prisoners. He calmed Haldimand down, but when he returned the home people demanded to know just exactly what was going on. They, also, were becoming suspicious. When the General Assembly met in Bennington in 1781 Ira Allen was asked point-blank to explain the cause of his trip to Canada. He told them that he had gone there to see about arranging an exchange of prisoners. "Fortunately I was successful," he said as he sat down.

Ira even went so far as to find out what Vermont could

expect under British rule. He was informed that they would have a governor appointed by the crown. Otherwise they would be given a great deal of autonomy.

The British now became more and more impatient for Vermont's answer. Ira Allen urged them to wait until the fall elections when the people could vote upon the matter. At length the British gave an ultimatum to the effect that Vermont must swear allegiance to the crown and join the military forces of England. Jonas Fay and Ira Allen, the visiting delegates in Canada, objected strenuously, but this time the British were ready for action. They stated their plan: When the Vermont legislature should meet in October they would move a fleet from the north up the lake and at the same time announce their 'terms in a proclamation offering the people of Vermont the chance to become a colony under the crown.

When the legislature met in October, 1781, Charlestown was full of men. Not fifty years before it had been a frontier fort distinguished by a number, not a name. Now it was one of the east-of-the-river towns that had been annexed from New Hampshire by the new state of Vermont.

On this autumn day its few taverns were filled. Even white-paneled doors, with fanlights over them, were kept swinging by the visiting delegations. It was the first meeting of the Vermont legislature in territory still on the map as part of New Hampshire.

The morning held the tang of frostiness, but by noon the sun made a drowsy warmth, filling the air with autumn haze. The delegates from over the mountains had traveled on a carpet of leaves as they came through the woods. The river, flowing peacefully past Charlestown, reflected the reds and yellows of the bordering trees. But among the delegates there was restlessness entirely out of keeping with the calm quiet of the October day.

There were sectional jealousies and personal spites and, underneath all, the growing suspicion of the leaders. The Allens, Chittenden, and Warner were all from west of the mountains. The newly joined "Eastern Union," severed from New Hampshire, had never been too sure of these men, though all concerned were Connecticut-born.

They were bound in their mutual desire for freedom from tyranny, but the conservative men of the river valley had always felt doubtful of the unorthodox Allens and their crowd.

Now had come news that St. Leger was moving from the north up Lake Champlain with his fleet, preparing to unleash the long-delayed attack. Groups stood around Charlestown's one street. They talked about strange doings, news of which had been leaking out for some time. The people of the Connecticut valley had begun to think that the Allen crowd had been selling out to the British. They weren't too reluctant to believe the worst of all the trips to Canada by Ira Allen.

On this day, with the enemy coming up the lake from the north, even west-side friends began to wonder about the Allens. "Yes," said one man, pushing through the crowd that was gathering outside the Town House for the legislative session, "Allen, how comes it that this British St. Leger is so cut up over the killing of that scout of ours? By Gad! he apologizes too much over killing an enemy."

Very calmly Ira Allen looked at the speaker in New Hampshire garb. "Mercy is sometimes present even in the foe," he said, as he turned to enter the hall. But that afternoon the session was electric. Ira's answers about the British comings and goings failed to satisfy the east-siders, who were, also, especially glad to find some reason for lessening the strength of the west-side influence.

The warm sun slanted through the colored leaves of the trees and through the windows of the rough building. Letters were read, questions were asked. Wavering delegates began to see there before them, in Ira Allen, a despicable enemy where they had thought stood a friend. The silence became too tense. From it there grew an ominous restlessness—the gathering of a storm which would break in action.

Ira wiped his brow. There was a clatter of hoofs on the bridge below the village. Someone was shouting. Then there was a single voice, high and excited: "Yorktown . . . !"

The door was jammed with excited men trying to get out; there was shouting that became a roar. Then the crowd heard the words: "Cornwallis has surrendered! Yorktown has fallen!"

Eventually St. Leger turned his fleet about and, catching the breeze, sped back toward his English haven. With him went the menacing sword that had hung over the head of the statesman Ira Allen.

It would almost seem that the persistent leaders of the struggling state might now begin to see light ahead, with the British menace apparently removed. But the battle again shifted. New Hampshire threatened force to get back her recalcitrant children on the east banks of the river. Likewise New York, aroused at last, tried to force those fourteen Hudson River towns to give up their unholy alliance. But the towns liked the ways of Vermont. No blood was spilled, but many words were.

At last on January 1, 1782, Governor Chittenden received a letter from General Washington in which he strongly intimated that Congress would look favorably upon

Vermont's desire for statehood if she would shed her two newly acquired wings—the Eastern and Western Unions. And Vermont did just that in a session of the General Assembly at Bennington in the winter of 1782. Of course there were repercussions along the Connecticut among the spurned towns, and also on the part of those on the Hudson. This feeling was more than ever bitter as the circumstances of weather had been such that only a small number of delegates from the Connecticut valley towns had been able to get over the mountains to the Bennington-held Assembly. It seemed obvious that the Vermont statesmen had not been unaware that this very probable situation would work to advantage in the course of action which they were seeking to bring about.

It was, however, full nine years more before the handful of indefatigable men saw their cause emerge in triumph. Meanwhile, as the years passed, there were frequent missions to Congress and to other states. Gradually local dissensions became less persistent as the new Vermont government grew in strength. While Thomas Chittenden, Jonas Fay, and Ira Allen were predominantly occupied with the affairs of state—judiciary, state finance, foreign relations—Ethan also had a finger in affairs in a less formative, but more spectacular fashion.

And he was capable of conducting business and romance in the same whirlwind manner. Shortly after the time when he took it upon himself to put the fear of the Lord (and himself) into the hearts of the reluctant people of Guilford, in Cumberland County, he became a widower. And within a year of widowerhood he saw the young woman he instantly intended should be his wife.

In the winter of 1784 the governor sent him as a delegate to the General Assembly being held in Westminster, where court was in session. Ethan had then been a widower for over a year, but it had not taken that time to make him forget. There had been no love between him and his wife for many years.

Fanny Buchanan, a young widow, born Montressor, had business to do with Vermont land left her by her stepfather, a former resident of Westminster. She was staying in some of the spare rooms of Stephen Bradley's mansion. Her mother, who also was a widow, was with her.

Fanny had a French father, who had been an officer in the British army. She was vivacious, pretty, and city-bred. The townspeople spoke of her imperious manner, but they liked to see her ride by in her brightly painted pung.

Ethan's fame had gone before him, and his appearance did not belie his reputation. The young widow was at once interested in the dashing hero, unlike any man she had ever seen. Ethan, himself, was smitten by Fanny Montressor at once.

He was not a man to dilly dally. He began a whirlwind courtship the very day after he met her. The tavernkeeper, John Norton, observing the situation, said to Fanny, "If you marry General Allen, Mistress Fanny, you will be queen of a new state!"

"If I should marry the Devil I would be queen of Hell," replied Fanny coolly. But she had never been wooed as the impetuous Ethan wooed her. She soon found that for all his bragging talk and swagger there was tenderness underneath it and a disarming gentleness.

On the morning of February 9, 1784, Stephen Bradley was entertaining the judges of the court at breakfast. He heard the bells of a sleigh that stopped at his door. Then Ethan strode into the room saying that he would wait upon the ladies who lived across the hall.

Hardly pausing for his knock to be answered, he opened the door of the room occupied by Fanny and her mother. Fanny was standing on a chair rearranging a china cupboard. "People don't usually make such early calls," she said.

"If we are to be married," replied Ethan, with only a nod of greeting, "now is the time for I am on my way to Sunderland."

Fanny may well have dropped the decanter in her hand at this blunt declaration. However, she didn't delay long in giving her answer. "Very well," she said, looking down at him, "but give me time to put on my Joseph."

Presently, they marched across the hall where Ethan amazed Judge Robinson with: "This young woman and I have concluded to marry each other, Judge, and to have you perform the ceremony."

"When?" asked the judge, looking doubtfully at Fanny. "Now," said Ethan. The astonished judge parried for time. "But, General, this is an important matter. Have you given it serious consideration?" "Certainly," said Ethan with some asperity. Then, glancing at Fanny, he added in a different tone, "But, after all, I do not think it requires much consideration."

The ceremony proceeded until the judge asked Ethan whether he promised to live with Fanny "agreeable to the laws of God." Ethan hesitated, and then looking out the window he said, "The law of God as written in the great book of Nature? Yes. Go on."

Just at noon Ethan put Fanny into the high-backed sleigh. He tucked her in with a big bear robe, and tied her trunk and guitar securely behind. Followed by the cheers of their friends they drove south along the winding river. They turned west, leaving the Connecticut valley for the long climb over the Green Mountains, now glistening white in the winter sun. The moon was rising as they drove up the valley of the Battenkill to the waiting farmhouse in Sunderland.

In the following years, which brought Ethan the deepest domestic happiness of his life, he must often have conferred and visited with Jonas Fay in Bennington and with Thomas Chittenden in Arlington.

Chittenden eventually found New York ready to make settlement with Vermont, for all of the land which she claimed, for the sum of $600,000. Finally they settled for half that amount. Then in February of 1791, George Washington, as president, and Thomas Jefferson, as secretary of state, signed the bill passed by Congress declaring that on March 4 Vermont should take its place as one of the United States of America.

On the 4th of March there was wild rejoicing along ice-bound Lake Champlain, and in the small settlements of the valleys of the Otter Creek and the Battenkill. And up and down the west banks of the Connecticut, its waters cold and black in its ice-edged channel, there was kindred jubilation.

CHAPTER XI

Missionary Zeal Along the Connecticut

U PON almost the exact date (February 17, 1789) of Ethan Allen's death the Association of Hartford County, at the instance and request of the General Association of Connecticut, was sending a missionary to the new settlements of Vermont.

This project was an attempt on the part of the Connecticut River valley divines to undo, or at least to mitigate, some of the irreligious influence which it was felt Ethan and his ilk were propagating in the new state. Perhaps the missionary zeal of these reverend gentlemen was also actuated by a fear that the irreligion of west-of-the-mountains Vermont might spread to the Connecticut valley and other states.

Ethan Allen had recently written a fearful and godless book according to their judgment. *Reason the Only Oracle of Man* had been published by Haswell and Russell at their

Bennington press. It had proved a deeply disturbing book to the Connecticut valley clergy. It had also proved disturbing to Ethan—but not for the same reasons.

The book's publication had proved to be a long and laborious process. It drew upon Ethan's finances to an extent he had not anticipated, and which he found difficult to support. He tried to raise a loan through his Onion River properties. Finally he sold out his right in the Sunderland farm to his brother Ira to secure some immediate cash.

He then took Fanny down to Bennington with him to board at Timothy Follett's. Very likely Fanny did not find the change an unwelcome one. The Sunderland farmhouse stood close against overshadowing Equinox Mountain. Soon snow and storm would be sweeping down upon it, burying it in winter loneliness. In November, 1784, while Ethan was bedeviling his publishers, Fanny bore him a son. Ethan named him Hannibal.

Money was again needed for the book, and late in the winter Ethan wrote to a merchant friend at Albany: "My system of philosophy is nearly half printed and the printers have proposed to me to take goods for their pay. I therefore ask the liberty of proposing a trade with you, to the amount of one hundred and fifty pounds lawful money, on terms of six or eight months credit, in which time I presume the Books will turn to money, to make remittance to you for the goods; besides I have considerable money due to me within that time. You will please to consider my proposition and act in the premises as may be consistent with your scheme of Trade."

But apparently Ethan's friend was not impressed by the revenue likely to accrue from the publication of *Reason the Only Oracle of Man.* So Ethan turned to another source of income. This time it was a certain one. Early in May, 1785, he made a trip to Philadelphia and collected the money due him for his service in the Continental Army. He and Fanny had a few gay weeks in New York and then returned home.

Money now began to come in a little more easily. Ethan sold some land and also made arrangements to dispose of Fanny's Westminster holdings. Summer passed and another winter approached. Finally, late in the year, the book was off the press. Ethan presented Fanny with the first copy and wrote a tender inscription to her on the title-page:

> Dear Fanny wise, the beautiful and young,
> The partner of my joys, my dearest self,
> My love, pride of my life, your sexes pride,
> And partner of Sincere politeness,
> To thee a welcome compliment I make
> Of treasures rich, the Oracles of Reason.

As soon as the book was published Ethan also sent presentation copies to two or three friends—Stephen Bradley in Westminster, at whose mansion he had courted and wed Fanny, Benjamin Stiles of Woodbury, and Saint-John de Crèvecœur, who had returned to Paris from his post as French consul-general in New York.

The Oracles, as the book became known, delighted the minds and convictions of freethinkers, it amused others, and it proved infuriating to the Congregationalist clergy of the Connecticut River valley.

When a fire broke out in Anthony Haswell's garret and destroyed many copies of *The Oracles*, which were stored there, pious people believed it was direct retribution sent by the Lord. Probably Anthony Haswell, after all he had endured at the hands of Ethan in the way of impatience, slow payment, and self-assured instructions felt that he had already received his share of retribution.

A good many copies of the book were circulated— abroad as well as in the United States. The Connecticut valley ministers and their General Association became more and more irate. Letters were written and published admonishing Ethan for his wickedness. The *Vermont Gazette,* printed in Bennington by the very men who had published *The Oracles,* carried the following advertisement:

> Just imported in the Balloon Sarcastic (Imported from France) and now opening for sale . . . by the Genius of Vermont at her store on the top of Mount Anthony in Bennington, a large assortment of valuable books, among which are the following . . . Deism Confessed and Good Manners Defended, with a chapter in favor of Oracles and a section on the heat of good blood near the grand clymacterice, and the animation of youthful charms. By E.A.
>
> And a sequel to be entitled: The Pleasant Art of Money Catching Reduced to Practise. I.A.

The advertisement was sent in by Dr. Lemuel Hopkins of Hartford, one of the distinguished divines of the Connecticut River valley.

Lemuel Hopkins, Lemuel Haynes, Ezra Stiles, Timothy Dwight, and Nathan Perkins, who were the outstanding ministers of the time, preached sermons against *The Oracles* and against Ethan Allen, its author, naming the latter as an infidel. Very probably Ethan enjoyed the excitement he and his book were occasioning.

As we have already observed, the men of the Connecticut River valley towns had long looked upon the Allens with disfavor. It was well known that west-of-the-mountains Vermont abounded in Deists and Separates. Both groups were abhorred by the Connecticut valley clergy. *The Oracles of*

Reason did little to help the situation. In fact it only fanned the flames of hostility to fiercer heat.

Ethan was a Deist. To the orthodox clergy Deism amounted to practically the same thing as atheism. On the day of Ethan's death the Reverend Ezra Stiles wrote in his diary: "Died in Vermont the profane and impious Deist, Gen'l Ethan Allen author of the Oracles of Reason a book replete with scurrilous Reflections, 'And in Hell he lifted up his eyes being in torments.'"

The Connecticut divines felt that Separates and Arminians were bad enough—the former refused to admit any civil or military coercive authority over religion and the latter were considered emotionally beyond the pale—but they were as nothing compared with the Deists. And Ethan Allen was, as everyone knew, the mouthpiece of the Deists.

Charles Miner Thompson, in his *Independent Vermont,* writes a couple of paragraphs which are especially interesting in relation to the furor which Ethan and his *Oracles of Reason* aroused in the breasts of the Protestant clergy of the Connecticut River valley. He says:

> Ethan would probably not have attained his bad eminence as an infidel had he been less vociferous and less witty. He did not care how offensive he was: he was tender to no man's susceptibilities, and his humor, though real, was coarse and profane. None of those whom he offended saw—in those days could not be expected to have seen—that the core of his doctrine was a belief in an overruling power and a metaphysical theory worthy of respect.
>
> If he were alive today, there would be nothing in his religious beliefs, however it might be with his manners, to forbid his being a guest at any reasonably liberal minister's or clergyman's table. In the best book on early American philosophy, he is set down as a forerunner of Emerson's.

Probably what stirred the divines of the Connecticut valley so deeply was especially Ethan Allen's deep hatred of the determinism of Calvinism. Freedom of the will was at the core of his belief. Love of liberty was the motivating force of his life.

He had first tried to get Watson & Goodwin, the Hartford publishers, to print his *Oracles*. This was natural since they had published most of his political pamphlets. He had worn a path from Vermont straight to their door. Certainly these documents were not orthodox politically. However, while they might be willing to print statements against New York, when it came to stepping on the sensitive toes of the Congregationalists of the Connecticut valley, they did not want to take a chance.

It wasn't so many years later that one of the bosom friends of the religio-political hierarchy of Connecticut was to deal his former cronies a blow along similar lines to those Ethan Allen had handed out.

Joel Barlow, one of the "Hartford Wits," companion of Trumbull and Timothy and Theodore Dwight, fell under liberal influences in France and there unearthed and had published Thomas Paine's *Age of Reason*. Forthwith anything Paine had done to save the country from dissolution was forgotten in the hysterical cry of "infidel."

That they felt the same insidious forces were moving in Paine's *Age of Reason* that permeated the *Oracles* of Allen is shown by the statement of a historian of a slightly later date to the effect that "long after the publication of Allen's book, which had fallen into oblivion, even with its readers, that vile reprobate Thomas Paine . . . filched from Ethan Allen the great body of his deistical and atheistical opinions, which from the time of Celsus, down to the age of Chubb Tindal and others, have been so often refuted by men of the utmost respectability of character."

Small wonder that when Thomas Jefferson was seated

in the presidential chair the old ladies in the Connecticut valley ,buried their Bibles or hung them in the well lest the godless destroy them.

To prevent the spread of the evil doctrine which they
felt was endangering the newer settlements up the river and
especially in western Vermont, the Reverend Nathan Perkins
(Princeton, 1770), with an honorary degree from Yale and
a Doctor of Divinity from his alma mater, was selected in
Hartford to go forth to the benighted regions.

On April 27, 1789, he wrote in ,his diary: "I left Hartford and set out for Vermont. Took leave of my family, a
tender companion and five dear children, with painful reluc-
tance and an anxious heart."

His description of the hardships of the journey, the poor
food—"no beef, no butter, no cheese anywhere"—and the
inelegance of manner are mingled with laments over the low
spiritual condition of the people in the smaller settlements. He
does not hesitate to call a spade a very black spade in the
"mean and nasty" homes where he was guest. In fact ,his physical discomforts call forth much more terrible indictments
of the people than their deplorable spiritual condition.

However, toward the end, he does see something in the
people he has been inveighing against. He admits that in
Vermont, "in ye wilderness—among all strangers—all alone
—among log huts—people nasty—poor—low-lived—indeli-
cate—and miserable cooks," he found people of worth. He
goes on to say: "All sadly parsimonious—many profane—yet
cheerful and much more contented than in Hartford—and
the women more contented than ye men." Perhaps being
"contented" was, in the mind of the Reverend Nathan Perkins, not a virtue but rather an evidence of sin.

CHAPTER XII

Travel on River and Shore

THE INDIANS had traveled on the river for generations. Probably their first craft was a floating log. Later several logs were fastened together to make a raft. In due time a single log was hollowed out with stone tools, or by burning, to make the first canoe. Instead of sitting astride of the log the navigator now sat in it. Then came that work of art, the birchbark canoe.

"Give me of your bark, O Birch-Tree!
Of your yellow bark, O Birch-Tree!
Growing by the rushing river.
Tall and stately in the valley!
I a light canoe will build me,
Build a swift Cheemaun for sailing,
That shall float upon the river,
Like a yellow leaf in autumn,
Like a yellow water-lily!"
　"Lay aside your cloak, O Birch-Tree!"

With his knife the tree he girdled;
Just beneath its lowest branches,
Just above the roots he cut it,
Till the sap came oozing outward;
Down the trunk from top to bottom,
Sheer he cleft the bark asunder,
With a wooden wedge he raised it,
Stripped it from the trunk unbroken.
   "Give me of your boughs, O Cedar!
Of your strong and pliant branches,
My Canoe to make more steady,
Make more strong and firm beneath me!"

Down he hewed the boughs of cedar,
Shaped them straightway to a frame work,
Like two bows he formed and shaped them,
Like two bended bows together.
   "Give me of your roots, O Tamarack!
Of your fibrous roots, O Larch-Tree!
My canoe to bind together . ."

From the earth he tore the fibres,
Tore the tough roots of the Larch-Tree,
Closely sewed the bark together,
Bound it closely to the framework.
   "Give me of your balm, O Fir-Tree!"

And he took the tears of balsam,
Took the resin of the Fir-Tree,
Smeared therewith each seam and fissure,
Made each crevice safe from water.
   "Give me of your quills, O Hedgehog!"

From the ground the quills he gathered,
All the little shining arrows,
Stained them red and blue and yellow
With the juice of roots and berries;

Into his canoe he wrought them,
Round its waist a shining girdle,
Round its bows a gleaming necklace,
   On its breast two stars resplendent.

Thus the Birch Canoe was builded
In the valley, by the river,
In the bosom of the forest;
And the forests life was in it,
. All its mystery and magic,
All the lightness of the birch-tree,
All the toughness of the cedar,
All the larch's supple sinews;
And it floated on the river
Like a yellow leaf in autumn,
Like a yellow water lily . . .

Whichever of these two canoes the red man used, it became as much a part of him as his hand or foot. Down the river he paddled, shooting most of the rapids with skillful abandon. But even he had to make a well-worn "carry" around the "white water" at Bellows Falls. The upstream journey required the constant use of the paddle. This took time and it was hard work. Nevertheless, the canoe was the last word in transportation for the Indian.

The white man had no sooner taken over the river than he began to figure how he could save time. Time was money —or its trading equivalent—an idea which never entered the red man's head. The white man wanted to use the river where it was easy to use it, and to overcome it where it put obstacles in his way. There was the great inconvenience of getting from one bank to the other. It seemed a silly waste of time to load oneself and goods into a boat simply to cross to a spot one could see with the naked eye. And the earliest ferries had no wires to guide them. "You had t' pull up-stream quite a stretch and then row like Sam Hill t' make t' other shore."

In 1784, Colonel Enoch Hale built the first bridge across the river, connecting Walpole, New Hampshire, and Bellows Falls, Vermont. The colonel used the rocks for foundation and built his bridge right over the raging torrent of the famous rapids. No doubt the shivers that ran along the spines of those who first looked down at the terrors beneath their feet enhanced the daring of the undertaking.

The *Massachusetts Spy* of February 10, 1785, hailed this new enterprise: "This bridge is thought to exceed any ever built in America in strength, elegance, and public utility, as it is in the direct way from Boston, through New Hampshire and Vermont, to Canada."

Of course this was a toll bridge. Colonel Hale at once put up a sign stating that a man on horseback could cross for three cents, if he rode in a chaise he should pay double. A chaise drawn by two horses cost twenty cents. Cattle went pounding across at lot rates; and the Boston market was increasing its demands for meat. Then, of course, the stage-coach passage added to the colonel's moneybox. In fact it soon became evident that this was a paying piece of property.

As usual there were those who coveted. Rudolph Geyer was such a one. He had lent Colonel Hale money and held a mortgage on the bridge. The papers were drawn in such a way that if payment day passed unmet, the property would immediately slip from the colonel's hands to those of Rudolph Geyer. Each day for payment found Rudolph Geyer hoping that something would happen to make the colonel late in his remittance.

One autumn day when he was waiting in his Boston

office for the colonel's payment his hope began to strengthen. As the day lengthened and the hands of the clock passed slowly around, his hope increased. There had been no money as yet from the colonel. He had never before left the payment so dangerously near foreclosure time.

Only three hours were left. Two hours. One hour! That night Rudolph Geyer went to sleep with a contented smile on his face. At last the bridge was his. Colonel Hale had not met his payment.

Next morning Colonel Hale's son rushed from the stage-yard in Boston. Disheveled and distraught he burst into Rudolph Geyer's office. In his hand he had the money from his father. But Rudolph Geyer was adamant. He would accept neither payment nor excuses. The bridge was his.

Young Hale had left Bellows Falls by stage in plenty of time to get to Boston before the fatal date. He had arrived at the inn where he was to put up for the night. Seated at supper he had suddenly discovered, sitting across the room from him, his wife from whom he had been estranged. In the peaceful comfort and isolation of the inn these two found that their differences didn't amount to much, after all. They were soon forgotten in the bliss of reunion. Forgotten also was the pressing engagement, which demanded an early departure next morning. Only by catching an early stage to Boston could the young husband reach Mr. Geyer's office in time to make the payment sent by his father.

And so the pioneer bridge builder of the Connecticut valley lost his bridge. It is to be hoped that the reunion established at such a cost was permanent.

The valley people wanted to travel up and down the river as well as across it. But there were those five or six places of white water. Those rapids were forever in the way.

The first rapids were Fifteen Miles Falls, not far below the Connecticut Lakes. To have called them Fifteen Miles Falls was an understatement. There were twenty miles of foaming, tumbling waters, which were, when they were calm again, three hundred seventy-five feet nearer sea level than they were at their beginning.

Later, when everybody in the region was excited over the idea of a network of canals stretching out on both sides of the river, it was this particular stretch of white water that put the quietus on one of the most ambitious schemes.

An anecdote about DeWitt Clinton's remarks, when he first viewed Fifteen Miles Falls, has already been mentioned. It will be recalled that his expert opinion had been sought regarding canal operations on the river. His remarks, after observing Fifteen Miles Falls, were highly discouraging. He did, however, prophesy their great usefulness to mankind upon some far distant day.

But even he would be staggered at the volume of water piled up behind the enormous dam which today successfully holds those once-foaming waters in servitude. From the powerhouse the high-voltage wires carry current to bring light and power to Greater Boston.

All the rapids, except those at Bellows Falls, could be navigated, even by loaded flatboats. But the upstream trip was as trying on muscles as the downstream trip was on nerves. The rocky gorge filled with swirling, angry waters at Bellows Falls had a reputation for danger and difficulty all up and down the river. It was said that the current was so swift "that it is impossible to drive an iron bar into it." Few ever survived a trip through its treacherous channel.

There is a story that an Indian squaw once found herself unable to get her canoe out of the swift current as she approached the rapids. She made a frantic attempt to reach shore. Finding it useless, she dropped her paddle and drained a bottle of rum. Then she threw herself on the bottom of her frail canoe and prepared for a quick voyage to the Happy Hunting Ground.

In due time her canoe was beached on the shore of the quiet water below the roaring rapids. In the bottom of the canoe was the squaw. She was completely intact, and completely intoxicated.

In 1792 ground was broken for a canal to circumvent those rapids at Bellows Falls. The charter for the first American canal was granted by Vermont's first legislature (after it had become one of the United States) legalizing a "Company for Rendering Connecticut River Navigable at Bellows Falls."

Three English brothers spent over a hundred thousand dollars and ten years on this difficult piece of engineering. That much was expected of this undertaking was noted in a London newspaper of 1797. The writer foresaw the canal becoming a "water communication with the river Thames—a glorious prospect for both countries—and a source of commerce and wealth to draw still closer between them the ties of amity." By way of contrast: a little more than a century after the completion of this project, it was abandoned as a canal but rebuilt as a hydroelectric development at a cost of four million dollars—all American money.

Of the six different canals, finally built to save time and labor for the river boatmen, perhaps the most interesting was the one at South Hadley, where for some years there were no locks whatever: It was a Yankee idea and of enough interest to attract Dr. Timothy Dwight even to the point of eliciting a fairly minute description of the contraption.

There was a solid piece of masonry rising from the lower level at the foot of the rapids to the height of the stream above the swift water. On the sloping surface of this wall there was a car large enough to take a river boat on board.

One of these boats, coming upstream, would find this car submerged in a pool at the foot of the incline. The boat would be floated onto the car and made fast. A cable ran from the end of the car to a cylindrical axle at the top of the incline. This axle revolved between two water wheels, on either end.

When the signal was given the water was turned onto these wheels. As they turned, the cable was wound around the axle drum and slowly the car, with its boat on deck, was hauled to the higher level. There, settling into another basin, the boat was floated off. Downriver boats were lowered by reverse methods.

The last canal to be finished was the one at Windsor Locks, where Adriaen Block had turned back on the memorable spring day when he discovered the river for the white man.

By now a new force was growing along the river—competition.

There were those who wished to improve the canals all along the river, and to clear out its channel so that shipping would be safe and sure. Soon a company was formed to have exclusive control of this enterprise. Rival companies planned to parallel the river with artificial waterways.

Engineers were sent out by the government following excited calls from capitalists and shippers in the upper reaches of the river. They had plans drawn by which the Connecticut and Lake Champlain were to be joined by one of three possible routes. As a newspaper writer, who covered a meeting at Montpelier, where these three plans were discussed, expressed it: "We most earnestly hope that the fever will not abate until the cooling waters of the Connecticut shall meet and mingle with those of Lake Champlain."

No doubt some application of cooling waters was indicated. Meanwhile another group was projecting a waterway straight across Massachusetts to Boston. A plan to use the Deerfield involved tunneling of the mountains where later the Hoosac Tunnel was bored through. The St. Lawrence and the Connecticut were to be joined, in another plan, via Lake Memphremagog. Hopes of new commercial grandeur bloomed in many an inland town where there was only a babbling brook.

The net result of all this excitement over canals was one real ditch, which was intended to be the beginning of a true rival of the river. This was the Farmington Canal. It was in operation from Northampton southward to New Haven and tidewater. This shunted trade from its natural downriver course and left the important business centers of Springfield and Hartford high and dry.

It was to overcome this that the last rapids, below which tides rose and fell, those at Windsor Locks, were circumvented with a canal. This was built by the businessmen of the lower river. It would keep the boats, loaded with goods from the north, passing down the river, in the way they should go if the income from trade was to continue for the valley cities, instead of being turned eastward at Northampton to the Farmington Canal.

During all these changes in the river there had been changes in the type of craft used upon it. From early days there had been sailing vessels on the lower river. Gradually shipbuilding assumed an important place in industry, and all along the shore boats of various kinds and sizes might be seen being built.

These tidewater boats carried goods not only to Boston, New York, and other southern ports, but often sailed to the West Indies and England. From small beginnings this trade had grown with the increasing needs of the valley.

From the newer settlements to the north came pipe staves and barrel hoops, furs, and later fleeces. From points lower down, salt fish—salmon mostly, with which the river abounded. Horses and cattle were part of the outgoing cargoes. When Governor Bradford's carefully nurtured apple trees had been spread abroad, cider was added to the exports. The first tobacco was being shipped by 1830 from the low-lying farms along the river. Soon the fragrant onion was beginning to make its way out of the valley.

On the return voyages the sailor-traders brought salt, and sugar, and hogsheads of molasses; for rum was in great demand. As fine houses began to appear along village streets and on the hills overlooking the river, certain luxuries for ladies found their places in incoming cargoes.

George Hall was advertising: "CHEAP, ELEGANT GOODS, Consisting of elegant cashmeres, yellow nankins, Chinese crepes, ginghams, and Irish linens."

Also there were advertised: "hardware, crockery and glassware, West Indies and New England rum, real cognac brandy, Lisbon port, genuine cider brandy, American gin and plug tobacco, Snuff, mould and dipp candles, brimstone, sulphur, etc." A Hartford merchant offered "looking glasses, stockings, hatchets, nails, firearms, cow bells and jews harps."

Obviously, as the towns grew in size and wealth many things which previously had been made at home, and probably were still fabricated in the settlements up the river, were now bought at the store. And the more that was bought at the store the greater was the demand for shipping.

Two other matters interested the river navigators who sailed the seas.

During the Revolution some of them had found privateering generally profitable. In 1812 a war was declared of which they did not approve. They felt it killed legitimate business; so they did not sit idly by. There were many tales of their trips far afield, of captures, of escapes, and of bloody battles. Not a few of these men went out from the river and never came back to tell their stories.

The other matter—an import which was never largely advertised in the river valley—was a well-known trade in slaves. That it never grew to large proportions was probably due to the fact that the valley was not adapted to slave labor. However, the owners of many of the fine mansions along the river had one or more black servants, who were frequently mentioned in last wills and testaments of the 1800's.

With the completion of the canals the types of boats used north of Springfield gradually changed—usually to fit the canal. The early flatboat was crude and strictly utilitarian. Not infrequently it made only one trip down the river and was then broken up for lumber. Others were made with considerable care, usually of two-inch oak planks, and generally with a cabin.

There were sails to help in the slow journey upriver. However, the chief reliance for locomotion in the tedious journey was placed in sturdy "polemen." These men, using long ash poles tipped with an iron point, literally pushed the heavily loaded craft upstream. Before the canals were built they also managed to get the boats through some of the rapids. In fact, at such places as Enfield Falls and Windsor

Locks there were always extra polemen waiting to be called into service.

In time these rivermen, crews of the flatboats, came to be known as river-gods. They were a picturesque lot, given to strong drink and singing, according to the old stories. When they stopped at towns overnight the taverns witnessed scenes of wild carousing. They, and the men who brought logs down the river in huge multiple rafts, furnished many a wild tale of strength and daring to be told to later generations.

The arrival of a boat at the landing places beside the river, from Barnet in Vermont as far as tidewater, was an important event and business became brisk. As many as fourteen flatboats were reported tied up at Wells River at one time. The town must have overflowed with rivermen, and with the merchants who came to buy from the cargoes.

All this time on the upper river, in Orford, New Hampshire, a young man, who has already been mentioned in the first chapter of this book, was puttering with steam. Samuel Morey had come up the river at the age of four in an ox cart driven by his father. First he made a spit, which turned the meat before the open fire by employing steam from the teakettle.

Then one Sunday morning in the spring of 1793, when the good people were at church, young Morey brought out another experiment with steam. Only a local blacksmith and a Yale professor knew what he had been working on for weeks during the cold winter.

It was a skiff, most of which was occupied by a steam boiler that left just room enough for a crew of one. The well-known water wheel was present too, but this time it was turned *in* the water and not *by* the water, and the propulsive force was steam.

Slowly the small craft got underway. It worked! The excited Samuel turned it upstream. It cut the current and went steadily on at five miles an hour. By the time the benediction in the churches on either side of the river had been said, the young inventor had his small boat tied up at the wharf opposite his Orford home. But in that short time history had been made on the quiet waters of the Connecticut.

For the first time steam applied to paddle wheels had been used to propel a boat. Six years earlier John Fitch, a native of Windsor, Connecticut, had built a boat, using steam to move paddles arranged in a row on each side of the boat, but neither he nor Morey knew of the other's experiments. It was fourteen years after Morey's Sunday morning voyage into history that Robert Fulton offered his steamboat to the world.

A year or two after his first trip in his little boat on the river, Samuel Morey made another boat in New York. With it he steamed from New York, through the Sound, and up the Connecticut to Hartford. It was the longest trip ever made by a steam-propelled boat up to that time.

His meeting with Fulton and Fulton's visit to Orford, as well as Fulton's later use of Morey's devices (some under patent), make a story in which Samuel Morey, disillusioned and disappointed, nevertheless showed qualities of greatness which Robert Fulton never possessed.

The introduction of steam-propelled boats at once aroused the commerce-minded men along the river. Again they saw a chance to save time—and more time was more money. First they got the river channel cleaned out under a company charter, which gave them control of the traffic that used the channel. It also gave them the right to charge there-for. It took them eight years to complete the job, and they charged boatmen accordingly.

It was not many years later when, on the lower river, a race was on between competing steamboat companies. Each one tried to produce a boat larger and speedier than its rival. Luxurious cabins made their appearance, and one company advertised separate cabins for men and women—the former placed up forward near the bar. Then they began to cut rates until, at one time, the usual $4.50 rate to New York from Hartford was pared down to 25 cents, meals included.

Then speed entered into the picture. Commodore Cornelius Vanderbilt sent boats scudding between New York and Hartford faster than anybody had dreamed possible. For a time he held supremacy. In due time, however, another company produced a speedier boat and the Commodore retired from the river. Needless to say, in this period of struggle for speed there were numerous burstings of boilers, with tragic results and there were holocausts that were remembered for generations.

On the other hand, there were leisurely trips down the quiet river with constant enjoyment of the scenery upon the shore. The stately white mansions set among great trees, the small villages almost hidden except for roofs, and pointing spires, slipped by until a region of busy wharves and factory chimneys was reached. Finally there was the voyage up the Sound, with gulls flying overhead. All this was a part of life along the river.

Above Springfield, Massachusetts, and along the Vermont and New Hampshire shores, the life of the river moved in a less majestic pattern. It was because the canals determined the pattern by which boats had to be cut for this region—the canals and the lessening depth of water. There were several

attempts to adapt the boats to the upper river, about all having been done that could be devised to adapt the river to the
boats.

The most successful style of steamer was a stern-wheeler
made by Thomas Blanchard, who had contributed a varied
assortment of Yankee inventions along the Connecticut. This
boat was said to be of such shallow draft that it would nav-
igate on a fairly heavy dew.

The various attempts to make Barnet, Vermont, the head
of river commerce resulted in several notable failures to reach
the goal. In the fall of 1826 one of Blanchard's type of boat,
drawing only two feet of water when loaded, was towed to
Hartford. She hopefully bore the name *Barnet*.

The Enfield Canal was not then completed and the
stretch of white water there offered the first obstacle. With
her engines sizzling to the bursting point and with extra
polemen straining every muscle, the best the *Barnet* could do
was to hold her own against the current.

Finally barges were lashed on either side of her, enabling
the polemen to dig into the riverbanks. Slowly these huskies,
whose jobs this new method of transportation was soon to
end, added the needed manpower to the boat's horsepower.
Thus the rapids were conquered. The little boat steamed into
Springfield with all the assurance of an ocean greyhound.

Up the river the Vermonters in Bellows Falls were preparing for a suitable reception of the pioneering *Barnet*.
There was to be a banquet at the Mansion House, with
speeches. Flags were spread to the breeze and back-country
settlers greased their wagon wheels and put fresh straw in the
wagon boxes.

On the appointed day the crowd gathered along the
riverbanks at Bellows Falls. They heard the new sound that

heralded the approach of the little wonder—the little wonder that was ushering in a new day of prosperity for the river.

With quiet dignity the *Barnet* steamed into the basin below the lower lock. That night in the crowded dining room of the Mansion House no less than thirty-two toasts were drunk and the new day about to dawn was not infrequently mentioned. "To the town of Barnet: may she speedily be gratified by the sight of her first born!" one speaker, slightly mixed in his vital statistics, proposed. Another, less poetic in his expression, shouted: "Let the Connecticut River be dammed, but never choked!" And so on, far into the night.

The new day dawned, but it was not the one the exuberent spirits of the night before had hailed. The *Barnet* would not go through the canal. She was too wide.

Others argued that the canal was too narrow. Just how it happened that the matter had not been looked into is still a mystery. Instead of doing what was done later with another misfit—loading the boat onto wheels and carting it through the town to get around the difficulty—the *Barnet* stuck to water.

After showing her prowess by whisking around in the still water below the canal, she turned her nose southward and sailed away trailing a banner of wood smoke across the December sky.

Not long after this journey the little boat overexerted herself and burst her boiler. Thus falling under suspicion she was next seen towing a barge filled with ladies and gentlemen, who were attending the ceremonies marking the opening of the Enfield Canal. They all felt safer to have the *Barnet* merely towing them.

Another boat tried to make Barnet, Vermont—still waiting for the sight of "her first born." It, too, failed. Then the *John Ledyard,* named for the famous Dartmouth student who had paddled down the river to the sea in a canoe he had fashioned from a log, got to within ten miles of the goal. But there, almost within sight of Barnet, it was stranded on a sandbar.

Someone, moved to verse upon the occasion, wrote a jingle about the ill-fated boat and its captain:

And further, and further, and further still,
The steamboat winding through the vale,
While cannon roared through hill and dale;
For this is the day when Captain Nutt
Sailed up the fair Connecticut.

After trying other boats, fitted to the various sections of the upper river, and finding the transfer costs too high, the whole dream of commerce faded away. Soon only rafts of logs, and here and there a canoe or rowboat, cut the waters of the upper river. Heavy freighters and swaying stagecoaches, along the highways, held the monopoly of the transportation business until the whistle of the new monster, the steam railroad engine, woke the echoes along the river's banks.

Charles Dickens described a short trip he took on the river during his American tour. He journeyed from Springfield to Hartford on a cold February day, when cakes of ice often surrounded the small boat in which he traveled.

It certainly was not called a small steamboat without reason. I omitted to ask the question, but I think it might have been a half pony power. Mr. Paap, the celebrated dwarf, might have lived and died happily in the cabin, which was fitted with common sash-windows like an ordinary dwelling house. These windows had bright red curtains too, hung on slack strings across the lower panes; so that it looked like the parlor of a Liliputian public house, which had got afloat in a flood or some other water accident, and was drifting nobody knew where. But even in this chamber there was a rocking chair. It would be impossible to get on anywhere in America without a rocking chair. I am afraid to tell how many feet short this vessel was, or how many feet narrow; to apply the words length and width to such measurement would be a contradiction in terms. But I may state that we all kept the middle of the deck, lest the boat should unexpectedly tip over; and that the machinery, by some surprising condensation, worked between it and the keep; the whole forming a warm sandwich about three feet thick. . . .

The river was full of floating blocks of ice, which were constantly crunching and cracking under us; and the depth of the water, in the course we took . . . did not exceed a few inches. . . . The Connecticut river is a fine stream; and the banks in summer time are, I have no doubt, beautiful, at all events I was told so by a young lady in the cabin; and she should be a judge of beauty, if the possession of a quality include the appreciation of it, for a more beautiful creature I never looked upon.

By the time the strange-looking procession of stage-coaches, drawn by a fiery steed known as the Iron Horse, had been moving fairly regularly between Albany and Schenectady, New York, in the early 1830's, the subject of steam railroads was much in the minds of the people of the Concticut valley. Especially in the minds of the people of the upper valley, where river traffic had proved a dismal failure in spite of the roseate dreams canals and locks and steamboats had offered. Now there was a vehicle driven by steam which was not dependent on the vagaries of the river. Farsighted men at once realized the possibilities of the upper valley's return to its pre-Revolutionary position as an important highway between Canada and the Atlantic seaboard.

By the time the first train steamed out of the valley, June 26, 1848, from White River Junction, Vermont, headed for Bethel, Vermont, track was being laid toward Burlington, on the Bethel end, and southward from White River Junction to meet other links along the valley.

The rail line across Massachusetts had been running for

some years from Boston to Albany, and lines had been spreading northward via Fitchburg and Keene to White River Junction, and also up the valley from Springfield, Massachusetts. A grand celebration, lasting three days, was held in Boston in September, 1851, attended by Millard Fillmore, president of the United States, Lord Elgin, governor general of Canada, Daniel Webster, and other dignitaries, to mark the opening of through traffic between the St. Lawrence River, at Montreal, and Boston.

Obviously considerable dirt had been flying during those few years. Many meetings must have been held along the river in schoolhouses and town halls, for local support was needed for the connecting links in the new railroad system. No doubt the market for wood, for which the new monster had an insatiable appetite, was a strong argument in the rural regions. To get the work done labor was imported from Ireland, and the eventual assimilation of these newcomers into the life of the region had a lasting influence upon its social structure.

By the time trains were running in the Connecticut valley, the early railroad cars, which suggested stagecoaches with flanged wheels, had given way to something resembling present-day coaches in general. The engineer and the fireman, who had been stationed on an open platform, were soon given shelter.

Even today few people fail to feel a slight thrill at the sight of a moving train. How much more must the early iron horses have filled the onlookers with awe. The Bellows Falls *Gazette* of January 4, 1849, gives an account of the arrival of the first train in Charlestown, New Hampshire. It had come up from the Western Railroad in Massachusetts over two connecting links and carried passengers from as far away as Boston. The item read:

THE CARS HAVE COME!

On Monday, January 1, much to the astonishment of some, and gratification of all, the first train of cars ever seen in this vicinity passed over the Cheshire road and Sullivan [road] to Charlestown, New Hampshire. The day was fine and a great assembly of people had collected here to observe the grand entree of the Iron Horse. The engine came up in grand style and when opposite our village, the monster gave one of its most savage yells, frightening men, women, and children considerably, and bringing forth the most deafening howls from all the dogs in the neighborhood. This day, Thursday, the Sullivan road is to be opened, with the usual ceremonies, to Charlestown, and then the arrival of the cars will be a common, everyday business affair.

It would appear that the notion that, immediately upon the arrival of cars as a daily occurrence, public interest would diminish was an attempt to assume a blasé and sophisticated pose. It took many years for the coming of the "cars" to be taken as a matter of course in the villages along the upper river valley.

In 1884 Springfield, Massachusetts, already an important railroad junction with northern and east-west connections, was joined by rail with Hartford, Connecticut. This piece of railroad building involved a sizable railroad bridge, fifteen hundred feet in length with a drawspan, across the river at Windsor Locks.

In Connecticut, the river held sway as a means of transportation for some years after railroads had surplanted it elsewhere. This was due to the zeal of the Connecticut Steamboat Company. Hartford and New Haven were joined by railroad fairly early, but it was not until 1871 that the lower river was paralleled by railway through to the Sound.

In passing it is interesting to note how some relics of former days were invariably retained in new undertakings. Just as the early railroad coaches were replicas of the horse-drawn stagecoach, so in the old railroad charters the pattern of the toll road was followed. Obviously it was expected that various companies would build adjoining sections of the road-bed and these facilities would be used by whatever steam car company desired to operate on them. So the builders were authorized to "erect toll houses, establish gates, appoint toll gatherers, and demand toll upon the road." In many cases the charter might "authorize any company to enter the railroad at any point."

So for fifty years the railroads along the river took over the valley's commerce except for the boat traffic which had its place from tidewater down.

Then came the period of consolidation, with the elimination of rival lines and the abandonment of others, the accent being more and more on through traffic. This was especially true in the lower valley where the meteoric rise of the interurban trolley took care of much of the local passenger traffic.

Meanwhile, in Springfield, Massachusetts, the Duryea brothers were experimenting with a gasoline buggy, which was destined to scare more horses than the iron monster on the rails had ever done, for this new means of transportation required no rails. If it was ever allowed on the highways, there would be no escape from it.

By 1896 this speed demon, which had already traveled at an average speed of a little over seven miles an hour, in a 50-mile road race, was being built in the first factory established for such a purpose. And at about the same time Hiram Percy Maxim had also got his idea of a gasoline-driven buggy out on the Hartford, Connecticut, highway. Unheralded, a new era was about to dawn—an era involving momentous changes that were then only faintly discerned.

The railroads are running up and down the valley connecting far ports. A few of them still are busy and prosperous, but for many the motorbus, the motor truck, and the private motorcar have made their long survival uncertain. Perhaps some of the various regulatory laws that have been suggested may make their situation more secure, by placing obstacles in the way of their rivals. But that such attempts can be permanently successful seems uncertain, to say the least.

These are the kinds of transportation the river valley, which has always been a highway, has known: First, it was the river itself that carried people and burdens; canoes, rafts, sailboats, and flatboats—and eventually steamboats—were its mode of transportation. Then the paths along the river's banks grew into roads. These became turnpikes on which swaying stagecoaches and freighters became the transportation system by way of land. Then came the era of steam-propelled modes of transportation: on the river the steamboat; in the river valley the railroads with their smoke-belching iron horses. Next there were smooth-running trolley cars for which the river often furnished power; and then appeared the gliding motorcars, and buses, and heavy trucks, moving on paved highways that the taxpayers demanded and paid for.

All these changes the valley, which is a highway, has seen. And overhead, perhaps, there is an airplane. It is flying high, but it is guided by the silver thread, far below, that is the river.

CHAPTER XIII

Parsons and Politics

IN ALMOST all the early settlements along the river there was a divine who shaped their ends even if at times a divinity seemed to be lacking. A town was not allowed to call itself such until it could support a church and have a settled minister. While not all inhabitants of towns were church-goers, those who were, ruled. In fact, it seems impossible to omit the church in any consideration of the early days of this country.

Our forefathers' arrival on the shores of Massachusetts was due, in large part, to their desire to worship God according to the dictates of their own consciences.

That did not mean, as many have thought, that they ever intended to allow everyone perfect freedom to form any kind of religious organization he might wish. The Puritan church was already in being when the group left Scrooby for Holland. They had it all arranged so that it was absolutely clear to anyone how their consciences dictated that God should be worshiped.

They desired to worship as their own particular brand of conscience dictated, not as some other congregation might find its mentor leading toward the heavenly throne. They evidently had no objection to a state church as such. They only objected to the one they were subject to in the mother country.

In this New World, the rules of the church being the rules one lived by since the law came from the Bible, there was naturally a close connection between the church and the government. To all intents and purposes, in the Connecticut River valley at least, there was an established church—the Congregational church. This was practically so in all of Connecticut and Massachusetts. Connecticut did not sever the ties that bound church and state together until its new constitution of 1818.

Even so successful a businessman and political leader as William Pynchon, founder of Springfield, Massachusetts, learned to his sorrow that the pulpit ruled. When after an outstanding career he offered some views on the Atonement which were contrary to the accepted Calvinistic beliefs, he found himself dropped from the magistracy. So deeply did he feel the treatment accorded to him by the Congregational powers in the valley that in sorrow and anger he returned to England.

For a hundred fifty years or more the fight against the state church in Connecticut and against theocratic control in Massachusetts and the general struggle to shake off the shackles of Calvinism continued. It offered the fighting instincts, which in earlier days had been given free play in struggles against the red men, a fresh field of endeavor.

While the process seemed devastating, the results were

on the whole beneficial. The splits in the Congregational church opened the way for other denominations with more liberal views. Then came a lessening of the exclusive interest in saving one's own soul from the fires of hell. There was an awakening to the social implications of Christianity according to the teachings of the New Testament.

Most important of all, the educational institutions that have made the valley of the Connecticut one of the most favorable spots in the country for the growth of fruits of the mind owe their origins, directly or indirectly, to the influence of religion.

Before the end of the century that brought the first colonists there had been a splitting away from the leadership of the clergy in many of the older settlements. The young people grew up and the graying minister found himself faced with the age-old problem of the younger generation. Church rows, not infrequently over the minister, resulted in the removal of small groups to another camping ground under a new spiritual leader. In the older settlements some of the pillars tired of carrying the burden.

We hear John Whiting's voice pleading in an election sermon for a return to the fold: "A rain of righteousness and soaking showers of converting, sanctifying grace sent from Heaven will do the business for us, and indeed nothing else."

The excitement incident to founding new settlements and the holy joy in the new freedom thus attained had lost considerable pristine potency in bloody struggles with the Indians and the necessary daily drudgery to keep body and soul together. These sobering matters tended to take men's attention away from exclusive thoughts of the soul's salvation in the hereafter. This world was verily too much with them, and a new generation was growing up.

So the Connecticut valley ecclesiastics through the General Court, the legislative body, tried to bolster up interest in religion by passing a law. It was a theological compromise known as the Half Way Covenant. In 1664 the General Court of Connecticut adopted a decision of the Church Council favoring it. By it the ministers hoped to hold young people in the church until they should be old enough to undergo a real conviction of sin and conversion. At once there was a split over it. Generally it seems to have failed to stimulate. Lyman Beecher, father of Harriet Beecher Stowe, referred to the move as "this anomaly in religion."

Later the power of government was again sought to bolster up matters pertaining to the church. A committee of laymen and ministers was appointed, and they brought forth the Saybrook Platform in 1708. It set up associations of churches and ministers. The Saybrook Platform gave members the power over the forming of new churches, the settling of religious disputes, and the licensing of ministers.

Immediately there was a storm of disapproval from the older leaders, especially from those who objected to any authority which interfered with the "sovereignty" of each congregation, which was, after all, the genius of the denomination. Then this new evidence of the close connection between church and state aroused growing uneasiness among those opposed to any such fusion.

Gradually the attempts to strengthen the church by law gave way to the idea of an inward rejuvenation, and the Connecticut valley felt the first of the long series of revivals; some of them local breezes, others of cyclonic proportions. They swept not only the entire length of the river valley, but all New England as well.

"The Great Awakening," a brief but widespread stirring

of the religious waters, started at Northampton, Massachusetts, in 1740. There the Reverend Jonathan Edwards revivified all the predestinational doctrines of Calvinism, with the perils of hell-fire and damnation vividly portrayed, thus bringing a large addition to his flock. "The noise of the dry bones waxed louder and louder," he announced.

The excitement spread up the river to the Hadleys, to Sunderland and Deerfield. Springfield also felt it. Jonathan Edwards's father was ministering to the church in West Hartford, Connecticut. He and a few others went to Northampton, Massachusetts, to see how Edwards the Younger wrought.

They found that the preaching was nothing new. Some were elected to be saved from the beginning, come what might; others were foreordained to eternal punishment, no matter how much they might try to avoid it. "Infants, if they are out of Christ are in God's sight young vipers, and infinitely more hateful than vipers." Preaching this doctrine Jonathan Edwards sired twelve spiritual possibilities.

Hartford was soon visited by the indefatigable Jonathan Edwards, who brought with him the English clergyman, George Whitefield. They, together with Eleazer Wheelock and others, stirred mightily the fires of religious zeal throughout the river valley. Emotional natures responded violently to their revivalistic methods and theological beliefs. The resulting outbursts were encouraged by some preachers, but by no means all of them. The coldness usually associated with religionists of that day was considerably warmed where the visiting clergymen operated.

It was inevitable that a strong opposition should eventually arise to outsiders like Whitefield going about and stirring up placid congregations. This was particularly true when such strangers attacked the minister of a congregation. In a few instances they even forced incumbents out of their pulpits because of a difference in theological opinion.

New groups came into being. There were the New Lights, and opposed to them, quite naturally, were the Old Lights. A third group of middle-of-the-roaders were called Moderate Lights. Each was trying not to outshine but to blow out the other.

Then there were those who denied and defied the authority of the state to take a hand in church matters—those who had been especially incensed by the legalizing of the Half Way Covenant and the Saybrook Platform. These objectors were called Separates. Of this group was Parson Dewey, the first minister of Bennington, Vermont. Later many of the Separates were absorbed by the Baptists.

Soon the New Lights found themselves pursued by the law. They were often arrested, jailed, fined, and excommunicated for even attending a Separates' meeting. This was done by the Congregationalists of the Old Light order. Many of the Separates now refused to pay taxes for the support of the state Congregational church, and were ousted from local offices.

Some clergymen who dared to occupy Separate, or even Baptist pulpits found their salaries withheld or themselves turned out from their church association. The Baptists gained not a few new members in this way. The Anglican church, which took no stock in revivals, also received many of the former supporters of the Congregational faith.

It was only natural that the upholders of the old order in matters theological should also be conservatives in matters political. In Connecticut and all along the river, generally, the proponents of Federalism and the leaders of the Congregational church walked together "like Moses and Aaron." They formed a powerful ruling class in the early part of the nineteenth century, which came to be known as the Standing Order. In this connection the powerful Timothy Dwight came to be known as Pope Dwight.

This conservative group looked upon tolerance in religion and democratic ideas in matters of a political nature as imports from France whence also came, in time, Deism and what they referred to as "other atheistic beliefs." Even the student body of Yale drifted into infidelism, leaving the men of orthodox beliefs in a hopeless minority. It took the reviving of Timothy Dwight, a grandson of Jonathan Edwards, to set the young atheists in the right way during the second Great Awakening of 1818, which eventually caused the separation of church and state in the lower reaches of the river; a result not at all desired or anticipated by its original leaders.

As a result of all these upheavals and soul stirrings the congregations of the newer denominations grew apace. They offered haven for the differing religious opinions that were evolving. Methodists, Baptists, and Anglicans found their numbers greatly increased. However, it was only after a struggle, at times bitter, that the Anglican church succeeded in getting a charter granted by the legislature of Connecticut which allowed the establishment of Washington College, later Trinity. This was started in Hartford in 1823, probably the first educational institution making the acceptance of no set creedal belief necessary for admittance. Eight years later the Methodist denomination started Wesleyan University down the river at Middletown.

It was at about this time that a sermon was delivered by Lyman Beecher, then serving the church in Connecticut, on the topic, "The Practicability of Suppressing Vice by Means of Societies Instituted for that Purpose." As a result of this sermon a society "for promoting good morals" was founded. This marked the beginning of an important and practical step by the church away from the narrow path of theology to the broader fields of everyday living.

There was the movement against intemperance, which found its first objects among the clergymen themselves. Cotton Mather, years before, had been concerned by the widespread use of alcoholic beverages among the ministry. "The consequences of the affected Bottel in that Colony [Connecticut] as well as ours [Massachusetts], are beyond all imagination." It was a good beginning, near home. A desire to spread the gospel grew apace and energetic souls longed to go forth into the wilderness to preach it.

"Lost! Lost! Lost!" had been the frequent cry of the soul struggling in agony. Timothy Dwight had stressed the use of "fire and the hammer." "Man must live at the foot of sovereignty to receive an undeserved favor," shouted another preacher. Even little children sang "A fallen creature I was born." Out of this theology, and nurtured in it, came a new leader—a leader toward the light.

Horace Bushnell, who at Yale had changed from the study of law to the study of theology, came to the North Congregational Church in Hartford, Connecticut, in 1833. He questioned both the idea of revival meetings and the value of the ideas they attempted to revive.

He could not stomach the idea of children being "vipers." He felt a child should grow up a Christian, never knowing himself to be otherwise. He emphasized the need for a Christian home where the child should grow in the happy atmosphere of trust and devotion. He wrote to his own child, "do not inquire so much what you are, whether truly a Christian in heart or not, as how you may come into the full Christian spirit." However dull this advice might be to a healthy youngster, it was certainly a radical departure from the agonizings demanded by the older Calvinists, which had wrecked the

childhood of many a sensitive soul. The Old Lights bestirred themselves and would have ousted the heretic Bushnell from his pulpit. But his church placed itself beyond their reach.

All these theological storms in the lower valley left their mark farther up the river. In general the conservatives held sway. In Massachusetts they held at bay for many years the growing power of Boston Unitarianism. Within the older churches they gave way only inch by inch to liberal ideas.

It will be recalled that in Vermont the early settlers, who followed the river valley northward, took their Connecticut conservatism with them. They looked askance at the Separates and Deists who had settled west of the mountains, and who allowed the "atheistical" writings of Ethan Allen to be circulated.

It will be remembered, perhaps, that when Vermont adopted its constitution it was the liberalism of the Pennsylvania constitution that went into it, due to the influence of Ethan Allen's friend and fellow Deist, Dr. Thomas Young.

Later the struggling orphan republic, unwanted as a state by its neighbors and unrecognized by the United States, adopted the laws as its own "as they stood on the Connecticut law book." The common law also was included according to the usage prevalent in New England. Thus Vermont had a most liberal constitution as related to its offers of freedom in matters of religious opinion; but the code of statute law it took from Connecticut was far otherwise. It has taken years to iron out the divergence.

In general in Vermont and New Hampshire, along the river, the social and religious pattern of Connecticut and Massachusetts was repeated. The newer sects occupied the other sections of Vermont and, to a less extent, of New Hampshire. Pope Dwight found the river valley men after his own heart—his Old Lights heart. "Steadiness of character," he said, "softness of manners, a disposition to read, respect for the law of magistrates, a strong sense of liberty, blended with an equally strong sense of the indispensable importance of energetic government, are all extensively predominant in this region." It is recorded that Timothy Dwight later referred to the west-of-the-mountains Vermont men as "a tobacco-chewing, swearing, Godless lot, who need the Gospel preached to them."

River towns backed the temperance movement with moderation. When the slavery question became a burning issue they favored the colonization idea rather than abolition. "Daniel Webster with his high tariff views and conciliatory principles regarding slavery became the idol of this wool-growing, church-going section."

Aristocratic Portsmouth and Exeter, to the east of the river valley, were not approved of by the valley people. So, at either side, the main river valley people found dissatisfaction in the over-the-mountain neighbors, who yet belonged to the same states that they belonged to.

Out of all these bitter quarrels and fights over theological matters there emerged all the educational institutions in which the river valley abounds. Yale was started so that certain theological ideas might be inculcated in the minds of the next generation of preachers. Trinity and Wesleyan came into being as a direct result of opposition to the Calvinistic ideas of the Congregationalists. Eleazer Wheelock was inspired to teach Indians and eventually to start Dartmouth by the revivalistic enthusiasm of the Great Awakening. Amherst's founders desired first to prepare young men for the gospel ministry, and it was a young clergyman named John Greene who in 1870 persuaded Sophia Smith of the need of a college for women, which became a reality in Smith College in Northampton in 1873.

Certainly it was religious zeal that prompted Mary Lyon to start the Female Seminary at Mount Holyoke in 1836. Springfield's American International College has the promulgation of Christian principles as a basic ideal. And there can be no doubt of what was in Dwight L. Moody's mind when in 1879 he began his famous schools at Northfield, Massachusetts. While the spiritual tempests that swept through the river valley gradually grew calmer, it is certain that the desire to propagate certain religious beliefs was inherent in each of the river's institutions of learning in their beginnings.

Out of the narrowness of the Calvinistic theology grew more liberal and more Christian ideas of God, and of man's relation to him, both within and without the Congregational church. Once men were freed from the engrossing struggle to save each his own soul from destruction, there grew up instead a social consciousness and an untrammeled interest in the material universe and its laws.

Over the years, thousands upon thousands left home in the Connecticut valley, carrying with them rich stores of the mind. The soul-saving slavery of the early days had given way to the freedom of the intellect. Man had grown up from a worm groveling in the dust to be a self-respecting son of God, with the right to interpret that phrase as he himself saw fit.

From those groups of vine-covered buildings, the colleges, universities, and the many schools of the river valley, all founded in faith and nurtured by unselfish devotion, have gone men and women possessed of those treasures of the heart and mind without which no nation can grow; lacking which civilization itself may be wiped out, even through its own scientific genius.

CHAPTER XIV

Mary Lyon Pioneers Along the River

COTTON MATHER probably voiced a common feeling when, writing of Harvard's founding in 1636, he said, "This colledge is the best thing New England ever thought upon."

Along the Connecticut River valley the interest in education seemed particularly to flourish. By 1825 there were, including Yale whose beginnings were intimately connected with several river valley towns, no less than five institutions in the Connecticut valley where men might receive collegiate education.

But there were no such institutions for women. Undoubtedly, in the minds of many men the females of the species were not equipped with intelligence sufficient to receive such training. They were certainly useful, often ornamental, but could not and should not try to be intellectual.

As a matter of fact, no boy was given higher schooling unless he planned to use it in his chosen field. Since preaching and the law and most teaching were taken care of by men, there was no reason why women should waste their time on something of no practical use to them.

There were a few women, yes, and a few men, who thought otherwise about women. There were two or three academies practically run by pioneering women, such as Catherine Beecher's Hartford Female Academy down the river, where, the theory practiced was that women should be given as liberal a mental training as men. The practical side was that educated women made better teachers—in the home, in training their own children, and in the primary schools, which gradually were being taught by women instead of men. One town, according to the records, awoke to the fact that "Females are a tender and interesting branch of the community, but they have been much neglected in the Public Schools of this town."

Mary Lyon, who had an insatiable thirst for knowledge, when she had drained the shallow cup of the available local schools, fortunately found a deeper spring—an experience too seldom possible for young women of her time.

In Mary Lyon's line was one Chileab Smith, who because he refused to support a church he did not attend saw his orchards uprooted and his land sold to pay his tithes. He and his sons fought it out for ten years, when at length the General Court came to his rescue.

Some of this dogged determination was passed on when Mary Lyon was born in Buckland, a small Massachusetts town, in 1797. "Her inheritance gave her a sound body, a dauntless spirit, a ventursome mind," says her biographer, Beth Gilchrist. To this was added "a merry heart." This added ingredient caused its owner, when she was doing her first teaching, some concern. Her inability to keep a straight face was, she found, bad for discipline.

Like most children brought up on a farm, Mary Lyon soon began her education. She had responsibilities. As soon as she was old enough to take her part, the comfort and well-being of the family were partly upon her shoulders.

She, with six sisters and a brother, were the support of a mother widowed when Mary was six. The mother had been left with a meager supply of this world's goods, and she needed all the assistance her children could give her, as the farm they owned would probably now be listed as a submarginal one.

Mary once wrote: "Want in that mountain home was made to walk so fairly and so gracefully within the little circle of means, that she always had room and to spare for a more restricted neighbor."

Mary learned the fundamentals. She took the wool clipped from their sheep, carded and spun it. This she wove into cloth, which she made into dresses. Not a formal education, perhaps, but a very real and practical one.

After a term at first one school and then another, after her mother had married again and moved away from the farm, Mary found herself at the Reverend Alvan Sanderson's school in Ashfield, Massachusetts. Mr. Sanderson was finally at his wit's end over his new pupil.

He couldn't keep her busy. She grasped knowledge by the handful and was always far ahead of the class. One Friday, in despair, he gave her a Latin grammar and assigned the first lesson for the following Monday. He excused her from her other classwork. On Monday afternoon when she was called on for the first lesson in the grammar she completely overwhelmed Mr. Sanderson. She not only recited the first lesson, which he had assigned, but she continued through the entire book: declensions, conjugations, and all, with hardly a slip. Despite this remarkable brilliance, her relationship with less gifted pupils was a happy one. Her biographer says, "It is not recorded that anyone disliked her."

That first term at Mr. Sanderson's she paid for her board with two coverlets, the wool for which she had dyed, spun, and woven. During later terms she paid her way by teaching.

After teaching a term or so in a small school in Buckland, she took some of her little inheritance and spent a term at Amherst Academy. It is written of her that "her homespun apparel, her extraordinary scholarship, and her boundless kindness, were about equally conspicuous."

At about this period she was also studying natural science under the Reverend Edward Hitchcock in Conway, Massachusetts. Mr. Hitchcock was later the president of Amherst College. His work as a geologist placed him high in his profession. Living in the Hitchcock family, Mary Lyon was taught some of the things which at that time were generally considered an essential part of any young woman's education as an accomplished female. She was instructed in painting and sketching.

Miss Gilchrist tells of the time of Mary Lyon's religious awakening. It seems to have been quite as unique, for that day, as was her mental development.

It occurred on her way home from church where she had listened to a sermon on "God's Government." "Her whole being seemed to open flowerlike toward the giver of the earth's life and her own. That such should have been her first personal experience of God, rather than some form of the agonizing self-torture, so prevalent at the time, is significant. Happiness always lay at the heart of her faith."

In 1821 Miss Lyon was attending a school run by the Reverend Joseph Emerson at Byfield, near Newburyport,

Massachusetts. Mary's old home at Buckland had been broken up after her mother's remarriage and her brother's removal to the West. She now made her home with the family of her friend Amanda White, in Ashfield. It was Amanda's father who because of his great interest in Mary and the family's deep affection for her made it possible for her to attend Mr. Emerson's school at Byfield.

Mr. Emerson had some unusual ideas about training women to be teachers. He had graduated from Harvard and been a tutor there. He discarded the usual reciting by rote of set lessons. "It is thinking, close thinking, that makes the scholar," he said. It was to this end that he successfully led his students. He strongly decried the prevalent notion that a woman must be delicate in body to possess delicacy of feeling.

Mary Lyon's roommate, Amanda White, wrote to her parents: "Mary is gaining knowledge by the handful . . ." She also declared that Mr. Emerson, whose school had students from all but one of the New England states, "is of the opinion that they [the young ladies] will profit more by spending considerable time in visiting and conversing with each other than to spend it all in study."

Presently Sanderson Academy, at Ashfield, thrust precedent aside and engaged Mary Lyon as an assistant and five years later made her preceptress. In the summer she assisted Miss Zilpah Grant at Adams Academy, in Londonderry (now Derry), New Hampshire.

During this period her reputation as a teacher to train teachers seems almost incredible. To whichever school she went, pupils flocked to her, even from other states. Experienced teachers sat under her to learn her methods. If one had been a pupil of Mary Lyon no further teaching certificate was demanded.

She introduced a degree of self-government into her classes, and it is reported that she promoted a "lively interest" in the study of grammar by her method of question and discussion.

The final phase of Mary Lyon's preparation as an educator was, again, under Miss Zilpah Grant at her new school at Ipswich, Massachusetts, which was to run both winter and summer and to offer a new degree of permanence.

Miss Grant's reputation as an educator assured the success of the new venture. Like a few others, she had "deserted the fashionable sands to build upon the rock of self-respect." The prevalent idea "that the proper young female should be taught to sing a few languishing airs, tinkle piano keys, lisp a few French phrases, and sketch impossible landscapes—an equipment which meant that once the stern realities of life were met, a girl and her education were soon parted" was not held by such women as Miss Zilpah Grant and her assistant, Mary Lyon.

There were courses, however, at the Ipswich school in some of the "accomplishments." There was seriously given instruction in painting and drawing for such students as were considered to possess sufficient taste and ability to warrant such training; and Mr. Lowell Mason came to give instruction in music.

Among the methods presented to Mary Lyon, for the teacher's use, at this new school was Miss Grant's belief that pupils should be led to feel that "text books contain only the elements of the study." Miss Grant had also systematized and simplified her curriculum until, as a rule, the students pursued only two subjects at a time.

All these theories and methods deeply interested Mary Lyon. Another thing that appealed to her at the Ipswich school was the ordered way of life despite the lack of any group of buildings. Students and instructors all lived beneath one roof. Often Mary Lyon pondered the dictum with which her superior had impressed her: "The government is intended to be *in* the students, rather than over them." "They need to have their views and feelings drawn away from self, and beyond the family; they need to learn from practice the true Christian philosophy of sacrificing private interest to public good," wrote Mary Lyon, after she had been experiencing this larger group living at Miss Grant's school. For that day, or any day, this was a liberal program for either sex.

At a time when denominational lines were likely to be strongly emphasized, Miss Grant and her asistant refused to make them important. "Not what you think, not what I think, but what is the *truth?*" was the question Mary Lyon put to her students.

The school grew rapidly. Many of its teachers had at some time been heads of schools of their own. Many of the students were teachers who had come to Miss Grant and Mary Lyon to learn new pedagogical theories and methods at this school of remarkable character and personnel.

Miss Grant was often absent and Mary Lyon had the entire charge of the school. Of her teaching methods, one of her pupils wrote: "She did not think so much of a perfect lesson, nor take so much time on the text books as many teachers do, but she made the hour one of delightful, improving conversation and exhilarating mental activity."

In teaching she aimed to make her pupils "bigger than their mothers or fathers." To her, religion was not so much a belief as a life. "God wants you to be happy," she told her students as she pointed out the naturalness of walking with God in his world. None of which sounds like the thunderings of Jonathan Edwards, even then echoing through the Connecticut valley.

The dream of a school endowed by the public, in which no one had any selfish pecuniary interest, where the expenses might be cut to even half of those usually incurred in the few adequate schools which then existed for women, and where the teaching should be of the best, gradually took form in Mary Lyon's mind.

She was handicapped by the taboo of the time, which forbade women's appearance in public as speakers—even in such a gathering as a public prayer meeting. She realized at once that she must make her plans and then get enough men interested in them to present them to the public.

Then came the matter of raising from twenty to forty thousand dollars, not—as might be easier—from one or a few men of outstanding wealth, but from the country's population. This would be a harder task by far, but a method of more value in planning the institution as regarded the minds of the parents whose daughters she wished to help educate.

In the spring of 1833, when Mary Lyon was thirty-six years old, she set about gathering a group of men—"a group of prospective trustees"—to promote her plan for a publicly endowed school for young women. The gentlemen assembled and listened to Mary Lyon's plan. Then they gathered as a group and took action at once. They voted to dissolve.

Through all her years of teaching, especially the latter years with Miss Grant who shared many of her convictions, Mary Lyon's mind had been going over and over the fact of the country's great need for trained teachers and the question of how best to procure that training for them.

knew their capabilities, their hunger for knowledge, and the inadequate fare available for them.

She knew how crowded and disorganized were the public schools and how inadequate and costly were the majority of private schools. She knew of the few whose leaders stood out as an advance guard in the matter of women's education. But she knew that, in this limited number of cases, the heads were always handicapped by uncertainties. They were necessarily overworked and had to depend on ill-trained and underpaid teachers.

Thirty thousand properly trained teachers were needed to take care of the children who were growing up with no schooling at all and an equal number were needed to replace the untrained and incompetent ones already teaching. Miss Lyon knew all this, and she knew that it was largely from women that her help in the matter must come.

Miss Gilchrist quotes President Hopkins of Williams College as saying, at the time, that a year in the girls' schools cost double, or more, what the whole four-year course cost in men's colleges. To meet the need for women's education the costs must be so low that daughters of the middle class could meet them and that those who would have to cover the expense by means of their own exertions could do so.

All of this was basic in Mary Lyon's intention. The need was obvious and the method of meeting it was clear in her mind. One school publicly supported would, she was certain, convince the country of the validity of the plan and method. So she gathered her group of prospective trustees—who met and voted to dissolve.

But by the next spring the resilient spirit of Mary Lyon, undaunted, opened the real campaign. She wrote a circular, with no name attached, and sent it to the friends of Ipswich

Seminary. In it she told of the country's need for educated and trained women and suggested that such a school as the one at Ipswich—a private institution—could be founded and maintained by the financial support of a Christian people as a public venture.

Her plan was plainly outlined:

1. Buildings for the accommodation of the school and of boarders, together with furniture and all other things necessary to outfit, to be furnished by voluntary contributions, and placed, free from incumbrance, in the hands of trustees, who should be men of enlarged views and Christian benevolence.

2. Teachers to be secured possessing so much of a missionary spirit that they would labor faithfully and cheerfully, receiving only a moderate salary compared with what they could command in other situations.

3. Style of living neat, but very plain and simple.

4. Domestic work of the family to be performed by the members of the school.

5. Board and tuition to be placed at cost, or as low as may be, and still cover the common expenses of the family, instruction, etc.

6. The whole plan to be conducted on the principles of our missionary operations; no surplus income to go to the teachers, to the domestic superintendent, or to any other person, but all to be cast into the treasury, for the still further reduction of the expenses of the ensuing year.

By the fall of 1834 the effects of this circular letter were being felt and much of the reaction to it, though by no means all, was favorable. The two local ministerial associations in Hampshire and Franklin counties passed favorable resolutions. This was important as up to date no New England college had been founded without ministerial aid and backing. Other associations were less than enthusiastic in their support.

Twelve eastern and central Massachusetts men met in

Mary Lyon's parlor at Ipswich on September 6, 1834. According to David Choate, they were there to inspect "a few small seeds which Miss Lyon was wishing to put into the ground *somewhere* and *sometime,* allowing us to have something to say as to the place and time and so forth, yet not wholly surrendering anything entirely up to any, and still allowing us the innocent fancy of thinking ourselves for the time being co-workers with her."

It is reported that, once Miss Lyon got under way on her plans, words tumbled out in a perfect torrent which could not be easily stemmed. She had a remarkable manner of persuading her hearers to her own devoted purpose and enthusiasm.

A committee of seven with Professor Hitchcock, four of them ministers, was selected to carry on, to choose a board of trustees, and to present the matter to the public until a charter and permanent organization could be obtained.

Miss Gilchrist records that twenty-eight years later Mr. Choate recalled the infant institution: "I shall never forget, I think . . . how gently we tried to rock its cradle, or how carefully we endeavored, at Miss Lyon's bidding, to carry it in our arms." "At Miss Lyon's bidding"—that was still the dominating note.

Miss Lyon was still the acting head of Ipswich Seminary, but she set forth at once to raise among women the thousand dollars needed for promotion expenses. From door to door she went, and few could resist her sparkling enthusiasm. Much of the money was hard-earned and all of it came in small amounts, but by the end of two months she had secured it, and many women had already become partners in the pioneer enterprise.

Feeling the need of rest, Miss Lyon found it in taking

a few courses at Amherst, notably geology under Professor Hitchcock. It is significant to note that he was a pre-Darwinian evolutionist.

Miss Lyon lived in the Hitchcock family. She went out from there, or gathered a few ladies around her in the Hitchcocks' parlor, to spread her gospel and expound her plans. She also found time to aid in the organization of Wheaton College and the induction of its first head, who was one of her former Ipswich pupils.

In progressing toward her goal she instituted several innovations which aroused criticism. One was the belief that each student at the prospective seminary should have a room of her own, opposition to which idea it is difficult to understand today, until we recall that Mary Lyon lived at the time when almost all families were large and the system of room sharing and "doubling up" was a matter of course.

Also there was skepticism about her plan to get teachers imbued with sufficient missionary zeal to persuade them to give their services for a nominal salary. Miss Lyon was to take only two hundred dollars for her own living expenses and she therefore felt justified in asking this sacrifice on the part of her teachers since they were all serving in a pioneering enterprise, in which any hint of gain for the personnel might injure or destroy the whole plan. She doubtless expected that once the general idea for the kind of women's college she was forwarding had proved itself, the proper remuneration for its teachers would be adjusted.

The great innovation of having all the household duties performed by students met with various objections. Miss Lyon was accused of really starting a trade school, which accusation she utterly repudiated.

While cutting expense had been her chief reason for

originally planning this type of co-operative housekeeping for her seminary, Mary Lyon kept finding other and better reasons for it. She disavowed any intention of teaching what would now be called domestic science. The girls, she believed, should learn such matters from their mothers in their own homes.

Nor did she plan to change the usual distinction between servant and mistress. To that end *all* the work at the seminary was to be done by the students. "As the exercise will be good for them, they will not find conditions differing from those at home, and they will not be burdened by utter dependence upon domestics," wrote Miss Lyon. Likewise, she believed that such co-operation would emphasize the principle of mutual helpfulness and usefulness, which she wished to have stressed among her students. Perhaps one of the most potent arguments in its favor as a program was that it answered a common question voiced in opposition to educating females: "When girls become scholars, who will make our puddings and pies?"

While turning to earlier recollections, in 1861, Professor Hitchcock said of Mary Lyon's educational venture: "To be its advocate in those early days, when most men treated the project as a quixotic dream, was quite a different thing from what it is now, when the plan has had the prestige of twenty-five years of successful trial, and the name of its founder is enrolled high among the wise and eminent benefactors of the race."

On February 11, 1836, the charter was granted for Mount Holyoke Female Seminary, to be situated at South Hadley in the Connecticut River valley.

Looking back upon its beginning we get a glimpse of the unbelievable obstacles Mary Lyon had to overcome almost singlehanded. Fifty years later William Tyler, who had been a professor at Amherst at the time of the founding of Mount Holyoke and was later to become one of its trustees, gave his recollection of some of the difficulties which Miss Lyon and her educational ideas endured:

> This whole idea, and every particular which I have enumerated, was disputed, repudiated, ridiculed, before this institution was founded. But now the idea and all the particulars are settled principles and established facts, and the credit of settling them belongs to Mount Holyoke Seminary.
>
> The objections to this idea of equalizing the educational advantages of the two sexes were many and various, and not always consonant with the courtesy due to the gentler sex. It was an innovation uncalled for, unheard of until now since the foundation of the world, and unthought of now except by a few strong-minded women and radical men, who would level all distinctions and overturn the foundations of the family, of society, of the church, and of the state. It was unnatural, unphilosophical, unscriptural, unpracticable, unfeminine and anti-Christian; in short all the epithets in the dictionary that begin with *un* and *in* and *anti* were hurled against and heaped upon it.

Hard times shrank the payments, the walls fell in, and the whole scheme for Mount Holyoke Female Seminary came tragically near to failure. But through it all Mary Lyon's persistence and courage won a victory. On October 3, 1836, the cornerstone was laid. A year and one month later Mount Holyoke Female Seminary was a going institution.

That interval had been far from calm for Mary Lyon and her trustees. She showed some of her genius in her selection of these men who should translate her plans into brick and mortar.

While the men were doing that, Miss Lyon was getting the women to send in the needed household supplies of furniture and bedding, and so forth. Likewise she was bolstering up the frequently despairing trustees, who were constantly worried about money matters.

Of course there were a few minor matters to be attended to: who would teach, where apparatus could be obtained, and what applicants should be accepted. The last-named matter Miss Lyon felt was really of utmost importance, for the first class would prove the advance guard of the new movement. If it should fail the entire plan might fail.

It was no wonder that in these days Miss Lyon wrote to her mother: "My head is full of closets, shelves, cupboards, doors, sinks, tables, and so on." Her thoughts and her body must have been occupied with unceasing effort and activity against the approaching day that should mark the opening of the Seminary.

In early November of 1837 the pupils began to arrive to add to the confusion of the situation, which presented an as yet unfinished building.

To many of the girls it was a far journey into a strange country; but any tendency toward homesickness must have been removed in a situation where everyone was at once set to work. Fathers, who brought daughters, were drafted for the heavier work. Girls were sewing, helping get meals. Each one was immediately made a necessary part of an organization where there was more than enough to do.

The trustees also were engaged in doing last-minute jobs that required men's strength and skill. The building, only part of which was finished, was 166 by 50 feet. There were four stories with basement, and two wings were later added. The dining room would hold four hundred people. There was a library, an assembly room, recitation rooms, and one hundred thirty-two private rooms.

An old record says of the day for opening: "The doors were without steps, the woodhouse was not covered, the furniture, delayed by storm, had not arrived, the stoves were not set up, and the bedding, pledged by the ladies in different towns, had not, nearly all, made its appearance."

Eighty rooms were ready for occupancy, but more than enough pupils to fill them were already there.

As soon as classes began there was the difficulty of arranging the domestic chores—about an hour's work a day for each student—so as not to interfere with recitations. To all these domestic arrangements Mary Lyon gave most of her time. She used to say: "The domestic work would prove a sieve that would exclude from the school the refuse, the indolent, the fastidious, and the weakly, of whom you could never make much, and leave the finest of the wheat, the energetic, the benevolent, and those whose early training had been favorable to usefulness, from whom you might expect great things."

That practical matters were made of educational value is proved by the solution of the seminary's difficulty with sour bread, which at first bedeviled Mary Lyon. She picked some of her most reliable pupils to help, studied every step in the process, and herself sat by the Rumford oven with her portable writing desk in her lap, keeping up her correspondence as the bread baked.

The first critical year ended with commencement in August, 1838, when Miss Lyon could say, "On the whole the success of our institution, in every department, is greater than I anticipated. . . ."

But these modest words of Mary Lyon's are not needed to attest the success of this first year of her Mount Holyoke Female Seminary. There is evident support of its success in the fact that four hundred girls, who applied for admission during the second year, had to be refused because of limited space and means.

In the following decade the institution grew enormously in physical aspects and in its influence and reputation. It was recognized, even so soon, as the unique and leading institution dedicated to the higher education of women.

In August of 1846 Mount Holyoke held its ninth commencement, or "Anniversary Day." The Boston *Daily Mail* of August 15 had this to say:

The stranger who looks at this institution, its splendid edifice, unsurpassed by any college building in the land . . . could hardly believe that it had all resulted from the persevering efforts of one Female, enlisting the benevolent energies of others. Yet such is the fact, and it affords a striking illustration of the power of mind, stimulated by motives of philanthropy. The object of its originator was to furnish the means of a thorough education to promising daughters of the poor, as well as of the rich; and this object has been entirely realized.

Mary Lyon lived until the spring of 1849, twelve years after the opening of the seminary's doors. Those twelve years were so packed with ceaseless effort and responsibility that it is not surprising that she died at the age of fifty-two. She had burned her candle at both ends; but she would rather have had it so if thereby the great cause that had germinated in her mind found its fruition.

She died in the midst of her work at her beloved school. Struck down by sudden severe illness, she lived only a week. Word of her death came as stunning, unbelievable news to her faculty, the student body, her associates all over the country, and even to the world across the sea.

But Mary Lyon had built too deep and firm a foundation of influence and purpose to have her death shatter her seminary—the visible embodiment of her belief in higher education for women. The institution she had given her life to create continued to grow and develop even though the earthly span of her existence was ended. Her unquenchable determination had been founded upon continuing truth.

Half a century after its founding, in 1888, Mount Holyoke Female Seminary became Mount Holyoke College. Of its pioneer service in women's education during those fifty years, President Seelye of Smith wrote:

> I should like at least to testify to the obligation which our higher schools for women are under to Mary Lyon and the institution which she founded. Most of them owe their very existence to Mount Holyoke Seminary; all of them are unspeakably indebted work which it has accomplished in the past fifty years in providing better and more abundant material for their work, in educating so many accomplished and self-sacrificing teachers, and in giving so clear and forcible expression to the truth that intelligence is as valuable in a woman's mind as it is in a man's and is as capable and as worthy of the highest cultivation.

Miss Gilchrist, Mary Lyon's most recent biographer, gathers the sum of her contribution to American society in these words:

> Probably no woman has laid a more persuasive hand on American society than she. Nor has her influence been the less compelling because its results have not always been accredited to her. She came upon a democracy in the making, and she left it more democratic than she found it. For Mary Lyon was typically American; the national strain of mingled idealism, pluck, persistence, and energy rose in her to high power. Her roots struck deep into the new world's history; her life is eloquent of its opportunity; her genius belongs to that practical order which has hitherto monopolized the transcendent expressions of its creative force. . . . Thus she moved, an epic figure through . . . the heroic age of higher education of women.

CHAPTER XV

Peddlers: Merchandise and News

THE Connecticut Yankee peddler was a unique character and his business was a unique institution. The period of his activities covered about three-quarters of a century. It began shortly after the Revolution and continued until the Civil War.

The Yankee peddler acquired an unenviable reputation for sharp dealing and chicanery; but, however that may have been, the Connecticut River valley was indebted to him for the expansion of its trade and for the marketing of the many commodities it manufactured. The rest of the country benefited by his distribution of countless wares that otherwise would have been unobtainable except through difficult and indirect means.

The peddler's profession was as old as civilization. It had existed at any time and in any region of the world where means of bartering or selling goods was limited.

Undoubtedly at the moment when the first Connecticut

Yankee peddler was setting out through the river valley, with his pack of wares, all the well-known divines in the valley could quote passages from Homer in the original tongue. In which circumstance they were familiar with the fact that even ancient Greece had had her peddlers. They might have recalled the incident when Odysseus, disguised as a peddler, sought out and discovered Achilles at the court of King Lycomedes.

During the War for Independence the ruse of using a peddler's guise to obtain secret information had frequently been used. Probably someone may have carried word down the river valley of how Gamaliel Painter of Middlebury, Vermont, had acted as a spy at Crown Point, got up as a feeble-minded peddler selling notions. Young Oliver Wolcott of Connecticut had slipped into the servants' quarters of the great DeLancey mansion on New Year's Eve, when British generals were sipping punch and joining in the minuet. Lounging in the kitchen, in his peddler's disguise, he had gained information from the servants who had passed trays of refreshments among the guests. Who was there? What was that that someone was quoting General Clinton as saying? Yes, the trick was fearfully dangerous, but it had worked many times.

Gathering information—secret or otherwise—was a large part of the Yankee peddler's stock in trade, but it was not his primary purpose. His purpose was to sell goods.

In the earliest days he carried his wares in a pack slung on his back and he traveled on foot. Very probably it was a one-man enterprise, and he was selling items he and his family had produced. His territory could not have been very extended.

When the number of salable commodities increased and

his load became too awkward and heavy, the peddler took to horseback and saddlebags. Finally, as the era of the peddler really became established, an ingenious and commodious cart was manufactured for his especial use. All up and down the Connecticut River valley, and throughout the country, the high, coachlike affair hung and packed with dozens of different articles became a familiar sight. Some industries employed fleets of peddlers, sending them out over well-marked routes with regular itineraries.

Setting out in the spring as soon as the roads dried out, they traveled all summer and autumn. They replenished their stock at certain centers. When snow began to fly they returned to the Connecticut River valley. If the business was a one-man concern, the horses and wagon might possibly be sold or the wagon was painted and set in condition during the winter months while the peddler and his horses rested.

Timothy Dwight, who was the moral arbiter for the valley of the early era, had a poor opinion of the peddler's occupation. In his *Travels* he says: "No course of life [as the peddler's] tends more rapidly to eradicate every moral feeling."

As early as 1793 some of the Connecticut newspapers published lists of articles which could be bought from peddlers. "Excellent good leather, brown, white, and striped towcloth of home manufacture, blue, white, and striped mittens, stockings, shoe thread, cheeses, butter, geese feathers, rags, rabbit skins and furs." "Good sweet rum" sold at five- and six pence a gallon and the best Jamaica rum cost one dollar and six pence a gallon.

Mr. William Gilbert Lathrop in his Connecticut Tercentenary Commission booklet on the *Development of the Brass Industry in Connecticut* has considerable to say of peddlers. The brass industry in the United States had its birth in the Naugatuck valley in Connecticut. Its subsequent development meant that an enormous trade in metal manufacture spread to the Connecticut River valley. Mr. Lathrop says:

All through the eighteenth century the general assembly was appealed to for assistance for various enterprises, many of which were unsuccessful. Brass making, however, was not to begin in Connecticut until after the close of the eighteenth century. Copper and brass utensils were, indeed, in use, imported from the Old World, but many of the arts in which Connecticut brass was later to have an important part were then being developed with other materials such as tin, wood, and pewter . . . There were, thus, to be found in the state shortly after the Revolution the beginnings of many industries which later raised the state to the high rank which it now occupies as a manufacturing center. These beginnings were, however, to be found in household industry rather than in more ambitious undertakings of the factory type.

The first in time as well as the most important, both because of its immediate history and because of its indirect influence upon brass and other manufactures, was the making of tinware. The manufacture of culinary vessels and household articles from sheet tin was begun . . . about 1740. After supplying their neighbors [the tinsmiths] reached out for a larger market. Their wares were sold from house to house . . . by pedlars whom they employed. It was easy to make a much larger product than the local market could absorb. . . . After the Revolution these pedlars extended the scope of their operations. At first on foot, then on horseback, and finally by wagon, they sold their wares all over the United States. After a little a special type of wagon was perfected for the trade. A one- or two-horse vehicle was developed, strongly built, to carry prominently displayed samples of wares to be sold. The pedlars traveled to Montreal and Quebec, to Charlestown and through the South, also far to the west, even across the Mississippi. They traded by sale or by barter, making use of every means which ingenuity could suggest to market the goods they happened to have. These Connecticut pedlars were for the West and South the original Yankees. The sharpness of their methods was well illustrated by the prevailing tradition, that they attempted, at least, to sell wooden nutmegs. It was the common practice to charge all that the traffic would bear.

After 1800 the selling of tinware was fully organized and for forty years Connecticut was the center of this industry. In 1810 two thirds of the product of the country came from that state. . . . The most valuable contribution which the tinware manufacture made to the industrial history of the state was the trade organization which it perfected. The itinerant vendors, who were at first mainly interested in the sale of tinware, found their occupation expanded in the sale of other small articles provided for them by Connecticut enterprise. The sale of the product was decidedly the more important end of the business. In 1815 single tin shops sent out as many as twenty or thirty pedlars, in some cases twice as many as the workmen in the home establishment. Until 1850 the pedlars of Connecticut merchandise were known all over the country and the part which they played in the marketing of the local manufactures of small wares can hardly be exaggerated. Several of the men who later made large contributions to the establishment of the brass industry gained their knowledge of the market by their experience as tinware pedlars. In 1850 the standard stock in trade, besides tin, copper, and brass wares, included clocks, hats, shoes, combs, axes, buttons, saddlery, and paper. These wares were even then generally made in small quantities in small establishments with limited capital, but the aggregate of production was large.

One of the items which netted the peddler large amounts was pins—what we call "common pins." But in colonial days and during the early 1800's all pins were imported. Mr. Lathrop says:

One of the items an estate left in Waterbury, Connecticut, in 1749, in company with wearing apparel, breeches, coats, knives, and a razor was a "paper of pins." In 1775 the provincial assembly of North Carolina offered a bounty of fifty pounds for the first twenty-five dozen pins of domestic manufacture equal to those imported from England. At this time pins cost seven shillings six pence a dozen. The cost of pins and their usefulness gave form and point to the phrase "pin money," designating the sum allowed a wife by her husband for the purchase of such necessary articles. Various attempts were made to introduce this manufacture in the United States, but until 1830 all pins were imported.

Then in 1831 a pinmaking machine was invented in New York. By 1841 it proved capable of turning out a pin with a solid head. Previously all pinheads had been made of wound wire. The old adage "See a pin and pick it up—all day long you'll have good luck" has especial significance after one reads these facts about pins. To save pins surely was a matter of wisdom and thrift.

There is an atmosphere of romance connected with the trade of the peddler and his jingling cart. Women and children began to listen for that pleasant sound as soon as spring came. Young girls saved money for some bit of finery, a few yards of dress material, a comb, or thread and needles for long-planned sewing. Matrons counted over their rags stored in the garret, carefully separating white from colored—the former brought more—and wondered how much they would bring in exchange when weighed on the peddler's scales; how many shining pans and pots would they buy?

Perhaps pewter or brass buttons were bought for a broad-cloth coat. Where money was plentiful brass and copper kettles were lifted out of the peddler's wagon, a set of pottery jars, or even a britannia tea service, a clock or a brass hand lamp. Where money was scarce, it may be that only a palm-leaf hat or a broom was sold.

The palm-leaf hat trade was a big one before the Civil War. The stuff to make the hats was shipped to many a small town and village in bales wrapped in a kind of palm-leaf fabric. It took two men to handle a single bale. The women and girls for miles around would take the palm leaf and braid it into hats—big work hats that all men wore in those days.

A woman who was a good hand at it could make several in a day. One woman wrote in a letter: "Made 14 pies and 8 hats today." A girl would have been as ashamed not to know how to weave a hat as not to know how to make a loaf of bread.

The man in the town—usually the storekeeper—who handled the hat business with the peddlers would hitch up his team and drive off into the surrounding country for a couple of days. He'd come back with his wagon loaded with hundreds of hats which he had gathered up in exchange for groceries. These he would store away to pass on to peddlers, who would sell them all over the country.

Colonel Israel Putnam is supposed to have introduced tobacco to the Connecticut River valley. It is said that when he returned from an expedition against Havana he brought cigars with him to be enjoyed by the inhabitants who were living in the valley in 1762.

However that may have been, it is true that the Connecticut valley people began raising tobacco in the late 1700's. The farmers' wives made crude cigars. Pretty soon these cigars began to be peddled around the countryside with other homemade products. Then in 1810 a cigar factory was started, and presently another was established. Roswell and Samuel Viets, who began these factories at East Windsor and Suffield, were enterprising men of vision. They hired a Cuban cigarmaker to teach the business to twelve women employees. By 1831 tobacco manufacture and tobacco raising were thoroughly established in the Connecticut valley. The early brands of cigars had intriguing names: Supers, Windsor Particulars, and Long Nines.

Experimentation made at East Windsor about 1830 with some tobacco seed brought from Maryland produced an unusually fine-textured and large plant leaf. This plant was worked upon until the famous Connecticut valley broad-leaf tobacco was produced.

In 1830 Warehouse Point—William Pynchon's old stand—was shipping great quantities of tobacco to Germany. The growth and development of the tobacco leaf industry in the Connecticut River valley from 1830 to 1890, and more especially from 1870 to 1890, was but a hint, a forerunner, of what the business was to become.

The invention of cigar machines made a revolutionary change in production. They made possible a great reduction in the cost of cigars, and it naturally followed that the demand for Connecticut tobacco leaf increased. But there was one serious possibility as to cigar manufacture facing the cigarmakers of Connecticut. The demand for cigarettes was constantly increasing. And cigarettes did not require broadleaf.

In 1910 eight and five-tenths billion cigarettes were manufactured and consumed in the United States, fifty-two billions in 1921, and twenty-four billions in 1931. As a result the market for Connecticut broad-leaf had a decided slump after 1920.

The tobacco situation was finally solved for the Connecticut growers when their long-leaf found a market in Cuba, where it was shipped to be used to make wrappers for Cuban-grown fillers.

But none of these situations existed to harass the cigar manufacturer during the heyday of the Connecticut Yankee peddler, who did a large and flourishing business in Windsor Particulars, Supers, and Long Nines. As the peddler sang and whistled along the country roads and lanes, as he drew up before some tavern or hotel at night, he was assured of a constant and growing market for his wares. He had the satisfaction of knowing that he was one of the indispensable institutions of the country. To the manufacturer he was all-important; almost more important than the employees who produced the wares he sold.

It was true that the past decades had seen a revolutionary change in the manufacture of many of the articles he sold; but what difference? It only meant that he had more to sell, and at less cost.

Take, for example, the brass and copper kettles hanging at the sides of his cart. They used to be cast or were imported. Then, when the process of rolling out sheet metal had been discovered, when the rolling mills began to appear, one by one, along the river, obtaining quantities of brass and copper utensils was a different matter.

Brass buttons too. Long ago they had been made in molds, head and shank cast in a solid piece, just as pewter buttons had been made. But as soon as sheet metal began to be used the brass and metal buttons were cut out by thousands from the sheets.

That discovery of rolling metal, of producing it in great sheets, had done all manner of things. It made new mills, with high chimneys and stacks, appear in the lower valley. It was responsible for making the manufacture of brass one of the foremost industrial enterprises in the Connecticut River valley.

Yet all these things, a meditative Yankee peddler might have cogitated, began with a few brass kettles cast at some small home-town, one-man plant; with the tow-cloth some housewife had woven on a loom in her big kitchen or attic; with the stockings and mittens she managed to knit in excess of those required by her family; with the saddles and harnesses made at some small local shop; with the tobacco rolled into cigars at some farm along the river.

Besides the merchandise the peddler had in his pack to supply the needs of his customers, he also carried from house to house news and, you may be sure, choice bits of local gossip: such vital statistics as deaths and marriages, and of course, most frequently, news of births.

Weather, and how the roads were, and how crops were coming in other parts of the valley offered chances for the peddler to be of use long before any newspaper was circulating in the smaller settlements.

The hard straits the landholders found themselves in at the close of the Revolution were still evident when the first foot-salesman began his trudging journey. Up the river he could give more news about the uprising around Northampton and Springfield in Massachusetts, where Captain Daniel Shays had led a rebellion when everybody was losing their land through foreclosure. Some of the peddler's customers had likely known the captain when he was serving in the federal army. The rumor was that he was still in hiding over the mountains to the west in Vermont.

If he was interested in politics the peddler probably wasn't all for the Federalists along in 1814. He might have spread some news about the Hartford Convention, where behind closed doors delegates from the New England states were planning to get a constitutional convention called to give the states more powers, or so it was rumored. And he'd give them the hush-hush lowdown to the effect that what the Federalists were doing was to get a movement started which might end in taking New England out of the Union. Those stiff-necked Congregational Federalists were certainly out to get the new element that Jefferson had led into power. Very likely the wary peddler would talk both sides until he found out how his customers felt. He could talk Federalist safely in Connecti-

cut but had to be wary when he got up into the Vermont and New Hampshire region. The Federalist influence up there was strong but new ideas on democracy had found a foothold.

There was one movement in which it is certain some of the later peddlers took a part. They must have known considerable about the mysterious travelers who came up the river at night, moving cautiously northward toward the Canadian border.

The question of slavery was gradually growing hotter and by the time most peddlers had taken to carts, lines had been drawn all along the river. In Vermont there was a clause in the constitution which outlawed slavery. Lower down the valley there were enough antislavery people to get the famous underground railroad to Canada going and over that route, by which the red man had taken his captives north to be sold, the black man was smuggled to freedom. On both sides of the river there were stations and untold numbers passed through them. It might well be that inside some of the peddlers' red carts there were black passengers.

Perhaps one of the itinerant merchants who came down from the upper valley may have told of hearing the church bell in Peacham tolling for three hours while he was hurrying around to make his last sales and get away before winter shut him in. It was December 2, 1859, and Leonard Johnson was tolling the bell as John Brown was being hanged in Charlestown, Virginia.

Another commodity which the Yankee peddler distributed, without charge, along his route was Yankee wit. He didn't charge for it but he found that a good story often helped a sale and a bit of juicy gossip made a friend.

These Yankee stories were sometimes plain folklore. Some of them were handed down in families with other heirlooms. Often they would contain some sound philosophy and be brought forth to help clear up some problem, usually with the introduction: "Well, you know what Aunt Mattie used to say" or "You remember what Uncle Charles remarked when he fell down cellar."

Yankee wit rarely had anything to do with exaggeration. It usually depended on understatement. It would be delivered without a hint that anything funny was being said showing on the face of the speaker. Timing had much to do with its success, too. There would be a pause and then the unexpected word or phrase that might seem to be an afterthought.

Having been brought up not to waste anything, naturally the Yankee didn't waste words. Nor did he allow himself to be led into verbal extravagance by any giving way to his emotions. He never overflowed. He held onto his emotions and everything else he had. So, when he was laconic under the most trying circumstances, it had the same effect as understatement.

Then he would rarely come out with a flat answer or even a positive statement—probably because his dependence on the weather had made him uncertain about everything. You might suggest that it was a fine day for haying. He'd likely say, "Seems 's though." Or one might remark on the oppressive heat and get the reply: "I guess there won't be no need fer a buffalo coat."

Of course stories which played one section against another would be especially valuable to the peddler.

For instance, there was the man from Middletown, Connecticut, who had made his living building small boats at the time boats were in much demand along the lower reaches of the river. Later in life he found himself living on a hill farm not far from Walpole, New Hampshire. His wife's parents had died and they had left the farm to the daughter.

One day two selectmen of the town drove into the former boatbuilder's yard. They told him they were in need of his services. One of the town charges had died suddenly. He was a very large man and the local coffinmaker had nothing on hand to fit. To make matters worse that worthy was laid up with the "rheumatiz."

"Knowin' as how you used t' be a boatbuildah, we thought mebbe you cud fix up a coffin fer old Elmah. Ed here's got th' figahs."

The boatbuilder thought he might get something together that would serve the purpose. He said he'd try to get it done by the next afternoon.

About four the next day the two selectmen drove into the yard in a lumber wagon. They were met by the boatbuilder.

"Well, she's done," he said, pointing toward the barn.

"It ain't jest such a job as I'd like t' done but mebbe it'll serve the puppose."

He led the way toward the barn. As he entered he began to chuckle. He shoved back his hat and said:

"They's jest one thing. By Jehosephat, afore I knowed it I'd gone and put a centerboard into 'er."

As the selectmen loaded the coffin into the wagon Ed remarked, "Well, I guess that centahboa'd don't make no mattah. Might make Elmah's trip ovah th' rivah a mite easiah."

Or, there was the fisherman who with his Vermont-born wife had lived in Saybrook. She had always hated the water and was only too glad to respond to the call of duty involving a return to the Vermont farm to care for her aging parents. Of course she dragged her sea-loving husband with her. In a few years—the neighbors said he pined away—he was laid to rest in the cemetery back of the meetinghouse on the Vermont hills.

The day of the burial there was a torrential rainstorm. As the friends were leaving the grave one of them stepped forward to shield the widow with her umbrella.

"Mis'able day to lay 'im away," she said, taking the widow's arm.

The widow stopped and looked back. "Well, it is wet but he wouldn't mind it a mite. He was always sailin' in leaky boats."

Then there was that Mrs. Gupple who moved up the river to Northfield, Massachusetts. She was very popular for the first year of her residence. She joined the Ladies' Aid, helped at all the Grange suppers, and made many friends.

Gradually her friends dropped away and after three years she sold her house and moved to New York State. Her criticisms of the town and its inhabitants were bitter. Some remembered they were quite like the remarks she had made about the town she had come from when she moved to Northfield.

She wrote to her only friend that she was most happily located among very congenial people, over in York State. Aunt Nancy heard this news with a thoughtful expression. Then she said:

"Well, she'll soon find a sarpent in her new Eden." She looked out the window a minute and went on: "The trouble is that wherever that woman goes she has to take Mis' Gupple with 'er."

Evidences of the especial brand of wit called Yankee often appear early. Witness Eddie Starks. Eddie's parents were very strict in all matters pertaining to religion. The Sabbath was set aside for churchgoing and quiet meditation or proper nonsecular reading. There were two growing children in the family, a boy and a girl, and the boy found the atmosphere of the first day of the week decidedly oppressive.

One Sunday afternoon he slipped out and was found by his mother engaged with another boy in playing Indian in the woods back of the house. She called him to her.

"Edward Starks," she said, her voice trembling with anger, "I'm ashamed of you, profaning the Lord's Day this way. Don't you know this is a day of rest?"

Eddie dug the dirt with his toe. "But, Ma, how is a feller goin' t' rest when he ain't tired?"

And it was another Eddie who worked in a store in Springfield in the early days. He didn't prove to be very much of a help to his employer. However small his salary, he consumed so much in the way of groceries and candy that he was an expensive employee. He admitted to his employer that "somehow I'm tired and hungry abaout all th' time."

One day the "setters" around the stove noticed that Eddie was absent.

"Eddie sick?" they asked the proprietor.

"Nope. He ain't sick. He's got through."

After a proper pause one of them asked, "Got anybody in mind t' fill th' vacancy?"

The storekeeper put a bolt of cloth back on the shelf. "Nope," he said over his shoulder. "Eddie didn't leave no vacancy."

As a rule the thrifty Yankee did not believe in "making" conversation. He could endure long silences without embarrasment. He felt that a loose tongue usually was hung in an empty head.

Ezra Hubbard of Lancaster, New Hampshire, felt that when he sat down to a "meal of vittels" he and all the others seated around the usually groaning board should attend strictly to the business in hand. Conversation at his family table was always limited to requests for food.

When Tom Kent came to work on the Hubbard farm he found the table an excellent place for talk. He had been told once that "your mouth was put on hot and run all over your face." At the Hubbard table he had a clear field and for a few days he made the most of it.

Then one day Ezra Hubbard decided it was time to put a stop to it. He interrupted Tom in the midst of one of his most important reminiscences.

"Say, did you ever stop t' think that every time a sheep blats it loses a mouthful."

In a day when religious questions were daily diet in many towns, rival factions fired verbal volleys at each other frequently loaded with sharp pieces of Yankee wit. There came a time when many towns found themselves overburdened with churches. Gradually the strong ones absorbed the weaker congregations, but usually not without a prolonged struggle.

Such was the case in a Massachusetts village where two churches had joined forces but the third had held out. It was supported chiefly by one deacon and members of his family.

One Sunday, during a period when they could get no settled minister, young Mr. Thomas, a student preacher, was asked to fill the pulpit. Knowing the great desire of the other churches to have this one join in the Community Church, the young preacher felt this was a God-given opportunity. He chose as his subject "Union." At the close he made a direct plea to the small group before him to surrender for the good of all.

The deacon hobbled down the aisle after the service was over. He shook the preacher's hand vigorously. "A powerful discourse, young man, a powerful discourse," he said in a high-pitched voice. Then recollecting himself he added, shaking his thin finger:

"But yew ner nobody else ain't agoin' t' unite me."

Perhaps it was in the same village that on a prayer meeting night the melodeon failed to let forth a sound. So the minister called on Sister Hoyt to pitch the hymn "Ten Thousand Times Ten Thousand." Taken by surprise Sister Hoyt started out so high that nobody could follow her. After a few bars she stopped and tried again. This time she got it pitched too low and she stopped again. A neighbor sitting back of her leaned forward and said, in an audible whisper, "Mebbe you'd better start with five thousand, Sister Hoyt."

In times past there were marked differences in the way the Yankees of different parts of the valley pronounced words. There are differences now but they are less marked and there is a blending of peculiarities. The broad "a" of the eastern section of Massachusetts stays broad along the river in that state but up the river it seems to get flattened somewhat by the Maine influence. You can usually spot a native of the Vermont and New Hampshire river valley by his use of the sound "ah" instead of "er," "ovah" instead of "over." Sometimes he puts an "r" in calf, making it "carf" and in general he talks with few gutturals.

A man from Connecticut met an up-the-river farmer going to the blacksmith's shop with a broken whiffletree in plowing time.

"Strike a stone?" he asked.

"No, sah. A stun."

So the Yankee peddler, whether he went through the valley on foot or on horseback or rode on a high red cart, was for many years not only the department store of the countryside; he was also the newspaper and the comic section.

CHAPTER XVI

Women and Politics

A WELL-KNOWN LAWYER, Chancellor Kent, and a friend were riding in the newfangled conveyance, a steam car. They had paid no attention to a young woman sitting opposite. She had paid little heed to them either, being absorbed with the novelty of the trip and the scenery scudding past the window at fifteen miles an hour.

Suddenly they attracted her attention. They (evidently wishing to discuss some very secret matter) were speaking in French. Without any hesitation at all the young lady said, "Excuse me, gentlemen, but I understand French."

With an appreciative smile the gentlemen thanked her and switched to Latin. Again they were interrupted.

"I am sorry, but I also understand Latin."

Somewhat nonplused they less smilingly acknowledged her remark. Shortly they began to talk in far from fluent Greek.

"I am afraid it is of no use," the young lady said, speaking easily in Greek. "Perhaps I had better change my seat."

That was too much for the chancellor. He exploded with "Who in the devil are you anyway?"

He wouldn't have been much wiser if she'd told him. She was Miss Smith.

She was Julia and she lived with her mother and father and four sisters in Glastonbury, Connecticut. Their home was a roomy old mansion built in 1739—one which had formerly been known as the Kimberly House.

They were an interesting family—those Smiths. The head of the family, Zephaniah Hollister Smith, had given up the ministry because he and his congregation could not agree. The young minister had come to the conclusion, no doubt after much soul searching, that it was not right for him to accept money for preaching the gospel. While his congregation probably provided him with little enough in the way of salary, they nevertheless were unwilling to agree to his theory in the matter.

So the shepherd forthwith cast out his entire flock from the fold. And then the flock, in turn, disowned their shepherd. He stuck to his belief that a preacher should not accept a salary. To maintain this conviction he finally gave up the ministry. To support his family he then became a merchant.

Later he studied law. It was after that that he moved with his family to the roomy old mansion on the elongated farm in Glastonbury. It was 22½ rods wide and ran along the Connecticut River for three miles.

The young woman on the train inherited her linguistic ability from the other side of the family. Hannah Hadassah Hickok, who had married Zephaniah Hollister Smith in the late 1700's, learned French when she was a child. Her children were well grown when she decided to read Italian. And so, no sooner said than done, she taught herself Italian. If we recall the general disbelief in education for women during the first decades of the 1800's, Hannah's undertaking was the more remarkable.

She had another accomplishment. She was sufficiently acquainted with the stars to make an almanac for herself. It was said that she could always set the neighbors' clocks right by studying the heavens. Probably she may have been thought a dangerous character by a few of the people of Glastonbury.

One other thing she did which showed further originality. She named her five daughters—we cannot think her husband had any part in this—Nancy Zephina, Cyrinthia Sacretia, Laurilla Aleroyla, Julia Evelina, and Abby Hadassah.

Not to avoid repeated spelling of all these names—which Hannah must have mustered to offset the commonplace Smith—but because it is Abby's and Julia's story, we are going to tell, we will skip over the years from the early 1800's to 1869.

By then the parents and three of the sisters had died. Abby was seventy-four and Julia was seventy-seven. Quite a way along in life to become heroines of a story. Yet that is what they suddenly became.

Abby was managing the farm with her usual energy and spirit, while Julia, who was more retiring in nature, spent more time with books. They did all their housework, handled their business affairs, and made butter and cheese; for they owned a fine herd of Alderney cows. The Alderney cows figure largely in their story.

Most of the neighbors liked the Smith sisters. To be sure they had strong antislavery opinions and some of the neighbors never could understand their interest in women's rights, whatever they might be! But in general, even though they didn't always agree with them, the people of Glastonbury knew how charitable Abby and Julia were, and how genial and kindly. Not the proverbial type of reformers at all. Yet that is what the Smith sisters turned out to be.

It was in 1873 that Abby, aroused by the fact that the property of voteless women in Glastonbury had been subjected to a raise in taxes while that owned by men remained the same, betook herself to a Woman's Congress in New York. Something she heard or felt while there stiffened the resentment that had been growing in the minds of the two sisters.

They were the largest taxpayers in town, but they had not one word to say as to how much should be assessed or how their money should be spent. So Abby and her sister repaired to the Glastonbury town meeting. Quietly and with dignity Abby told the voters what she and her sister thought about taxation without representation.

The hundred-odd male population of the town was assembled for that sovereign right—the foundation stone of the great American experiment—Town Meeting. They had stood outside the Town House discussing crops, swapping yarns, and chewing tobacco. Gradually they had drifted into the hall where the legal authority of the town had already ascended the platform. The voters stood around the wall, their caps on, their jaws still moving.

There was a stir outside just as the moderator rapped for order. A carriage had driven up and from it stepped two ladies. One was slightly above medium height and walked with a firm carriage and an air of independence. Her sister was shorter and slimmer. They nodded to the men still standing outside the Town House door.

As they hurried into the hall and walked forward, a sudden hush fell on the room. A few of the citizens removed their caps. One man, who hadn't removed his, nudged his neighbor and grinned. Here were those Smith sisters butting in again.

The moderator looked down on the two women before him. "We ask to be allowed to address this meeting," Abby said in a firm voice. "I know of no reason why I should permit it," the moderator answered. "We will go on with the regular business of this meeting."

"Your treatment of us is not just, Mr. Moderator," Abby insisted as she and Julia turned to go. "Especially since my sister and I have paid more in taxes for this hall than anyone in it."

A few of the men, feeling the sisters should have been heard, followed them out. Before they reached their carriage someone called: "Give 'em a chance to have their say. 'Taint more'n right." Those who had remained outside in the sun, more interested in talking than in voting, began to move toward them.

"Get up on that old ox cart, ma'am!" someone cried. "Give 'em a hearing!" shouted another. People near the door of the hall looked out and saw the ladies standing on the rickety ox cart. A group was gathering around it. Soon a fair part of the voters were outside listening to the pleas of the disfranchised sisters, who asked for an equal voice with the male taxpayers.

They didn't harangue. They argued. They declared their intention. They would pay no more taxes without representation.

There was no cheering when they finally drove away, but there was little jeering either. Thoughtfully, some went back to the Town Hall. Probably the lank, easygoing farmer leaning on the fence near the door spoke for the majority: "Thank God, my woman ain't eddicated!"

Then things began to happen and Glastonbury became

the Mecca for curious travelers. The old brick Kimberly House was the center of interest. Newspaper reporters took the uncomfortable winter trip just to interview the sisters.

"Is taxation without representation, which was wrong in Boston in 1774, right in Glastonbury in 1874? That is the issue forced upon the intelligent, justice-loving people of Connecticut . . . by these women." So editorialized Samuel Bowles in the Springfield *Republican*.

What had brought this all to a head was the New Year's call (by no means social) of the tax collector at the home of the Smith sisters. He had allowed their unpaid taxes to slide for a time. They would be drawing 12 per cent, and not a few citizens thus borrowed from the town. But the tax collector did not allow matters to go on in the case of Abby and Julia Smith as he did with the rest. Maybe he found that funds were getting short, and the Smith sisters' tax was not inconsiderable.

At any rate he proceeded to remove seven of their choice Alderney cows, worth $400 of anybody's money, for payment of a tax of $101.39. That night there was only one cow to be milked on the Smith place. In due time there was a sale. The cows were put up at auction to satisfy the claims of the town against the Smith sisters.

Of course, with all the talk, there was a crowd. When the Smith sisters came there was a little drawing back and the buzz of conversation stopped for a minute. One or two loyal friends stepped up to speak to them, but the atmosphere was hostile.

Miss Abby wrote the whole story, after it was over, in a peppy and pithy pamphlet entitled: *Abby Smith and Her Cows. With a Report of the Law Case Decided Contrary to Law*. In spite of many things that happened later she couldn't get this January day's doings out of her mind. In her pamphlet, written two years afterward, she says that all she saw at the sale were "forty men waiting to buy an Alderney cow cheap." It looked at first as though they would get them cheap, too, but then a steadfast friend stepped in and bought them all. He no sooner paid for them than he turned them over for the same price to the sisters, who drove them home in triumph. The Smith sisters still hadn't paid the tax collector. The principle, they felt, had been upheld.

The whole story was soon spread abroad. One reporter braved the "Connecticut icebergs" and sought that usual source of information, the country store of Glastonbury. He found the proprietor full of stories of the kindness of the Smith sisters. He cited cases where they had helped with purse and with hand.

Outside the store the reporter got the other side. Evidently this informant saw the proverbial strong-minded reformers in these two campaigners. He was certain they'd been bottled up since the slavery issue had died down. They'd "been watching and waiting for something to take its place, and for that reason the suffrage movement was a godsend to them."

The Alderneys came in for plenty of attention from the press, too. Letters and poems and even money made the Glastonbury postmaster considerable extra business. But, as a later writer remarked, "The Smith sisters were not the kind to let sleeping cows lie." And this despite the fact that they were seventy-five and seventy-eight years old.

Of course another tax soon came due. Again payment was refused by the indomitable sisters. This time the tax collector overstepped. He had a right to take their cows and other personal property. But this time he took the best part of the sisters' farm. Worse than that, he sold it, not at public auction as the law required but privately to a neighbor who

had long had his eye on it. And he sold it to him for $60—
land worth $4,000 at least!

The fat was in the fire. The town fathers, however, felt
that they had been made goats of long enough. Here were
outsiders—newspapers like the Springfield *Republican*—mess-
ing into their local affairs! One paper had started a defense
fund. Money was coming in to the embattled sisters. At first
they refused to take it; but finally accepted it to use in the
cause of women's rights.

It seemed like a clear case against the tax collector. But
the Smith sisters' lawyer deserted them under political pressure and another refused to come to their aid. Undismayed
they studied the case and prepared to be their own counsel—
these two elderly women. Just then they secured a lawyer
of courage and ability.

There was a row of teams in front of Justice Hollister's
house that day when the case of the Smith sisters against the
Glastonbury tax collector came up for trial. His small parlor
was filled with witnesses, the town officials, and the nervous
tax collector. Even Justice Hollister, "a quiet homespun gentleman . . . chewed a lead pencil and nervously rubbed his
chin." The most collected people in the room were the two
Smith sisters. "Abby is the taller of the two, thin and straight
as a lath, she sits erect in her cane-bottom chair through
tedious hours with less signs of weariness than a modern girl
in her teens would show. Julia, the elder, is more petite, and
shows less indication of age, if anything, than her sister. Notwithstanding her eighty years, her face is still bright and ex-
pressive, and she evidently entered into the occasional humors
of the affair more heartily than Abby." So reads a contemporary story of the notable affair.

Justice Hollister decided that it was a clear case. The tax
collector was ordered to pay damages of $10 and costs—little

enough for such a breach of law. Naturally it was expected
that he would appear again at the Smith house, and it was
rumored that this time it would be furniture that would go.
Instead of that, the case was appealed and the scene shifted
to Hartford. There in the following February the trial took
place. It lasted three days. Each night the indomitable sisters
drove back from Hartford to their home in Glastonbury.
"The weather was very cold and bad," Abby wrote, "but we
drove home every night. We thought we would continue to
sleep in our own house—while we had a house to sleep in."
"While we had a house to sleep in"—what steadfast devotion
to a principle!

Probably to the delight of some Glastonbury officials,
but certainly even to their amazement, the judge of the
Appellate Court reversed the decision of Justice Hollister.
Not only that, he withheld his opinion until it was too late
to get an appeal into the March court; and even then the
Smith sisters' lawyer could get no reason from him for his
action. All they ever obtained was a statement that the papers
had been lost and that in the opinion of the tax collector no
personal property could be found at the sisters' home upon
which to levy a tax.

Obviously there was something rotten in the judicial department of the sovereign state of Connecticut, and there was
a general outburst of enraged public opinion through the
press far and near. The *Woman's Journal* of November 18,
1876, printed one of the milder excoriations, saying in part:

Nothing more dastardly can be found in all the records of
Southern violence . . . The Smith sisters are old ladies, well educated, intelligently maintaining at any cost the rights which our
Revolutionary ancestors died to establish. Connecticut . . . has just
paid Centennial honors . . . to these ancestors, but not a single
official in that state, from the Governor down, has . . . given these

sisters the least help, but has left them to be plundered of their property . . . and the principle they defend to be trampled under foot.

Perhaps the beleaguered sisters managed to get a little quiet fun out of it all. When, later, the Alderneys were again seized and an auction advertised, they put a notice in the Hartford *Courant* inviting their friends to come to the auction and to have tea with them. Again the cows were bid in by friends. Next, bank stock was seized and auctioned off in front of the Hartford State House.

Meanwhile, the sisters had appealed the case against the overzealous tax collector, who had seized their land, to the State Supreme Court. In November, 1876, this court gave the aging sisters their dues by reversing the appellate verdict. The last sentence of Abby's account of this trial reads: "We must hold in remembrance we only yielded up our property, when, for the same principle, our . . . forefathers gave up their lives."

Perhaps by then Glastonbury began to see the light. At any rate there seems to be no record of further visitations from the tax collector, nor of suits against the sisters. They continued to the end in their crusade—these still energetic old ladies. They addressed innumerable meetings and conventions; they sent formal petitions to the adamant Connecticut legislature; and they even appeared before a committee of the United States Senate.

But these Smith sisters had been doing something else, quietly at home, even before they took up publicly the cause of women's rights. It had begun when they were middle-aged. They had felt that the translations of the Bible they read were not adequate. When the Smith sisters were not satisfied with things, they generally did something about them.

So we find them poring over a Hebrew grammar for weeks. When they had sufficiently mastered it, they proceeded to translate from the Hebrew the entire book of Holy Writ. Not satisfied with their first translation they made a second one from the Hebrew. And, incredible as it seems, they then made two from the Greek and one from the Latin Vulgate. "We don't like the way the Bible has been translated; we are going to see if we can make one we like better." Such was their simple purpose, and at the end of seven years, although they originally had no thought of publication, their Bible was published—the first and only one to have been translated and published by women.

In 1877 Abby, the younger and more aggressive of the sisters, laid down her burden. She left Julia, then eighty-five, to live alone in the big house on the elongated farm. Past that farm the Connecticut River flowed ever toward the sea. Perhaps Julia looked out upon it now and saw in the river's ceaseless moving toward its inevitable goal something comforting.

Julia wasn't one to sit down and mourn her loss and bemoan her solitude. But everyone knew what her loneliness must be. When help came to relieve her sadness she accepted it with gratitude. It came in this wise:

At the Smith house one of the much-read volumes on the old shelves in the library was a book of *Recollections*. It was written by Judge Amos Parker, who during Lafayette's farewell tour in 1825 had become his intimate friend and companion.

The book, which the Smith sisters had read so often, told of this farewell trip of the French marquis. It told of his visit to Hartford where he took the steamer to the Sound. The author remarked the simplicity of the hero's dress. He listed his nankin pantaloons, his swan's-down vest, and his blue broadcloth coat with gilt buttons. "And without any insignia of rank or office on his person."

Perhaps the Smith sisters felt that they learned something of Judge Parker too as he told what had impressed him in the Marquis de Lafayette. Maybe that was how it so easily came about that Judge Parker, who had long been a widower and lonely, found Julia Smith a sympathetic and interested friend. It was probably a reason for her reliance upon his judgment and taste.

He was eighty-five and she was nearing ninety when they were married in the old Smith mansion. Yet to the people of Glastonbury, who long ago had grown to expect unusual things from the Smith sisters, it may not have seemed too strange or ill-advised a step that Julia was taking. Very likely they had all worried about her, more or less, and felt her loneliness as a vague responsibility. They knew enough, also, to realize that Judge Parker was a gentleman of distinguished attainments. In her own way, they probably admitted, Julia was a woman of unusual attainments too. More than one parlor table held the large plainly bound book that bore in gold letters the words "The Holy Bible," translated by Julia E. Smith. On the title page there was a little more information: "The HOLY BIBLE containing the OLD AND NEW TESTAMENTS; translated literally from the original tongues. . . . Hartford, Conn.: American Publishing Company. 1876."

After all, Abby had lived to see it published. With her quick sense of fun she must often have mentioned her and Julia's two publications with an amused smile. *Abby Smith and Her Cows* and *The Holy Bible* translated by Julia E. Smith. The two publications, however, were indicative of the deepest traits in their remarkable characters.

Judge Parker and Julia Smith were a distinguished couple as they led the procession out to the dining room of the old mansion after their wedding ceremony. A fire blazed in the big fireplace. Friends escorted them to the head of the table.

"This cup," said Julia, holding up the one at her place, "and the one beside you, my dear, are brought out in honor of this occasion."

The judge lifted the delicate china cup beside him and looked at it.

"They've been in my family—yours now as well as mine —for over two hundred years. They belonged to Governor Saltonstall."

"Well, Julia, they are remarkably preserved."

"Yes," replied Julia with a smile, "almost as well as you and I."

After the supper there was music in the big room, and dancing began: polkas and quadrilles. The judge watched the figures intently. He kept time with his foot to the lively music and followed the more stately measures with a gentle swaying of his shoulders. He and Julia were urged to dance a figure.

The judge agreed to do so if his wife would consent. Julia hesitated a moment. Then she said, shaking her head, "No, Amos, I guess I'd better not. It would get into the papers." The judge said he didn't see what harm there would be in that. "Well," Julia said, smiling at him, "I wouldn't want people to think I'd gone to pieces completely."

After eight years of pleasant living with her husband Julia's days came to a close. Younger hands had taken up the torch which the Smith sisters had borne so valiantly.

CHAPTER XVII

The River's Industrial Contribution

SMOKE rising along the river has always been important. In early days it marked the campsites of the Indians. Then it marked the hearthstones of the white pioneers as they spread northward along the banks.

Today black smoke pouring from thousands of tall stacks tells the story of industrial development which has come to the river valley. These tall monuments to industry, many of them in the lower reaches of the river—darkening the sky with their outpourings—and scattered in small towns throughout the northern sections, have replaced the water wheels whose power came chiefly from the feeder streams which tumble into the Connecticut throughout its length.

The industrial story of the valley no doubt started around the huge fireplaces in cabins that were winterbound. There, on long winter evenings while their wives sat knitting, men engaged in the ancient art of whittling.

There are no records to show how many a laborsaving

gadget emerged from a piece of a tree, cut in the settler's very dooryard, while flames roared up the wide-throated chimney and the kettle sang on the crane. Inventive genius was inborn with those New England Yankees.

So it was natural that there gradually grew up on the streams headed for the river small woodworking shops. This was true especially on the New Hampshire side of the upper river. Out of the material at hand—the wood of the surrounding forest—were made many things later formed of metal. It was in metal that the contribution of the valley to the world's industrial development was made.

Since America has become the world's greatest industrial nation and since our industries resulted largely from a method developed along the river, the story of its growth certainly belongs here.

It is chiefly the story of the interchangeable system of manufacture, which Professor J. W. Roe defines as "the production of complete machines or mechanisms, the corresponding parts of which are so nearly alike that they fit into any of the given mechanisms."

To produce these interchangeable parts in vast quantities and with great accuracy demanded the invention and making of innumerable machine tools, and in this toolmaking industry the river valley has led the world. Old England, around 1800, saw the birth of the machine-tool industry; New England developed and refined it.

In those early days when a shooting iron was a household necessity, the village gunsmith was an important member of society. Probably no implement was in more general use than the musket, and it is natural that the industrial development should begin with that. As the local shop turned out muskets, they were as individual as the men who made them. When a part broke another had to be made by hand and fitted into that particular gun.

When Thomas Jefferson was representing his country in France he wrote home about one La Blanc who had plans for making guns in such a way that the various parts—such as the hammer or trigger—would be made so alike that they would fit any gun. In spite of Mr. Jefferson's interest, La Blanc seems not to have developed this idea.

In 1781 Eli Whitney, of cotton gin fame, secured a contract from the government for the manufacture of muskets. He built a plant in New Haven, Connecticut, and turned out thousands of guns approximating his original plan, which was something new and startling: "To make the same parts of the different guns—as the locks for example—as much like each other as the successive impressions of a copper plate engraving."

Later in the same year Simeon North secured a contract for pistols from the government, and he was the first along the river to put into use methods of mass production for interchangeable parts. He was also the first to have this production method stipulated by government contract. To carry out the necessary change from handwork to fabrication by machines, in whose operation no particular skill was demanded, required the invention and development of a whole array of new tools and standard gauges.

The river saw another important step taken in its industrial development when, in 1848, Samuel Colt came to Hartford, Connecticut, to build a factory to produce his famous revolver. This was to be a factory the like of which the world had never seen.

To make it a reality he picked Elisha K. Root, already known as a successful mechanic and manager, to organize the factory. Root equipped the Colt factory with more than 1,400 machines, and spent for the special tool and gauge equipment—much of which he developed—more than the cost of the machines. Colt invented the revolver; but that is now growing obsolete. But Root's methods of making it have spread throughout the industrial world.

Likewise, as Odell Shepard suggests, these new methods of production made possible the "factory as we know it, the labor problem, over-production, modern capitalism, modern warfare and the class struggle. In its triumphant strides through these fourteen decades it has crushed the individual artisan . . . and has invaded even the sacred territories of the mind and spirit. Our business, our propaganda, even our system of education, are now imitating the method by which North and Whitney taught us to speed up production, minimize costs, and turn out always a perfectly standard article which could be readily and cheaply replaced in every part without depending upon human intelligence."

While this momentous change in human economy was going on in the lower valley, there had been some signs of budding Yankee ingenuity along the northern reaches of the river. For some obscure reason these centered in and about Windsor, Vermont, where there happened to be water power.

There, Lemuel Hedge had operated his invention for ruling paper, from which he later developed still other machines for the rapid and accurate marking and numbering of rules and mechanics' scales—indispensable necessities in the machine-tool industry. Out of Lemuel Hedge's small beginnings grew other companies, with plants at several places down the river. True to form, Hedge had started out as a worker in wood.

The chief Windsor industry was built up from a failure.

In 1827 John Cooper of Guildhall, well up on the river, had built a rotary pump. This, in time, was backed by the $100,-000 capital of a Windsor company, and there many of the pumps were made and sold. But there were serious defects, and eventually the company failed. It looked bad for Windsor, and probably nobody ever thought that a certain young fellow, one Asahel Hubbard, who was running a combination sawmill, gristmill and machine shop on Mill Brook at the foot of Mt. Ascutney some three miles from Windsor, would have any part in preserving the town's industrial reputation.

He had seen the defects in the Cooper pump and had built a wooden model of another design which he knew would not only work but wear. Capital being tied up with the rival pump in his home town, he took his pump over the mountain to Jabez Proctor of Proctorsville. There in 1829 they incorporated the National Hydraulic Company.

Jabez Proctor, like many of his descendants, was active in politics. As a result he got Asahel Hubbard appointed warden of the Vermont State Prison at Windsor. At the same time he got the prison authorities to install a steam engine—the first one in the upper valley—and a machine shop. There the National Hydraulic Company moved in 1830, employing prison labor in part.

This was a progressive move when one recalls that in that day prison reform was something mostly in the brains of reformers, and that the ball and chain were as yet acceptable means of correction. It is said that when their time was up many of the prisoners at Windsor remained on the regular payroll of the National Hydraulic Company.

This company began the production in quantity of Hubbard's hydraulic engines by the interchangeable system of manufacture. Here was one of the early applications of the

method first used only in gunmaking. Of course it also demanded the development of many machine tools.

That it was successful is attested by the company's growth. Its reputation soon spread across the country. When the city of St. Louis was installing a water system, to Windsor went the order for a "huge" pump which was to raise water 104 feet from the Mississippi. When the pump was finished it started on its long journey under the personal escort of its builder, Asahel Hubbard. First came the rough wagon journey over the Green Mountains to Albany. Then canal and lake boats to the small village named Chicago. Then by wagon and river boat to its final destination.

In due time, under Hubbard's direction, the pump was put to work. It was perfectly satisfactory; but the St. Louis water company found itself short of funds. Public-spirited citizens passed the hat. Still there wasn't quite enough. Finally, as a last payment, the homesick Hubbard accepted a beautiful pure-white saddle horse. With the cash payment in gold in his money belt, he set out on the long return journey to Vermont. Ultimately he rode into town on his white horse and was joyfully received by his friends and family.

Among the family who greeted him was a daughter. For some time she had been receiving attention from the son of the village blacksmith. He was known as N. Kendall, the "N" standing for Nicanor. He had served in his father's smithy after school hours and then had learned the gunsmith's trade in a local shop run by Asa Story, who made turkey and squirrel rifles to order. During his courtship, N. Kendall demonstrated that romance as well as necessity can mother invention.

On a bright winter afternoon N was taking his girl for a sleigh ride on a quiet country road. As usual he had one of Story's side-hammer percussion rifles under the buffalo robe between them. He saw a squirrel in a near-by tree and reached down to pull the gun out. The exposed hammer caught on the robe and there was a deafening explosion. The muzzle was in his hand and it was pointed toward Miss Hubbard. Thinking that his right hand had been blown to bits, Kendall thrust it under the robe, and, horror stricken, turned to the young woman, expecting to find her wounded or dead.

She was white with fright but unhurt. She had turned to one side to look back just in time. Not saying anything about his crippled hand, Kendall drove at once to the doctor's. There he found that his hand was burned but otherwise uninjured. The ball had passed between his fingers. The resulting mechanical improvement in guns, born of this almost tragic experience, was the Kendall underhammer lock, in which trigger and hammer are equally protected.

Having married Miss Hubbard, N. Kendall was employed by his father-in-law in the National Hydraulic Company and got him to produce the new underhammer gun. These new guns journeyed far. Texas was, as Vermont had been a few years before, struggling as an independent republic and was at war with Mexico. To arm her forces she ordered a quantity of the new Kendall underhammer guns. The Windsor company, using the interchangeable parts method, could turn out these guns at about half the price of the regular army musket. By now Windsor was gaining a reputation that belied its size. It continued to build both reputation and machines.

Asahel Hubbard had gone west. He sold rights for the manufacture of his pumps to other New England states. Improved and adapted, but essentially Hubbard's, they are still being made by these, or descendant, firms. About 1838 the National Hydraulic Company was changed to N. Kendall and Company.

And at about this time (1838) there came to Windsor a young man who was destined to play an important part in the history of American industry and to add to the fame of the small town on the river. He fired three shots from the village doctor's squirrel rifle which re-echoed around the world. The young man was Richard S. Lawrence, who had learned his trade in Asa Story's gunshop.

He had been doing some wandering, but returned to Windsor when he was twenty-one. He put up at Dr. Story's —a brother of the gunsmith. The doctor was naturally interested in guns, and he had a pet squirrel rifle which his guest suggested would be improved by a little cleaning. He took it to the place he was so familiar with—Story's gunshop—and there he forged and installed a peep sight on the doctor's rifle. It was a gadget never before seen in Windsor. The doctor was well pleased with the look of his rehabilitated favorite and at once wanted to see how it would work with the new peep sight.

Lawrence, all confidence, paced off twelve rods from a maple tree and pointed out a hole in the trunk, that had been bored for a sap spout the previous spring. That, he said, would be his target. He shot twice. The excited doctor examined the target and, with some feeling, announced that the bullets had not even hit the tree. Chagrined and puzzled the young gunsmith said that he still had one more charge, and that he would try again. The doctor was shaking his head at the seemingly untouched target when Lawrence peered over his shoulder. His better eye discovered that the hole was plugged with lead. All three shots were in the small target.

The very next morning the delighted and amazed doctor took the young man to the shop of N. Kendall, located in the state prison. Impressed by the doctor's story, Kendall hired the young man for two years at $100 per year. He not only worked at the various phases of gunmaking, but he also locked the prisoners in their cells, cleaned out the boilers, and in spare time did some of the bookkeeping. In six months he was superintendent. So began a career whose influence extended, through numerous associations and in various companies, down the river and even to the birthplace of the machine-tool industry in England.

Incidentally, one of Kendall's workmen carried on the manufacture of underhammer sporting rifles in Cornish, New Hampshire, until 1877. David H. Hilliard there employed no great number of men, but they were so well trained that many of them later filled important positions in the large armories of the country.

To continue with the Windsor machinists: Through various changes in partnership the Kendall firm eventually became Robbins and Lawrence, Kendall having sold out his interests. By developing machine tools this firm produced thousands of rifles for the government. Their success led them to place a small display of their arms in the Crystal Palace Exhibition in 1851.

Even at that late date English arms were produced by the old methods, and the military authorities were immediately taken with the American display and the method of production.

Their famous toolmaker, Nasmyth, referred to this as the "American System"—no slight honor to be brought to this country by the small plant on the river.

There followed a visit to Windsor by a British commission, which not only placed an order for a large number of Enfield rifles, but also ordered some 150 machines for production. Not many months later the products of Connecticut River genius were starting an industrial change in Great Britain which had far-reaching results.

In passing, it is interesting to note that later Lawrence was building the famous Sharps rifles in a new plant built by a new company by whom he was employed, in Hartford, Connecticut. Occupying that same plant had been the Weed Sewing Machine Company; and in it was started the Hartford Machine and Screw Company, indirectly connected with the old Robbins and Lawrence Company.

The Weed Company then was building the Pope bicycles of the high wheel variety. Later in the same plant the Pope Manufacturing Company produced its own safety bicycles and motorcycles, and the Pope automobile. Now it is part of the Pratt and Whitney plant—which company, years ago, followed the old Robbins and Lawrence concern as the leading exponent of the interchangeable system of manufacture. They now have been turning out most successful airplane engines.

A few miles below Windsor, on the Black River, is Springfield, Vermont. In 1888 there came to that town, located on the falls of the Black River, the Jones and Lamson Company, a lineal descendant of Robbins and Lawrence, which after a varied career in Windsor found the available capital in Springfield to keep its machine shop in operation.

To them came a mechanical genius of the first order, James Hartness. He had a new idea for a turret lathe. Men employed under the stimulating influence of Hartness developed new machines or improvements on the old ones, and from time to time set out to carry out their own ideas in their own plants.

Gradually Springfield, Vermont, became the industrial center of the upper river and one of the most important tool-building centers in the world. Among its names famous in the industrial world, in addition to Hartness, are Fellows, Gridley, Flanders, and Bryant.

So, in ever-widening circles, influence from the upper Connecticut valley shops spread out like a genealogical chart, touching plants all along the river in Springfield, Massachusetts, in Greenfield, Massachusetts, and in Hartford, Connecticut, to mention only a few, to say nothing of other localities in New England and throughout the country.

The river valley produced not only machine tools but men. Professor Roe, speaking of Robbins and Lawrence, states that this small Windsor, Vermont, company during the 1850's produced more great mechanics than almost any other plant in the country—all of them conspicuous in the field of interchangeable manufacturing. Thereafter for nearly a third of a century these and other New England manufacturies, most of which had some men trained in the early plants, equipped armories for almost every government in the world.

Why two small towns tucked away in the upper Connecticut River valley should stand out so prominently in the industrial world, holding their own against competition with places nearer raw materials and nearer markets with infinitely better shipping facilities—for Springfield, Vermont, is not even on a railroad—is an interesting question.

The answer the leaders themselves give in one word: "Men." They have drawn their workmen from the farming regions surrounding them. These men have grown up where there was almost daily demand for initiative and ingenuity. They have been entrusted with responsibility from the time they were old enough to fill the woodbox. In times of depression they turned again to the farms. So, through good times and bad, these small-town plants more than held their own, manned by such men.

The importance of all this history of the river's pioneering in interchangeable manufacture may be better realized when we consider that, owing to the introduction of that method, innumerable necessities and comforts of everyday life have been made possible for us. Clocks, and then watches, became available to new thousands through mass production methods. Sewing machines in homes and factories were made possible by it. The automobile is used by thousands instead of by the richer few. Today airplanes and tanks are rolling from assembly lines, all the result of this American system of production born on the river. To it and its handmaiden, the machine tool, can be traced almost every mark of our civilization. "Everything we use at work, at home, at play, is either the child or grandchild of a machine tool."

As Professor Joseph Roe concludes: "The output of interchangeable manufacture is better in quality, cheaper in cost, and more useful than would be possible without it. It constitutes one of the greatest contributions of the machine age, and we may well be proud that when the British introduced it into England they called it the AMERICAN SYSTEM."

The clacking of machines in knitting mills, the staccato tapping of typewriters in thousands of offices, the purring of motor cars on highways the country over, the fast-fading throb of the airplane as it eliminates all boundary lines; yes, and the hellish roar of the destruction-dealing tank, and the deadly rattle of the machine gun, and the screech of the falling bomb, and the quiet ticking of the clock on your mantel —all these are telling the story of the river's contribution to industrialized America.

CHAPTER XVIII

An Industrial Postscript

ONE CITY on the river has the unique distinction of continuing as an industrial center under a plan a hundred years old. For that reason a brief account of Holyoke, Massachusetts, which leads the country in the manufacture of writing paper and envelopes, deserves special mention in any story of the river valley's industrial history.

It will be recalled that Hadley Falls, north of Springfield, Massachusetts, offered one of the greatest obstacles to shipping in the early days of commerce on the river. There was a fall of sixty feet within a fifth of a mile, which obviously presented a serious problem to comfortable navigation.

In 1795 a canal was built with an 11-foot dam across the river. It was there that the ingenious device of an inclined plane with a pulley, to lift boats to a higher level, was first used instead of the locks that were later installed.

In 1848 a company was formed to make use of this water power, which was largely going to waste. It was an enormous undertaking for that day, both physical and financial.

The plan was to build a dam across the river above the falls. A mill town was to be built in the bend on the west bank. At the time there was on this site a small rural community, part of West Springfield, known as Ireland Parish, although its inhabitants were of English stock, to a man.

The river was to be diverted to run into canals, which would be so arranged, according to a circular written at the time, "that the whole Connecticut River can be used over *twice*, by sets of mills on different levels."

This plan was altered to allow the use of the water *three* times, instead of only twice, by the construction of three, instead of two, canals.

First the water entered the upper canal. There was a row of mills and raceways between it and a parallel canal, on a lower level, which received the water that had poured through the mill wheels. This water powered the mills on the second level, and passed to the third canal.

While engineers were figuring out this difficult and unique system of water power, plans were being drawn for the buildings needed in the town. There would have to be stores, boardinghouses, and tenements, for the use of the mill-workers.

The rural landholders of Ireland Parish were persuaded with some difficulty to sell property. They were doubtless skeptical of this sudden display of wealth; they probably were only remotely interested in large money-making schemes. They were farming people and they didn't put much stock in grandiose enterprises.

For $300,000 a group of men from Boston and Hartford became the owners of some twelve hundred acres of

land, and to the water rights to the greatest potential industrial development in New England. Associated with them
were railroad men, who only a few months before had built a
railway line from Northampton, south through Ireland Parish, to Springfield.

To top it all, they organized a company capitalized at
$2,450,000, at a time when capital was not too plentiful.
Only one Boston bank had a capital of as much as $3,000,000.

At once plans were carried out. The first dam—1,000
feet across and 30 feet high—was finished in November,
1848. It was built of hemlock timbers riveted to bedrock and
faced with boiler plate.

When the dramatic moment for the filling of the dam
arrived it turned out to be a tragedy. Leaks developed and
this laconic report reached the Boston office: "Dam gone to
Hell by way of Willimansett." But, nothing daunted, within
a year a new dam was successfully holding back the impatient waters of the Connecticut.

Ten years later the company failed and the stockholders
received $1.34 for each hundred dollars they had invested.
The main difficulty seemed to be that the supply of power
was in advance of the demand for it. New enterprises to use
it failed to come in in sufficient numbers to bring in the
necessary revenue. The time was not quite ripe for the use of
so much power. A few mills were set going, but labor troubles, disturbed economic conditions, and poor management all
conspired to wreck the company.

A new company, the Holyoke Water Company, under
wiser management took over affairs. It had a capitalization of
$350,000. Gradually, in addition to cotton mills, which were
at first expected to be the chief industries, there were wire

mills, various textile mills, and a plant where mill machinery was produced.

Almost from the beginning there had been a paper mill. There was plenty of power to run the machines, and a volume of pure water, a factor essential in the manufacture of fine paper. Gradually more and more paper companies, discovering these great advantages to be had at Holyoke, began to come in. There were offshoots of old companies, and then consolidations, until the city's pre-eminence as a center for producing fine writing paper and envelopes was established.

Naturally, with the growth of the small hamlet of Ireland Parish, with its three thousand inhabitants of English stock, into the thriving city of Holyoke, with around eighty thousand people, there were growing pains. The introduction of Irish, Scotch, Belgian, German, and French-Canadian people produced social problems that threatened the very life of the community.

Housing, sanitation, social life, and labor-management relations: all these matters had to be handled. Unfortunately, it was usually after serious consequences of their neglect had forced the growing community to attention that action was taken. The assimilation of people of foreign birth, speaking different tongues, often with diverse social and religious customs, posed problems heretofore little known in the river valley.

Complicating it all was the private ownership and control of water power; private ownership and control of the lifeblood of the community. The planning and development of the city's power were not public enterprises, and profit and private interest was their motivating force.

Here is a city in the very heart of New England, yet with no New England traditions, no prominent original families, and little stock of inherited wealth. However, in its century of existence it has epitomized the changing modes of life and readjustments of thought forced upon America by the coming of the machine age. It is the history of industrialism with all its social consequences.

While all this industrial center was flourishing at Hadley Falls because of the power potentialities of its geographic location, up the valley in settlements like Windsor and Springfield, Vermont, to mention only two, there were successful developments due largely to the genius of a few men. They had ideas which they turned into useful machines. The success of their enterprises did not depend on the investment of large sums of money or the importation of large groups of laborers. The industrial contribution of the upper river valley was individualistic, native, and distinctly Yankee. In its growth it did not produce problems, because it was a natural growth, perhaps, rather than a planned economy.

CHAPTER XIX

"From . . . Tempest . . . Earthquake, Fire, and Flood"

WHEN the first Pilgrims and Puritans arrived in the Connecticut River valley (1633-1635) we know that no matter what other possessions they may have left behind them they brought the Holy Bible with them. Words from the Scriptures interlard their earliest records, their lawbooks and legal documents, their diaries and journals, their letters and narratives, and their "Accounts of Remarkable Escapes and Preservations."

But there was one book which these Pilgrim and Puritan settlers thought well to have left behind them in England. A book they rigidly eschewed: the *Book of Common Prayer.*

However, in its Litany there were words of supplication which, had they known them, would often have come to their lips during their and their descendants' habitation in the Connecticut River valley.

"From lightning and tempest; from earthquake, fire, and flood; from plague and pestilence, and famine; from battle and murder, and from sudden death, Good Lord, deliver us."

Here, aligned in awesome order, were the catastrophies that might occur: the elemental forces, unfathomable circumstances, and violence of man, which might sweep down upon them and lay them low. And such was their fate that they had no more than built their cabins when all these catastrophies began to afflict them.

In 1635 the little settlement of Windsor, Connecticut, underwent famine. That was the winter when more and more people, from Dorchester, in the Bay Colony, were encroaching upon the land which the Pilgrim group of 1633 had held to be exclusively their own. There was not sufficient land under cultivation to supply food for so many people. When winter came the food that had been hoped for from the autumn harvest was destroyed. There was not even that limited supply to be depended upon.

In August flood and hurricane had denuded the river valley. The Indian corn upon the pocconocks had been lost. It lay flat and broken upon the ground, buried in silt.

Not only had the river overflowed its banks, in the terrible flood that washed away and buried the corn crops, but the terrific tempest that accompanied the flooding waters had demolished the settlers' cabins. It had uprooted giant trees and broken them into great shambles of fallen timber. No wonder many of the unwelcome people from Dorchester were glad to return to the Bay Colony by any means they could manage.

An *Early History of New England* published in Concord, New Hampshire, more than a century ago, relates:

On the 15th of August, 1635, New England was visited by a tremendous storm, or hurricane. It is thus described by Morton. "It began in the morning, a little before day, and grew not by degrees, but came with great violence in the beginning, to the great amazement of many. It blew down sundry houses, and uncovered divers others; divers vessels were lost at sea, and many more were in extreme danger. It caused the sea to swell in some places to the southward of Plymouth, so that it rose to twenty feet right up and down, and made many of the Indians to climb into trees for their safety. It threw down all the corn to the ground, so that it never rose more. . . . Had the wind continued without shifting, in likelihood it would have drowned some part of the country. It blew down many hundred thousands of trees, turning up the stronger ones by the roots, and breaking the high pine-trees, and such like, in the midst; and the tall young oaks and walnut-trees, of good bigness, were twisted as a withe by it,—very strange and fearful to behold. It began in the south-east, and veered sundry ways . . . it continued not in extremity above five or six hours, before the violence of it began to abate; the marks of it will remain for many years, in those parts where it was sorest."

In this same book there is an account of the arrival of the Bay Colony people at the Windsor settlement following the August flood and hurricane. They could hardly have chosen a less auspicious time at which to arrive. The account continues with the conditions of that famine-beset group upon the river.

On the 15th of October, 1635, about sixty men, women and children, with their horses, cattle, and swine, commenced their journey, through the wilderness, to Connecticut River. After a tedious and difficult journey, through swamps and rivers, over mountains and rough ground, which were passed with great difficulty and fatigue, they arrived safely at the respective places of their destination. They were so long on their journey, and so much time was spent in passing the river, and in getting over their cattle, that, after all their exertions, winter came upon them before they were prepared. This was an occasion of great distress and damage to the plantation.

The winter set in this year much sooner than usual, and the weather was stormy and severe. By the 15th of November, Connecticut River was frozen over, and the snow was so deep, and the season so tempestuous, that a considerable number of the cattle could not be brought across the river. The people had so little time to prepare their huts and houses, and to erect sheds and shelters for their cattle, that the sufferings of man and beast were extreme. Indeed, the hardships and distresses of the first planters of Connecticut scarcely admit of a description. To carry much provisions or furniture through a pathless wilderness was impracticable. Their principal provisions and household furniture were, therefore, put on board several small vessels, which, by reason of delays and the tempestuousness of the season, were either cast away or did not arrive. Several vessels were wrecked on the coasts of New England, by the violence of the storms. Two shallops laden with goods, from Boston to Connecticut, in October, were cast away on Brown's Island, near Gernet's Nose, and the men, with everything on board, were lost. A vessel, with six of the Connecticut people on board . . . was cast away.

By the last of November, or beginning of December, provisions generally failed in the settlements on the river, and famine and death looked the inhabitants sternly in the face. Some of them, driven by hunger, attempted their way, in this severe season, through the wilderness from Connecticut to Massachusetts. Of thirteen, in one company, who made this attempt, one, in passing a river, fell through the ice, and was drowned. The other twelve were ten days on their journey, and would have perished had it not been for the assistance of the Indians. Indeed, such was the distress in general, that by the 3rd and 4th of December, a considerable part of the new settlers were obliged to abandon their habitations. . . .

The people who kept their station on the river suffered in an extreme degree. After all the help they were able to obtain, by hunting and from the Indians, they were obliged to subsist on acorns, malt and grains . . . a great number of cattle perished . . .

It is difficult to describe, or even to conceive, the apprehensions and distresses of a people, in the circumstances of our venerable ancestors, during this doleful winter. All the horrors of a dreary wilderness spread themselves around them. They were encompassed with numerous, fierce and cruel tribes of wild, savage men, who could have swallowed up parents and children at pleasure, in their feeble and distressed condition. They had neither bread for themselves nor children; neither habitations nor clothing convenient for them. Whatever emergency might happen, they were cut off, both by land and water, from any succor or retreat. This was once the condition of those fair opulent towns on Connecticut River.

This same little *History* records the terror that was caused three years later by a series of earthquakes felt throughout New England and along the river valley.

Several earthquakes are noticed in the early history of New England. The first, which was on the 1st day of June, 1638, is spoken of by Trumbull as "a great and memorable earthquake." His description of it is the following. "It came with a report like continued thunder, or the rattling of numerous coaches upon a paved street. The shock was so great, that in many places the tops of chimneys were thrown down, and the pewter fell from the shelves. . . . The duration of the sound and tremor was about four minutes. The earth at turns was unquiet for about twenty days. The weather was clear, the wind westerly, and the course of the earthquake from west to east."

The next earthquake of any considerable violence, of which a particular account is left on record, was on the 29th of October, 1727. . . . Rev. Mr. Gookin, of N.H., gives the following account . . . "The shake was very hard, and was attended with a terrible noise, something like thunder. The houses trembled as if they were falling; divers chimneys were cracked, and had their tops broken off . . . When the shake was beginninng, some persons observed a flash of light running on the earth: the flame seemed to them to be of a blueish color. These flashes, no doubt, broke out of the earth; otherwise, it is probable they would have been seen more generally, especially by those who were abroad. . . . It is hard to express the consternation that fell both on men and beasts, in the time of the great shock. The brute creatures ran roaring about the fields, as if in the greatest distress. All of us saw the necessity of looking to God for his favor and protection; and I would hope that many did, not only look to God in that time of their distress, but did truly and heartily return to him. Many are now asking the way to Zion with their faces thitherward."

All nature must have conspired to fill the river valley pioneers with awe, for in 1719 there was a great display in the heavens.

A phenomenon singular at the time, and still unsatisfactorily explained, alarmed the people in 1719. This was the Aurora Borealis, first noticed . . . on the night of the 17th of December. It began about eight o'clock in the evening and filled the country with terrible alarm. It was viewed as a sign of the last judgment. It is thus described by a writer of the time. "There arose a bright light in the north-east, like that which arises from a house when on fire; which soon spread itself through the heavens from east to west and was unusually broad. It streamed with white flames, or streams of light, down to the horizon, very bright and strong. When I first saw it, which was when it extended itself over the horizon from east to west, it was brightest in the middle, which was from me north-west; and I could resemble it to nothing but the light from some fire. I could plainly see streams of light redder than ordinary, and there seemed to be an undulating motion of the whole light; so thin that I could plainly see the stars through it. Below this stream, or glade of light, there lay in the horizon some thick clouds, bright on the tops or edges. It lasted somewhat more than an hour, though the light of its red color continued but a few minutes. About eleven at night the same appearance was visible again; but the clouds hindered it being accurately observed as I could wish. Its appearance was now somewhat dreadful—sometimes it looked of a flame, sometimes of a blood-red color, and the whole north-eastern horizon was very bright, and looked as though the moon had been near her rising. About an hour or two before the break of day, the next morning, it was seen again, and those who saw it say it was then most terrible."

Surely "tempest . . . earthquake, fire and flood" had visited the river valley as well as "battle, murder and sudden death."

In 1735 it experienced one of the epidemic disorders that so often afflicted the pioneers with pestilence and death. In this terrible experience it seems to have been children who were the chief sufferers. Many families were left entirely childless. The throat was always affected, greatly swollen and inflamed, and thus it is recorded in the early annals as "the throat distemper."

This particular epidemic lasted for several months and it is stated that in one township alone ninety-nine persons died, of whom eighty-one were children.

In 1816 there occurred in New England, and along the Connecticut River valley, what was known as the "Poverty Year" or the "Cold Year."

During every month in that year there was heavy frost, and in many cases there was a fall of snow as well. In June a depth of snow fell that amounted to a blizzard in some places. It is recorded that a man was frozen to death while searching for his sheep in the storm.

In Walpole, New Hampshire, Squire Thomas Bellows had more corn than he needed for his own use. Most people's crops had failed because of the long-continued cold and many had not even the necessary seed corn for another year's planting.

Squire Bellows therefore offered his surplus corn for sale in small quantities. He asked no more for the corn than its

price would have been in years of plenty. When a purchaser could not give cash in payment, the squire accepted labor.

One day there appeared a customer who said he would like to buy all the corn the squire had left for sale. The squire replied: "You cannot have it. If you wish a bushel for your family, you can have it at my price but no man can buy of me to speculate in this year of scarcity."

The winter of 1826-27 was as erratic in temperature as had been the Cold Year of 1816, when snow had fallen in the summer time.

In the spring of 1826 there was a severe freshet along the river, and there was average rainfall until June. Then there followed a long summer of drought. It was intensely hot and a pest of grasshoppers assailed the land, ruining crops and forcing farmers finally to gather in what they could, before it was even ripe for harvest. No rain fell to relieve the situation until September 10. Then for days it fell steadily and slowly.

The weather was so warm that a new, thick growth of grass rapidly sprang up. All along the river valley the farmers had their flocks out at pasture. They were able to keep them there until January 8, 1827.

Although snow then fell heavily, there was no frost in the ground. In Walpole, New Hampshire, men were plowing in the fields by the end of February, while snow covered the mountains.

Freshets and floods along the Connecticut River valley have been a constantly recurring portion of its history ever since it has been known to man who could make a record of what he experienced and observed.

And the terrible cost in loss of life and property, which the river's floods have wrought during the years, has brought about the steadily mounting efforts, private, state and federal, to construct methods of flood control for the Connecticut valley.

After that earliest recorded flood of 1635 we find frequent mention in old histories and journals of the havoc that ever and anon occurred along the river as a result of torrential autumn rains and spring thaws, which poured thousands of tons of melting snow and ice into the river at its headwaters and along its tributaries. Dams constructed at such places as Bellows Falls, Turner's Falls, Hadley Falls, and Enfield Falls, often broke under the terrible strain of gathering waters, ice and snow that pressed behind them.

When the dams went out the waters would tear, snarling and roaring, down the valley. The rapidly rising water level would sweep away great bridges, and barns and farmhouses close to the shores of the river. Cattle were drowned in their stalls. Land was ruined by wreckage and by being buried in silt or eaten away by the gnawing force of the waters. People were marooned, drowned, and injured. Financial loss was tremendous. To some farmers it proved a financial bankruptcy.

Anyone living in the river valley can vouch for the fact that the Beautiful River, "the Smile of God," that flows so peacefully in "elegant meanders" can overnight become a raging, destructive torrent, a wild, elemental force, rushing like a mad creature upon every obstacle in its course, ready to devour and obliterate.

Another flood, of larger proportions, occurred in the valley in 1815. In 1840 the roaring river cut the old town of Hadley in two, making an island of part of it and threatening its entire life. Funds were raised by Hadley, and supplemented by the state, to build a protecting rampart about that portion of the town which stood in such constant peril.

In 1862 the river rose to the highest level it had ever reached in the Flume below Bellows Falls. At Brattleboro the tollhouse on the bridge across the river was washed away. And four years later the river, at flood height, carried away the old Windsor-Cornish bridge.

When the great flood of 1927, which centered in the Vermont area, swept the Connecticut valley, twenty-one lives were lost. It was caused chiefly by heavy November rainfall at a time when the ground was frozen, resulting in an extremely high runoff. The total direct damage in this flood was approximately $15,000,000 divided between the four states as follows: Vermont, $11,000,000; New Hampshire, $1,800,000; Massachusetts, $2,200,000; Connecticut, $600,-000.

In March of 1936 there was another disastrous and terrible flood in the river valley. Eleven lives were lost. The flood occurred in two parts, March 9-13, and March 17-19, and set an all-time record for floods in the valley. The chief causes were the rapid depletion of an extremely heavy snow cover, due to continuous high temperature, and heavy rains, yielding phenomenal runoffs which, combined with disastrous ice jams along many sections of the river, caused tremendous damage. The total direct damage caused in this flood amounted to approximately $35,000,000; Vermont, $2,000,-000; New Hampshire, $2,500,000; Massachusetts, $19,-000,000; Connecticut, $11,500,000.

In addition to these direct losses, almost $25,000,000 in indirect damages was sustained because of loss of business, income, delay, rerouting of rail and highway traffic, and other intangibles. Further, and in view of recent developments, an even more important loss has been that due to depreciation of property subject to flood damage. This has been estimated by careful survey, based on reduced values since the flood, to be about $75,000,000, making a grand estimated total of the loss due to the 1936 flood upward of about $135,000,000.

The disastrous flood of March, 1936, crystallized public opinion and demand for flood control became intense. Almost immediately plans for flood-control dams on tributary waters were under the consideration of government engineers. Some of these dams are now constructed and others are in process of being built.

On September 21, 1938, New England, and the Connecticut River valley in particular, were striken by hurricane. The great storm roared its way from the West Indies. It first threatened Florida, then turned north past Cape Hatteras, and suddenly swooped into Long Island and New England.

The result was death and destruction. A region prepared for hurricanes might have been ready as the result of past experience. But the last previous hurricane that had struck New England was in 1815. The United States Weather Bureau was able to give only meager advance warnings because there were few points to report the progress of the storm north of the Atlantic Coast. Barometers foretold a disturbance but the information was not widely available.

The storm, following a low-pressure area as the course of least resistance, was unable to swing westward because of a high-pressure area which had developed over the Middle Atlantic states—fortunately for that region.

Unfortunately for Long Island and New England, another high-pressure area had developed over the Atlantic. Between these two areas was a valley of low pressure. A Valley of Death which was a dagger pointed into the heart of New England. Into the valley, or trough, went the hurricane, now sweeping along at more than sixty miles an hour.

The Connecticut River rose in its might during the hurricane. It did not quite meet the high-water mark of 1936 but it drowned out railroads and made highways utterly impassable. Even a place like Bellows Falls was as isolated from the rest of the surrounding country, on the day following the hurricane, as though it had been the early pioneer settlement of Windsor after the storm of 1635.

This time wind combined with water to wreck the beauty and prosperity of the river valley. For miles and miles forests of trees were lying in hopeless shambles that not even charges of dynamite could disentangle, avenues of great trees were snapped off midway in their trunks, or lay uprooted, their enormous spread of roots torn up as easily as one would pull up a garden vegetable from the soil. Towns were denuded of the beautiful trees that had composed their magnificent setting for centuries and whole mountainsides were stripped of their verdure, their timber lying for miles in broken, tangled masses.

It was one of the most terrible evidences of the destruction wrought by the unrestrained forces of nature that can be imagined.

Flood control—yes. But who can stay the wind?

CHAPTER XX

Some Writers and Other Artists

NATURALLY the most prolific writers of the early days along the river were the clergymen. In our day much of their writing is of interest only to students of theological history. Often their publications were tedious theological treatises, which had been delivered as sermons. A notable exception, perhaps, was Jonathan Edwards' scholarly volume on *The Freedom of the Will,* which is still read with profit.

The early historians, too, were commonly ministers, who did not always write their stories without bias; and they rarely lost an opportunity to interject a paragraph of pious propaganda.

In Hartford, however, in the 1780's a group of young men took up writing of a different sort. They were graduates of Yale College and there had begun their interest in writing. They came to be known as the Hartford Wits. They were versifiers and satirists.

One of them was John Trumbull, whose cousin became

famous as the painter of the American Revolution. In 1782 the publishers, Hudson and Goodwin, who were established near "the Great Bridge," brought out John Trumbull's satire in verse on the Tories. It was called *M'Fingal*. Evidently it was well received in its day, for it went through thirty editions in this country and England.

Another member of the group was Colonel Humphreys, who had won his title fighting under General Washington. When he retired from his military occupation he resorted to writing poetry, which seems not to have been too good. He later was sent as minister to Portugal. Returning, he brought with him a hundred Merino sheep, which very likely had more lasting influence in America than his verse.

The Reverend Timothy Dwight and his brother Theodore also were of the Hartford Wits, as was the latter's brother-in-law, Richard Alsop. The latter ran a book shop. Probably finding even at that early date that books exclusively produce a precarious living, Mr. Alsop sold tea, coffee, and rum, which do not go so badly with books. Very likely the back room of the Alsop bookshop saw many pleasant meetings of the Wits.

One of the most widely known of all these young writers, whose outpourings were received with considerable attention, was Joel Barlow. Before he had taken up writing he had been a chaplain under General Washington. His next interest was journalism; and he started a newspaper, the *American Mercury*. This effort failed within the year. Then he took up the law. However, he was diligently writing much of the time and in 1787 published his long narrative poem, containing some five thousand lines, which he called *The Columbiad*. Later in life, after he had accrued a comfortable fortune, Joel Barlow brought out an elaborate edition, which he called *The Vision of Columbus*. This edition was notable for its illustrations drawn from designs by Robert Fulton.

The discovery, settlement, and glorious future of America was the story this book told. The following is the impression the Connecticut River made on Columbus in his vision, according to the poet:

> Thy stream, my Hartford, through its misty robe,
> Played in the sunbeams, belted far the globe.
> No watery glades through richer vallies shine,
> Nor drinks the sea a lovelier wave than thine.

In France, soon after the publication of this poem, Joel Barlow's political ideas were nourished by his association with many of the leaders of revolutionary thought. He wrote numerous articles on the political affairs of the time and one of them was banned by the British government. Its title was *Advice to the Privileged Classes*, and it greatly strengthened his position among the liberals in France.

After a period of comfortable living in America, Joel Barlow returned to Europe on a mission for the government. It involved a meeting with Napoleon, who was then in the midst of the disastrous retreat from Moscow. Waiting to meet him in a small Polish village, Joel Barlow died of exposure.

He left one other poem, which is perhaps best known today. He wrote this poem while he was in France when he was served with the dish from which the poem takes its title: *The Hasty Pudding*. It was a dish he had known well at home in America. The poem has a racy spontaneity which is in sharp contrast to the long, dreary passages of *The Columbiad*, which are enlightened too infrequently by passages of real beauty.

Joel Barlow had done one thing which had finally alienated his Connecticut friends. His liberal political views were enough to make them cast him off. When he unearthed the manuscript of Thomas Paine's *Age of Reason* and had it published he became an outcast from the old circle.

In the early days Barlow had gone along with Trumbull and the Dwights and the others. He had revised the hymns of Watts and agreed with them in their Calvinist and Federalist beliefs. Now he was almost as bad as Thomas Paine. He had gone over to the very French infidels and democrats whom the original group had met to fight.

The others of the group, remaining strong in their political and religious feelings, were interested in literature as such and produced some good verse and real wit.

Probably better known than the rest was Timothy Dwight, who in spite of the fact that he rarely ventured outside of New England managed to see enough of interest there to fill several volumes of travel. While he perhaps failed to arouse deep interest in his readers he did collect in his four volumes a great deal of factual matter which is of great value to the reader of today.

Timothy Dwight was also a poet. It is unfortunate that he did not use some of his poetic gifts in writing of his travels. However, he left numerous hymns which are sung even today, and a pastoral poem, *Greenfield Hill,* which showed his real feeling for the hills and valleys of his native land.

While Barlow, in his early days, was trying to get his newspaper started, he had as a collaborator a Yale classmate. The classmate was Noah Webster. Of all Joel Barlow's contemporaries he made the most lasting contribution to the growth of a distinctly American culture.

of a new spelling book, which he finally published along with a grammar and reader. This he called *A Grammatical Institute of the English Language*. In these he kept away as far as he could from anything not strictly American. His spelling book, which over the years sold in the millions, used no imported illustrations of usage. It was all strictly American. It gave the population a uniform spelling, which was sadly needed.

Supporting himself and his family largely on the speller, Webster at various times practiced law in Hartford, started a newspaper in New York, and also undertook a magazine. He was a man of original ideas and he used books, pamphlets, and his newspapers to spread his gospel abroad.

Finally, at the age of forty-eight, he set to work on the thing he had long dreamed about—a full and comprehenive dictionary of the English language. His announcement shows his determination to stir up a real national pride in the hearts of Americans:

However arduous the task and however feeble my powers, a thorough conviction of the importance and necessity of the undertaking has overcome my fears and objections, and determined me to make an effort to dissipate the charm of veneration for foreign authors, which fascinates the minds of men in this country and holds them in the chains of illusion. In the investigation of this subject great labor is to be sustained, and numberless difficulties encountered; but with a humble dependence on Divine favor for the preservation of my life and health, I shall prosecute the work with diligence, and execute it with fidelity suited to its importance."

For twenty years Webster worked at his task, in New Haven, in Amherst, Massachusetts, and finally in Cambridge, England, whither he went to consult books unobtainable in America.

The year 1828 saw the first edition of this momentous work off the presses. Twelve years later there was a revision, and when Noah Webster died in 1843 he was still at work on further revision. The first edition contained 12,000 words. Webster's Dictionary is still published on the Connecticut, at Springfield.

While the Wits were beginning their careers in Hartford, far up the river two men were sending regular contributions to *The Farmers' Museum,* published in Walpole, New Hampshire. Their column was headed: "MESSRS. SPONDEE AND COLON, Wholesale Dealers in Verse, Prose, and Music." While their names did not appear, the writers were Joseph Dennis and Royall Tyler. They were sending their contributions down the river from the thriving Vermont town, Guilford, to which town of 2,800 souls they had moved from Boston.

Guilford was the town that had, a few years before, been visited by Ethan Allen when he came to remonstrate because of its lack of interest in the struggles of Vermont to become a state, free of New York's hampering influence. He had then threatened, it may be recalled, to lay Guilford "as waste as Sodom and Gomorrah."

Little is known of Joseph Dennis, but Royall Tyler had already gained fame when he moved to Vermont. The same year that Barlow's *Vision of Columbus* had been published, 1787, had seen a play by Royall Tyler staged—*The Contrast.* This play had the distinction of being the first American comedy to be played professionally on the American stage. The "contrast" was drawn between the sturdy character of the native American and the artificialities of foreign manners. In the winter before he wrote the play Tyler had been one of the pursuers of Daniel Shays and his supporters after they had attacked the arsenal at Springfield, in what is now known as Shays' Rebellion.

Even before the success of *The Contrast*, Royall Tyler had written another comedy, *May Day: New York in an Uproar*, which was America's first musical comedy.

In Guilford, Tyler wrote a novel which he named *The Algerine Captive*, and, oddly enough, this became the first American novel to be republished in England.

Removing to Brattleboro, the town adjoining Guilford, Royall Tyler added further to his fame by becoming the chief justice of the state of Vermont. His volume of court decisions is the only book from his pen that bears his name. Perhaps this was due to extreme modesty. On the other hand, it may well be indicative of the uncertain position the early writers, especially play writers and novelists, held in the society of that day.

Hartford, Connecticut, continued to be the center of literary life in the river valley. During the century beginning with 1764 some one hundred periodicals were published there for a longer or shorter period.

There, in 1830, George Dennison Prentice was publishing the *New England Review*, a weekly literary magazine. He engaged a young man of Quaker ancestry, John Greenleaf Whittier, to be its editor. While Whittier was thus engaged his first volume of verse came out: *Legends of New England*.

If at some time the *New England Review* did not receive and print verses by Lydia Huntley Sigourney, the magazine was a rare exception, for in her prime the "Sweet Singer of Hartford" was contributing regularly to more than twenty publications. In fact, editors engaged in fierce struggles to get something from her prolific pen.

So successful was Mrs. Sigourney as a writer that she supported her less successful merchant husband. In her later years she lived in comfort and dispensed charity with a generous hand. She even managed a trip abroad. Ever after she spoke and wrote of the contemporary English writers as her intimate friends. She freely told of her enthusiastic reception by the literary lights of England and the Continent. That that was far from the real state of affairs was made known by some of her avowed intimates, but Lydia Sigourney utterly ignored these repudiations of friendship.

Not a year was complete without at least one new volume of Mrs. Sigourney's sobbing stanzas. "Her literary coterie abounded in the balmier mental graces, soft as the breath of gazell." Sigourney Circles enveloped feminine New England. Many a hand, worn with toil, briefly rested while its owner found release in the sentimentalities of the Sigourney paradise.

These verses were filled with directions for obtaining passport to the everlasting joys of heaven. Let anyone among her friends enter these blessed precincts, Mrs. Sigourney's pen was sure to be dipped in tears and to inscribe forthwith some sad, sad verses. So certain were the verses to appear that one wag remarked that Mrs. Sigourney "had added a new terror to dying."

Life was hard in those days and there is no doubt that the Sigourney verse offered the comfort of escape to many. When it came time for Mrs. Sigourney to lay down her own burden, which for her seems to have been fairly light, she had produced no less than sixty-seven volumes.

Even before a suitable stone had been erected over Lydia Sigourney's grave, these volumes were gathering dust in attics. Yet for some time Hartford must have remembered her as a person, for no visitor from abroad came to Hartford—and it was sure to be on the itinerary of any visitor of note—without having met Hartford's Sweet Singer.

To her house went the Marquis de Lafayette at the time of his farewell visit to America. Hartford had given a brilliant reception for him, and Mrs. Sigourney had read verses which she had written for the occasion.

In 1842 Charles Dickens, who had come down the wintry river by steamboat, called to pay his respects to Mrs. Sigourney. He wrote of the boat trip, but he did not mention his call on the city's famous poetess.

In fact, Mr. Dickens didn't mention anything or anybody connected with Hartford as a literary center. He did comment favorably on the Asylum for the Insane, where he had conversation with some of the inmates. In his *American Notes* he has this to say: "I shall always entertain a very pleasant and grateful recollection of Hartford. It is a lovely place and I have many friends there." Certainly a very satisfactory bread and butter note from Mr. Dickens.

Up the river at Springfield, Massachusetts, Mr. Dickens stopped in at the editorial office of the *Republican* to see Samuel Bowles, who had taken over his father's paper soon after it had been made a daily at his insistence.

Young Samuel Bowles had become one of the few great newspapermen in the country when Mr. Dickens visited his office. For many years a training on his paper was the goal of aspiring young journalists, and many were the men so trained.

Samuel Bowles combined a knowledge of the kind of local news the people roundabout liked to read, and an ability to get the larger affairs of the world served up in a form to attract readers. His chief fame rested on his editorials, which had "often confused the functions of the *Republican* with those of the recording angel," but his honesty of purpose got him a hearing.

In 1849 J. G. Holland, having given up the practice of medicine, was assisting in getting out the *Republican*. Some of his contributions came out in a book under the title *Timothy Titcomb's Letters*. This was the first of a number of books including prose and verse, quite popular in their day but now mostly forgotten. He was one of the founders and long-time editor of the *Century Magazine*.

Samuel Bowles's interests were not only those of a newsman. He was interested in writing in general and he had a keen eye for talent. He went up to Amherst from time to time to call at the home of his friend Edward Dickinson, the treasurer of Amherst College. There he would sometimes share with the family a new manuscript that had come in, perhaps from a new writer. He found the older daughter of the family, Emily, an interested listener and sometimes a discerning critic.

Later, after Emily Dickinson's unhappy experience at Miss Lyon's Seminary, where she found the interpretation of religion too exacting, it was Samuel Bowles who encouraged her in the writing of poetry. In 1862, when she had so strangely and utterly withdrawn from the world, she used to speak to him, as to others, from the shadowy realms of the upper hall in her home.

A recluse at thirty-two, she devoted the remainder of her life to writing hundreds of verses. Few of them were published until six years after her death. In spite of the fact that new collections have appeared from time to time, there are still many poems which have not been published.

The Springfield *Republican* was not the only newspaper in the valley to achieve a strong position in the life of the day. From 1826 to 1837 the Hartford *Times* had the strong hand of Gideon Welles to guide it.

The *Connecticut Courant* was the Hartford *Courant* when Charles Dudley Warner was shepherding it. In it appeared a series of papers by him, which he published in a book in 1870. The title was *My Summer in a Garden*. It was an early example of the story that deals with the more or less humorous experiences of gardeners. He was soon an author who was widely read. He was the first editor of the series of "American Men of Letters" to which he contributed the Life of Washington.

Of all the books of Charles Dudley Warner perhaps the story of his boyhood in *Being a Boy* is the most revealing. It is a fit companion for Thomas Bailey Aldrich's *Story of a Bad Boy*.

Not far from the Warner home was that of Harriet Beecher Stowe and her white-bearded husband, Calvin. They lived in an eight-gabled house which Mrs. Stowe had built following the great success of *Uncle Tom's Cabin*. There she wrote *Old Town Folks* and a great number of articles and stories for magazines.

Hartford had been growing into a publishing center chiefly through the great success of the American Publishing Company. This enterprising company had adopted the selling technique of the Connecticut Yankee peddler. It was not such a radical change from the door-to-door peddler to the rather slicker young man with a black case hidden under his coat.

Once he got his foot in the door the unwary householder was well on the way to signing his name on the dotted line. After all, people were getting more interested in reading and, even if they weren't much given to reading, it was well to have a few nice volumes on the parlor table beside the Bible.

Moreover, when the subscription book was contracted for, the buyer was fairly sure of getting something worth while, for some of the best books of the time were sold that way.

Under the leadership of Elisha Bliss the American Publishing Company had an excellent reputation. It was to see Mr. Bliss, about a new manuscript he was working on, that Samuel Clemens first went to Hartford.

By the time Elisha Bliss had persuaded his directors (by threats of leaving them and taking it over himself) that *The Innocents Abroad* was not too shocking for their public, Samuel Clemens had become very fond of Hartford. This, in spite of the fact that the conservative directors of the American Publishing Company felt that the first title he had suggested for his book—*The New Pilgrims' Progress*—was close to being sacrilegious, and had insisted upon relegating it to the position of a subordinate subtitle.

There were still many members of New England's literary, cultured class who were disturbed by this bushy-haired westerner, Mark Twain, the like of whom they had never seen or heard. Eventually their suspicions of the literary stranger must have been somewhat allayed by the fact that one of his first friendships in Hartford was with the Reverend Joseph Twichell and his wife. They had been introduced by Elisha Bliss, and at once liked one another. Samuel Clemens had not been at the Twichells' house many times before he confided to Mrs. Twichell what he feared was his hopeless devotion for Miss Olivia Langdon, of Elmira, New York. However, Miss Langdon became Mrs. Samuel Clemens not so very much later, in spite of the gloomy forebodings that had been poured into Mrs. Twichell's sympathetic ear.

Charles Dudley Warner was another person who made

Hartford attractive to Samuel Clemens. With these friends—the Blisses, the Twichells, the Stowes and the Warners—waiting to welcome them, the Clemens family moved to Hartford in 1870. The new house they built soon after their arrival was always open, and usually filled with visitors and friends.

They moved in amid carpenters and plasterers. The house was unusual in appearance and it caused considerable comment. People wanted to know why Mr. Clemens had had the kitchen placed on the street side of the house. Mr. Clemens replied, "So the servants can see the circus go by without running out into the front yard."

By this time Hartford had become a sort of shrine for all literary visitors, and other notables as well, whether of America or from overseas.

William Dean Howells recalls a visit to the Clemens house when Thomas Bailey Aldrich and Charles Dudley Warner were there. "We had two such days as the ageing sun no longer shines upon," Howells wrote. "After two days of talk, talk, talk, I came away as hollow as one of those locust shells, which you will find sticking to the bark of trees at the end of summer."

Over the fireplace in the Clemens house there was a brass plate with an inscription: "THE ORNAMENT OF A HOUSE IS THE FRIENDS WHO FREQUENT IT." Certainly no house was more richly ornamented than the Hartford home of Olivia and Samuel Clemens.

About the time Samuel Clemens moved to Hartford (1870) another literary spirit moved into Brattleboro, up the river in Vermont. "Spirit" is used advisedly. As a matter of fact, it was an itinerant printer named T. P. James, who drifted into town and soon was the recipient of a visitation. He was sought out by the spirit of Charles Dickens, who ordered the bewildered printer to arise and, as "the Spirit Pen" of Charles Dickens, complete Dickens's unfinished novel, *The Mystery of Edwin Drood;* the book upon which Dickens had been laboring when he was stricken with apoplexy and died within twenty-four hours.

Submissive to the demand of Dickens's spirit the printer gave up his occupation, engaged a room in a secluded spot in Brattleboro, and went to work. For many months he worked, writing and casting away, until paper was stacked about him.

The newspapers heard of what was going on in Brattleboro. In due time Sir Arthur Conan Doyle was investigating the strange mystery of the tramp printer who had written the last half of Dickens's book in a fashion so completely duplicating the author's style that even experts could not tell where the Spirit Pen began and where Dickens's own pen had actually ended, as far as any difference in characteristic writing was concerned.

After the most minute investigation Sir Arthur Conan Doyle, along with hundreds of other investigators, was completely at a loss to explain the situation. That it was not a hoax was proved without doubt. The writing was done in a state of trance, it was substantiated, but it was all the more mysterious because T. P. James had never written even a paragraph of his own composition before the time he took up the Spirit Pen of Charles Dickens. The book was published in 1873 and received favorable, as well as bewildered, approval from Dickens students.

Not many years before this the people of Brattleboro had been stirred, not exactly by a spirit but by something akin to it, an angel.

Larkin Mead, whose family had moved from Chesterfield, New Hampshire, to Brattleboro soon after his birth in

1835, had been a clerk in a local hardware store. He attracted the attention of various people in the town by his unusual ability in carving small figures from marble. Some of the visitors at the near-by Water Cure became interested in him and ended by sending him to New York to study sculpture. Two years later he was back in Brattleboro giving lessons in drawing.

One bright January morning passers-by were arrested by a large angel done in snow at the street intersections. It was soon discovered that this was the work of the young drawing teacher who used to work in the hardware store down the street. The cold weather held, and soon people were coming from neighboring towns to view the Snow Angel and to wonder at its beauty. New York papers sent a correspondent up to see it. Before the sun had destroyed it Larkin Mead was being acclaimed as a sculptor of great promise. In the words of Charles Crane, "On the wings of this angel, young Mead rose to fame."

Today he is best remembered in New England for his statue of Ethan Allen in the portico of the Vermont State House at Montpelier, and for another one of Allen in the National Hall of Statuary in Washington. Better known, perhaps, is his statue of Lincoln in Springfield, Illinois, and "The Father of Waters" in Minneapolis.

Larkin Mead's wife was a sister of William Dean Howells. He met Miss Howells while serving under her brother, who was then American consul at Venice. Another member of the Mead family, a brother of Larkin, became equally famous as an architect. He was William R. Mead, a member of the firm of McKim, Mead, and White.

Still another sculptor and patron of art was born and grew up in Brattleboro. He was William Morris Hunt, who first showed talent by working in marble and also making busts of his friends out of a yellowish substance which he procured from the bleaching vats of the Lowell, Massachusetts, mills.

He left Brattleboro and was studying drawing and sculpture in Rome in 1843. Later, in Paris, he fell in with Jean François Millet, "the sincerity of whose work took possession of him." Hunt bought many of Millet's paintings just at the time when the artist most needed help and encouragement.

In 1856 William Hunt brought his bride to Brattleboro. They lived there for some years, and later moved to various cities where Hunt influenced many young painters to study the then new Parisian style.

His efforts were not always welcomed, however. His own painting of "The Prodigal Son" was received with open hostility in Boston. To prevent him from becoming utterly discouraged his mother bought the picture and hid it away in Brattleboro, at her death bequeathing it to the Brattleboro Library. Later an exhibition of his work in Boston attracted thousands of people, and his mural in the Albany Capitol, "The Flight of Night," was held in high esteem.

It was not the literary or artistic atmosphere, nor the fact that it had long been a printing center, that brought Rudyard Kipling and his bride to Brattleboro. Mrs. Kipling was bringing her husband to visit her grandparents and her brother, Beatty Balestier, in the place of her birth.

Only a few months earlier another brother, Wolcott Balestier, for whom his sister Caroline had been keeping house in London, died very suddenly while on a business trip on the Continent.

Wolcott Balestier had been a publisher's agent in London and had become an intimate friend of Rudyard Kipling. Together they had written *Naulahka*. Through her brother, Kipling had come to know Caroline Balestier, and, in time, to love her.

Soon after Wolcott's death Caroline and Rudyard Kipling were married. In February, 1892, they sailed for a visit to America, and her old home, where she and Wolcott had grown up.

It was a wintry landscape that greeted the Kiplings. Vermont was buried deep in snow. But Rudyard Kipling, singer of the sun-baked East, liked the snow-covered hills. He liked to look at Monadnock rising dark above the snow-clad hills of New Hampshire, across the river. He liked the cold air "as keen as a newly-ground sword."

By spring they had decided that they would like to live in Vermont. They bought land in the neighboring town of Dummerston. The next winter found them, with their baby daughter, settled in their new house, built like a ship and named *Naulahka*. Across the river Monadnock kept watch, and Kipling did his first writing in his new home.

In his study on the Vermont hills Kipling wrote the stories collected in the volume *The Day's Work*, and in *Captains Courageous, The Jungle Books*, and *The Just So Stories*.

Train travelers in the upper Connecticut valley recognized something very familiar in the story "How the Whale Got His Throat." When the shipwrecked mariner is making his submarine voyage, you may recall, he was told to be prepared to disembark "when the whale opened his mouth wide and wide and wide and said, 'Change here for Winchester, Ashuelot, Nashua, Keene, and stations on the Fitchburg road.' And when he said FITCH the mariner walked out of his mouth."

To the neighbors Mrs. Kipling seemed more English in

her speech and manner of life than her husband. She liked to drive through the main street of Brattleboro behind a pair of prancing horses, driven tandem, by a coachman in a striking costume. Brattleboro people were used to seeing her brother Beatty drive down the same street in a sagging buckboard, followed by a large and varied collection of dogs.

Perhaps in some ways the brother and sister were too much alike to be able to get along comfortably together. At any rate, there arose family disagreements which in time grew into a real quarrel involving alleged threats and a consequent lawsuit brought by Beatty Balestier against his famous brother-in-law. The whole matter was made odious to the conservative, somewhat retiring Kipling by its exploitation and exaggeration in a new type of journalism, which was just beginning to yellow the horizon.

After four years, most of them happy ones, the Kiplings in distress and distaste, sailed for England, leaving forever the river valley, and *Naulahka*, the shiplike house that still rests at anchor in the Vermont hills.

No doubt the departure of the Kiplings from Brattleboro, and from America, was especially felt by the group of artists and writers who had been growing in number in the New Hampshire hills about Cornish, across the river from Windsor.

There, five years before Mr. and Mrs. Kipling's arrival in this country, Augustus Saint-Gaudens, rapidly coming to fame as one of America's great sculptors, was learning for the first time the charm of life in the country.

His name and fame had already come to the river valley, for in 1887 the people of Springfield, Massachusetts, were gazing intently at the striking statue he had sculptured of Deacon Chapin as "The Puritan." About the same time his famous statue of Lincoln was placed near the Chicago Library.

Saint-Gaudens's letters, written in these early years, are full of the joy he felt in the countryside, and it was inevitable that he should soon gather friends about him. There was Daniel Chester French, a native son of New Hampshire who at the age of twenty-three, after a year of study abroad, had been commissioned to create the statue "The Minute Man" which was unveiled at Concord, Massachusetts, on the centenary of the battle.

From then on, Daniel Chester French's place as an American sculptor was made more secure with each succeeding work. One of his best-known pieces is in the Forest Hills Cemetery, Massachusetts, erected there for the tomb of the sculptor Martin Milmore and called "Death Staying the Hand of the Sculptor." Daniel French also made the statue of Lincoln in the Lincoln Memorial in Washington.

It was a son of Vermont, Judge Wendell Safford, who wrote peculiarly fitting words concerning that great Memorial Temple in which the statue, created by a New Hampshire sculptor, is enshrined:

> More proudly will Potomac wind
> Past thy pure temple to the sea;
> But, oh, the hearts of men will find
> No marble white enough for thee!

Maxfield Parrish also came to live and to paint in Cornish, above the river. And Winston Churchill, the American novelist, came to work there too. But it was Saint-Gaudens and his son, Homer, who drew them and others to the spot of such beauty and inspiration, above the quietly flowing river, across which they looked to Mt. Ascutney. They must often have known it in its tempestuous moods, as well as its peaceful ones, but to Saint-Gaudens's mind it was beautiful in all its moods, although often terrifying.

First in the old barn and later, after a disastrous fire, in his new studio, Saint-Gaudens turned out sketches, heroic statues, bronzes, designs for United States coins, and medallions and reliefs in marble and in bronze.

He loved the river and the surrounding hills. "It is very beautiful," he said a few days before he died, as he looked out at a sunset behind Mt. Ascutney, "but I want to go farther away."

The studio filled with casts of his best-known work was arranged as a perpetual memorial through donations by thousands of the sculptor's admirers. It met the same fate that overtook the earlier studio. With its priceless treasures it was completely destroyed by fire not many years after it had been opened to the public.

A native American culture and artistic genius has emanated from the river valley. To this American culture many besides those mentioned in this chapter—writers, editors, preachers, actors, musicians, painters, sculptors, and statesmen —have made their contributions.

The modern poet, Witter Bynner, who spent some summers at Cornish above the river, under the spell of that experience, wrote his long lyric poem *The New World*. In it are lines that express the contribution of mind and spirit that some of the writers and other artists of the river valley have made to America.

> To share all beauty as the interchanging dust,
> To be akin and kind and to entrust
> All men to one another for their good,
> Is to have heard and understood,
> And carried to the common enemy
> In you and me,
> The ultimatum of democracy.

Acknowledgments

WHOEVER writes a book is under obligation to many people. An idea here, a slant there, a little coloring, unconsciously registered in the writer's mind, becomes a part of his writing. Obligations are registered somewhat in the bibliography in a book such as this. However I am deeply conscious that I am omitting many names which should by right appear in these paragraphs. To all such I herewith extend my thanks and offer a blanket apology for neglecting to add their names to this list.

I will always remember with warm gratitude the patient and painstaking help which Stephen Benét gave me, as one of the editors of the River Series. Later when his place was taken by Hervey Allen, he too gave generous and kindly criticism and much help along the way. Each of these was always aided and abetted in his helpful ministrations by the other editor, Carl Carmer. Watching over it all were the kindly and discerning eyes of Jean Crawford, Associate Editor, and Faith Ball, Art Editor.

I am indebted to Professor Eldridge Jacobs, of the University of Vermont, and Vermont State Geologist, for what is, in a very real sense, fundamental information, both through his state reports and through his advisory letters. Dr. Joseph Wickham Roe has also been an enthusiastic supporter. To him I am indebted not only for his book, listed in the bibliography, but for his painstaking review of the toolmaking chapter, and for the loan of valuable magazine material. Thanks are also due to Professor Homer Woodbridge of Wesleyan University and to friends there to whom he introduced me. Harold Rugg of the Baker Library at Dartmouth and members of the staff were most kind, as was Anna Buck of the Mark Skinner Library in Manchester, Vermont. Earle Newton of the Vermont Historical Library in Montpelier gave needed aid as did Charles Crane of Montpelier, and Marion Hooper, of Brattleboro.

The various historical societies along the river, state publicity bureaus, public service companies and various commissions, all have had a part in furnishing material. I am indebted to the late P. W. Whittlesey and members of his family for the use of the manuscript on the Smith Sisters of Glastonbury. To all these and many more my sincere thanks is herewith registered.

Bibliography

ABBOTT, KATHARINE, *Paths and Legends of the New England Border*. Putnam's, 1909.

ADAMS, JAMES TRUSLOW, *The Founding of New England*. Atlantic Monthly Press, 1921.

—— *Revolutionary New England*. Atlantic Monthly Press, 1923.

—— *Epic of America*. Atlantic Monthly Press, 1941.

ALLIS, MARGUERITE, *The Connecticut River*. Putnam's, 1939.

ANDREWS, G. R., *The Connecticut River from Hanover to the Sea*.

BACON, E. M., *The Connecticut River and Valley of the Connecticut*. Putnam's, 1907.

BAIN, GEO. AND MEYERHOFF, HOWARD, *The Flow of Time in the Connecticut Valley*. Hampshire Bookshop, 1921.

BEARD, CHARLES AND MARY, *Basic History of the United States*. Blakiston, 1945.

BEERS, HENRY A., *Connecticut Wits and Other Essays*, Yale University Press, 1920.

BENÉT, LAURA, *Come Slowly Eden*. Dodd Mead, 1942.

BOWLES, E. S., *Let Me Show You New Hampshire*. Knopf, 1938.

BROOKS, VAN WYCK, *The Flowering of New England*. Dutton, 1937.

—— *New England Indian Summer*. Dutton, 1940.

—— *The World of Washington Irving*. Dutton, 1944.

CLARK, GEORGE, *A History of Connecticut, Its People and Institutions*. Putnam's, 1914.

CRANE, CHARLES, *Pendrift*. Daye, 1931.

CUTTS, MARY, *Life and Times of Hon. William Jarvis*. Hurd & Houghton, 1869.

DUNBAR, SEYMOUR, *History of Travel in America*. Bobbs Merrill, 1915.

DWIGHT, TIMOTHY, *Travels in New England and New York*. Baynes & Son, 1823.

FOX, D. R., *Yankees and Yorkers*. New York University Press, 1940.

GILCHRIST, BETH, *Life of Mary Lyon*. Houghton Mifflin, 1910.

GREEN, CONSTANCE, *Holyoke, Massachusetts*. Yale University Press, 1939.

HAIGHT, GORDON, *Mrs. Sigourney, The Sweet Singer of Hartford*. Yale University Press, 1930.

HARLOW, A. F., *Steelways of New England*. Creative Age Press, 1946.

HART, ALBERT B., *American History Told by Contemporaries*. Macmillan, 1897.

HARRINGTON, POMEROY, *The Background of Wesleyan*. Wesleyan University Press, 1942.

HAYWARD, JOHN, *New England Gazetteer*. Boyd & White, 1839.

HAYES, L. S., *History of the Town of Rockingham*. Vermont, 1907.
—— *The Connecticut River Valley in Southern Vermont and New Hampshire*. Tuttle, 1929.

HITCHCOCK, E., *Life of Mary Lyon*. American Tract Society.

HOWE, HENRY, *Prologue to New England*. Farrar & Rinehart, 1943.

HOOPER, MARION, *Life Along the Connecticut River*. Daye, 1939.

HUBBARD, WILLIAM, *Hubbard's History of New England*. Mass. Historical Society, from original of 1815.

JONES, MATT, *Vermont in the Making*. Harvard University Press, 1939.

LUDLUM, DAVID, *Social Ferment in Vermont*. Columbia University Press, 1939.

MILLER, WILLIAM, *The Geological History of the Connecticut Valley*. Hampshire Bookshop, 1942.

MORISON, SAMUEL, *The Puritan Pronaos*. New York University Press, 1936.

PAINE, ALBERT, *Mark Twain*. Harper, 1912.

PALFREY, JOHN, *Palfrey's History of New England*. Little, Brown, 1890.

PARKES, HENRY, *Jonathan Edwards*. Minton Balch, 1930.

PELL, JOHN, *Ethan Allen*. Houghton Mifflin, 1929.

PERRY, RALPH B., *Puritanism and Democracy*. Vanguard Press, 1944.

POWELL, LYMAN, *Historic Towns of New England*. Putnam's, 1898.

ROBERTS, *Historic Towns of the Connecticut River Valley*.

ROE, JOSEPH W., *English and American Toolmakers*. McGraw, 1926.

RYDER, FREEMONT, *Two Forgotten Connecticut Feminists*. Original paper unpublished.

SAINT-GAUDENS, AUGUSTUS, Edited by HOMER SAINT-GAUDENS. *Reminiscences of Augustus Saint-Gaudens.* Century, 1913.

SHEPARD, ODELL, *Connecticut Past and Present.* Knopf, 1939.

SIEBERT, WILBUR, *Vermont's Anti-Slavery and Underground Railroad Record.* Sparkes & Glenn Co., 1937. (Privately printed.)

STEWART, GEORGE, *Names on the Land.* Random House, 1945.

SYLVESTER, H. M., *Indian Wars of New England.* Clark, 1910.

THOMPSON, CHARLES, *Independent Vermont.* Houghton Mifflin, 1942.

THWAITES, R. G., *Epochs of American History.* Longmans, 1915.

TYLER, ROYALL, *The Contrast.* Houghton Mifflin, 1920.

WEEDEN, WILLIAM, *Economic and Social History of New England.* Houghton Mifflin, 1894.

WHITE, HENRY, *Early History of New England.* Boyd, 1842.

WHITTLESEY, C. W., *Crossing and Recrossing the Connecticut River.* Putnam's, 1939.

WILBUR, JAS., *Ira Allen.* Houghton Mifflin, 1928.

WILLISON, GEORGE, *Saints and Strangers.* Reynal & Hitchcock, 1945.

WILSON, FORREST, *Crusader in Crinoline.* Lippincott, 1941.

WILSON, R. R., *New England in Letters.* A. Wessels Co., 1904.

WILSON, WOODROW, *A History of the American People.* Harper, 1918.

The American Guide Series of the Federal Writers Project for Vermont, New Hampshire, Massachusetts and Connecticut. Houghton Mifflin, 1937-38.

Reports of the Massachusetts State Planning Board.

Publications of the Committee on Historical Publications of the Tercentenary Commission of the State of Connecticut. Yale University Press, 1936.

Various publications of the Vermont Historical Society.

Various publications of the Connecticut Valley Historical Society.

Magazine articles including those in the *Granite State Monthly, The Vermonter, New England Magazine.*

Private diaries, papers and pamphlets in the Vermont and other state Historical Societies.

Booklets, pamphlets and reports from various Chambers of Commerce, Public Service companies, state publicity bureaus and others.

Index